LIBERIA

PORTRAIT OF A
FAILED STATE

LIBERIA

PORTRAIT OF A
FAILED STATE

JOHN-PETER PHAM

Reed

PRESS

Published by Reed Press™
360 Park Avenue South
New York, NY 10010
www.reedpress.com

ISBN: 1-59429-012-1

Library of Congress Cataloging-in-Publication Data

Pham, John-Peter.
    Liberia : portrait of a failed state / John-Peter Pham.—1st American ed.
        p. cm.
    Includes bibliographical references (p.).
        ISBN 1-59429-012-1 (alk. paper)
        1. Liberia--Politics and government--1980- 2. Liberia--History. I.
    Title.
DT636.5.P47 2004
966.6203--dc22

                                                                2003023000

Book Design and compositon by John Reinhardt Book Design

Printed in the United States of America

10 9 8 7 6 5 4 3 2 1

For my family,
with gratitude for having seen me through
my West African sojourn.

When Freedom raised her glowing form on
On Montserrado's verdant height,
She set within the dome of Night
'Midst lowering skies and thunderstorm
The star of Liberty!
And seizing from the waking Morn
Its burnished shield of golden flame
She lifted it in her proud name
And roused a nation long forlorn
To nobler destiny.

From "The Lone Star Forever"
by EDWIN JAMES BARCLAY,
President of Liberia (1930–1944)

CONTENTS

PRINCIPAL ACRONYMS AND OTHER ABBREVIATIONS

PRINCIPAL ACRONYMS AND OTHER ABBREVIATIONS

ACS ....American Colonization Society, officially "American Society for Colonizing the Free People of Color in the United States"

AFL ....Armed Forces of Liberia

AFRC ....Armed Forces Revolutionary Council (Sierra Leone)

ALCOP ....All Liberian Coalition Party

APC ....All Peoples' Congress (Sierra Leone)

APP ....Alliance of Political Parties

ATU ....Anti-Terrorist Unit

AU ....African Union

CRC-NPFL ....Central Revolutionary Council of the NPFL

ECOMIL ....ECOWAS Mission in Liberia

ECOMOG ....ECOWAS Cease-fire Monitoring Group

ECOWAS ....Economic Community of West African States

IGNU ....Interim Government of National Unity

INPFL ....Independent National Patriotic Front of Liberia

LAP ....Liberian Action Party

LDC ....Liberia Development Company

LDF ....Lofa Defense Force

LFF ....Liberian Frontier Force
LNP ....Liberian National Police
LNTG......................Liberian National Transitional Government
LPC ....Liberian Peace Council
LPP ....Liberian People's Party
LUP..........................Liberia Unification Party
LURD......................Liberians United for Reconciliation and Democracy
MINUCI..................United Nations Mission in Cte d'lvoire
MJP ....Mouvement pour la Justice et la Paix (Côte d'Ivoire)
MODEL ....Movement for Democracy in Liberia
MOJA ....Movement for Justice in Africa
MPCI ....Mouvement Patriotique du Côte d'Ivoire
MPIGO..................Mouvement Patriotique du Grand Ouest (Côte d'Ivoire)
MSCS ....Maryland State Colonization Society
NAACP..................National Association for the Advancement of Colored People
NDPL......................National Democratic Party of Liberia
NPFL......................National Patriotic Front of Liberia
NPP..........................National Patriotic Party
NPRAG..................National Patriotic Reconstruction Assembly Government
NTGL......................National Transitional Government of Liberia
NTLA......................National Transitional Legislative Assembly
OAU..........................Organization of African Unity
PAL ....Progressive Alliance of Liberia
PDG ....Parti Démocratique de Guinée
PPP..........................Progressive People's Party
PRC ....People's Redemption Council
PUP..........................Parti de l'Unité et du Progrès (Guinea)
RDA..........................Rassemblement Démocratique Africain (Côte d'Ivoire)
RUF..........................Revolutionary United Front
SCSL ....Special Court for Sierra Leone
SLPP ....Sierra Leone People's Party
SMC ....ECOWAS Standing Mediation Committee
SSS............................Special Security Service
TWP ....True Whig Party
ULAA......................Union of Liberian Associations in the Americas
ULIMO..................United Liberian Movement for Democracy
ULIMO-J ....ULIMO-Roosevelt Johnson Faction
ULIMO-K..............ULIMO-Alhaji Kromah Faction
UNDP......................United Nations Development Program
UNIA......................United Negro Improvement Association
UNOMIL................United Nations Observer Mission in Liberia
UNAMSIL..............United Nations Mission in Sierra Leone
UNOMSIL..............United Nations Observer Mission in Sierra Leone
UP............................Unity Party
UPP..........................United People's Party
USAID....................United States Agency for International Development

PREFACE

IN ONE OF THE EARLIEST literary accounts of travel in Liberia, *Journey Without Maps*, which chronicled his 1935 trek through the country's interior, Graham Greene lamented that:

It would have been easier if I had been able to obtain maps. But the Republic is almost entirely covered by forest, and has never been properly mapped…I could find only two large-scale maps for sale. One, issued by the British General Staff, quite openly confessed its ignorance; there was a large white space covering the greater part of the Republic, with a few dotted lines indicating the conjectured course of rivers (incorrectly, I usually found) and a fringe of names along the boundary. These names have been curiously chosen: most of them are quite unknown to anyone in the Republic; they must have belonged to obscure villages now abandoned. The other map is issued by the United States War Department. There is a dashing quality about it; it shows a vigorous imagination. Where the English map is content to leave a blank space, the American in large letters fills it with the word "Cannibals." It has no use for dotted lines and confessions of ignorance; it is so inaccurate that it would be useless, perhaps even dangerous to follow, though there is something Elizabethan in its imagination. "Dense Forest"; "Cannibals"; rivers which don't exist, at any rate anywhere near where they are put; one expects to find Eldorado, two-headed men and fabulous beasts represented in little pictures in the Gola Forest.[1]

In recent months, I have had the sensation that history was repeating itself. As the increasingly beleaguered Liberian leader Charles Ghankay Taylor faced first two rebel movements and, then, mounting international pressure, including an ultimatum from United States President George W. Bush, to resign, images were flashed around the world of hundreds of thousands of desperate Liberians besieged in the capital of Monrovia, the government's last redoubt, cut off from humanitarian supplies bottled up in the city's Freeport, which was held by the rebels. A clamor arose, driven by editorial writers and other media pundits, demanding "action"—without, of course, defining what sort of action. Having just returned to the United States from a diplomatic assignment covering Liberia (as well as Sierra Leone and Guinea), I grew increasingly frustrated with the quality of the information—or better, the misinformation—constitute the standard fare, not just in popular news coverage, but in policy making circles. I had the distinct impression that momentous decisions were being made on the basis of information little improved since Graham Greene traipsed through the Liberian countryside. Some policy makers seemed as poorly informed as the mapmakers at the British General Staff—but at least the Britons had had the honesty to admit their ignorance. Others, especially among the interventionist advocacy groups, behaved more like the U.S. War Department described by the British author and relied on erroneous information—that is, if one adopts a charitable interpretation and refrains from both imputing on them ulterior motives and speculating on the origins of false reports—and filled in the gaps with flights of fancy designed to whip up righteous indignation among those with sensitive consciences. In any event, all-too-many pundits during the stampede to "do something" would have fallen under the late Israeli statesman Abba Eban's proscription against commentators who "have a tendency to imagine the past and to describe the future"[2]—they invented an idyllic Liberian past under the supposed sponsorship of the United States, demonized the Liberian president as the primary obstacle to a West African *utopia*,

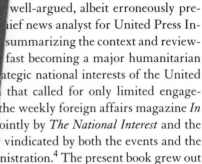

be brought about by the intervention

well-argued, albeit erroneously pre-
ief news analyst for United Press In-
summarizing the context and review-
fast becoming a major humanitarian
ategic national interests of the United
that called for only limited engage-
the weekly foreign affairs magazine *In*
ointly by *The National Interest* and the
y vindicated by both the events and the
inistration.[4] The present book grew out

ne that the principal reason the public discourse on Liberia was so poorly informed by facts and, consequently, driven by emotion—rather than the detachment required by statecraft has less to do with modern technology's ability to broadcast vivid images in real time so much as an old-fashioned lack of information. While several excellent histories of Liberia were written in the first half of the twentieth century,[5] more contemporary publications suffer from one of several shortcomings that render them less useful in a fast-paced policy debate. Some works, while remarkable scholarly treatises, are specialized works whose appeal to already-pressured policy makers—to say nothing of general readers—is limited.[6] The same critique could be applied to most journal articles. Other works, prescinding from any consideration of their academic value, have been authored by persons with direct interests in political outcomes and, hence, lack a certain objective detachment from the events they analyze.[7] Still other works, while moving personal accounts, offer very few elements to inform geopolitical analysis and strategic decisions.[8]

The present book is an attempt to fill the gap in the literature, presenting a general panorama of the context and issues involved without weighing it down with too many scholarly devices. It is, admittedly, the result of my own familiarity with the vast array of historical and contemporary scholarly literature that has preceded and to which I am indebted, having studied many of these earlier publications as a part of my preparation for and continuing interest in the part of Africa that was until recently my diplomatic responsibility. Originally, I had intended to treat the subject in greater depth at a later moment, after I completed another work

I have been laboring on. However, the press of current events came as a summons to contribute to an important public discussion, one that I had no right to sit out given the privileged access to the principals I had enjoyed. Consequently, the book is less a definitive scholarly endeavor than the product of my own journey into the "heart of darkness" when I had to confront some the issues that make up and characters who play a role in the contemporary tragedy of Liberia and the West African subregion. Thus the writing of this book helped me make sense of some of these experiences as well as contribute to the current policy discussions.

In addition to providing an overview of the historical and social background and political and military consequences of the recent Liberian crises, this book also uses that context to explore the question of state failure and its implications for the international community in general and the United States in particular. Far from being an exceptional phenomenon, the "failed state" has been one of the hallmarks of the post-Cold War era as the previous, relatively static balance of power gave way to a more dynamic order. And while countries that have imploded like Liberia, Sierra Leone, Somalia, Zaire/Democratic Republic of Congo, and others, have oftentimes been remote, the geopolitical implications of the collapse of their states have reverberated across the globe. Whatever the precise causes of each conflict, overall effects are remarkably similar, both in terms of human misery and displacement of the political equilibrium. By learning the lessons of any one instance–Liberia being the case at hand–one develops certain conceptual categories and analytical tools which are helpful in understanding other emergent challenges and has the opportunity to hone the response mechanisms–economic, cultural, diplomatic, and military–with which to deal with them. Consequently, while the conflict in Liberia–aside from sensationalist accounts in the popular media—may not necessarily loom large as a threat to U.S. national interests, it can nonetheless provide a microcosm of the violence and unrest that lay just beyond the horizon of the strategic core of the modern day American *imperium*– the stable group of largely developed and democratic nations of North America, Western and Central Europe, Northeast Asia–in the failed or potentially-failed states of Africa, the Middle East, and other regions. Whether their interests eventually necessitate a military intervention or dictate another form of direct involvement or even no engagement, the United States and other prosperous nations will find the international environment in the near future teeming with crises like Liberia's. In assessing what the future has in store and determining what options may be available, one does well by casting a close look at the recent past.

In conclusion, I must acknowledge a number of debts, absolving as I do so all those mentioned and unmentioned from any responsibility for the judgments expressed—much less for any errors contained—on the following pages. Dr. Nikolas K. Gvosdev, senior fellow in strategic studies at the Nixon Center and editor of *In the National Interest*, took a chance in publishing my commentary on the Liberian crisis at a time when my views went very much against the current of editorial opinion. My literary agent at the Spieler Agency, John F. Thornton, who was already working with me on another project, enthusiastically took up my tentative proposal and helped turned it into reality in a very short time. I am grateful for his patience and confidence. I appreciate the faith that Nicholas Weir-Williams, publishing director of Reed Press, had in this work even when its author was proposing to challenge conventional wisdom. It has been a pleasure working with Nick and his staff, especially Fiorella deLima, production coordinator, whose creativity and diligence rendered the final result a far more pleasant encounter than the piles of unattractive paper I waded through—and produced—in the process of writing this book.

I am grateful for the friendship and innumerable kindnesses of colleagues in the *Corps diplomatiques* in Monrovia, Liberia; Freetown, Sierra Leone; and Conakry, Guinea. During my mission in the countries of the Mano River Union, the members of the United States missions in the three countries, especially the embassy in Guinea, were a tremendous personal as well as professional support to a fellow American whom circumstances landed there under an international flag. I regret that the conventions of diplomatic discretion do not permit me to mention names, but the interested parties—Americans and others in our tight-knit expatriate circle—know who they are. I am also grateful to a group of loyal friends back in the States—in particular, Dr. Linda Atherton, Gary Caster, David Erickson, Mary Hazen, and Richard Soseman—who generously assisted me in bringing a measure of succor to the lives of some of the most innocent victims of the West African regional tragedy, the orphans of the scourges of war and AIDS. Finally, upon my return to the United States, my dear friends, Gabriel and Emmanuelle Riedel, aided me in more ways than one in making the transition from life as a diplomat in Africa to life as a civilian in that jungle that is Manhattan.

This book is dedicated to my family, especially Tom, who loves Africa with a purity born of innocence and who constantly tried to get me to look beyond the parameters of *Realpolitik*; Tara, who shared the earlier adventures of Niger and Ghana with me and who, understanding the unique pressures of life amid strife in Africa, dragged me off to a much needed break after my misadventures during the LURD offensive in 2002; little Kaitlin, who prayed every night for her uncle in Africa; and, of course, Mom and Dad, without whose support I doubt I would have made it through my sojourn in a place "so long forlorn."

J.P.P.
New York, October 15, 2003

ENDNOTES

1. Graham Greene, *Journey Without Maps* (1936; New York: Penguin Books, 1980), 45–46.
2. Abba Eban, *Diplomacy for the Next Century* (New Haven/London: Yale University Press, 1998), 11.
3. Martin Sieff, "The Liberian Gambit," *In the National Interest: Weekly Commentary and Analysis on Foreign Policy* 2/27 (July 9, 2003), at www.inthenationalinterest.com/Articles/Vol2Issue27/Vol2Issue27Sieff.html>.
4. J. Peter Pham, "A Realistic Commitment: Balancing National Interests and American Ideals in Liberia," *In the National Interest: Weekly Commentary and Analysis on Foreign Policy* 2/28 (July 16, 2003), at <www.inthenationalinterest.com/Articles/Vol2Issue28/Vol2Issue28Pham.html>.
5. See, *inter alia*, Charles S. Johnson, *Bitter Canaan: The Story of the Negro Republic*, edited with introduction by John Stanfield (1987; New Brunswick, New Jersey/London: Transaction Publishers, 1992); and Nathaniel Richardson, *Liberia's Past and Present* (London: Diplomatic Press, 1959). Johnson, a pioneering and influential African-American sociologist, wrote his historical-sociological account of Liberian society in 1930 and revised it in 1948, considering it his best work. However, for a variety of reasons, most having to do with *Bitter Canaan*'s challenge to accepted conventional wisdom on its subject matter, the work was not published until 1987.
6. See, *inter alia*, Stephen Ellis, *The Mask of Anarchy: The Destruction of Liberia and the Religious Dimension of an African Civil War* (1999; New York: New York University Press, 2001).
7. See, *inter alia*, Amos Sawyer, *The Emergence of Autocracy in Liberia: Tragedy and Challenge* (San Francisco: Institute for Contemporary Studies, 1992); and Lester S. Hyman, *United States Policy Towards Liberia, 1822–2003: Unintended Consequences* (Cherry Hill, New Jersey: Africana Homestead Legacy Publishers, 2003). Sawyer, a Liberian academic long involved in opposition politics, was president of the failed Interim Government of National Unity from 1990 to 1993. Hyman was retained by Liberian warlord-turned-president Charles Ghankay Taylor as his government's counsel and lobbyist in Washington from 1997 to 1999.
8. See, *inter alia*, Arthur F. Kulah, *Liberia Will Rise Again: Reflections on the Liberian Civil Crisis* (Nashville, Tennessee: Abingdon Press, 1999); and Gabriel I.H. Williams, *Liberia: The Heart of Darkness* (Victoria, British Columbia: Trafford Publishers, 2002).

INTRODUCTION

THE FAILED STATE
OF LIBERIA

N OWADAYS, WHEN ONE MENTIONS the term "failed state,"[1] Liberia almost immediately comes to mind. The snapshots of the brutal Liberian civil conflict such as the vivid images captured in an especially memorable dispatch by African-American journalist Keith Richburg, then Africa bureau chief for the *Washington Post*, virtually cry out "failed state":

Welcome to Liberia, scene of one of the wackiest, and most ruthless, of Africa's uncivil wars. It's a war with a general named Mosquito, a war where soldiers get high on dope and paint their fingernails bright red before heading off to battle. It's a war where combatants sometimes donned women's wigs, pantyhose, even Donald Duck Halloween masks before committing some of the world's worse atrocities against their enemies. It's the only war that hosts a unit of soldiers who strip off their clothes before going into battle and calls itself "the Butt Naked Brigade." It's a war where young child soldiers carry teddy bears and plastic baby dolls in one hand and AK-47s in the other. It's a war where fighters smear their faces with makeup and mud in the belief that "juju," West African magic, will protect them from the enemy's bullets.[2]

Nor did the government that emerged from the internationally supervised elections in 1997 do much to ameliorate the situation. Rather, the man elected president of Liberia, Charles Ghankay Taylor, had not only fired the first shots in the civil war, but was generally held responsible for having expanded the conflict into a regional conflagration that engulfed neighboring Sierra Leone as well as Guinea and Côte d'Ivoire. Moreover, Taylor has subsequently been implicated not just in extensive human rights abuses at home and the continuing subversion of neighboring states but also in a conspiracy involving financial ties with Islamist terrorist groups, including al-Qa'eda.[3]

While reports such as these paint a heart-wrenching picture of a country where responsible government institutions have essentially imploded, they are not sufficient to construct a complete picture, let alone to explain—to say nothing about laying the foundations for a model from which a practical solution might be developed. For many observers, the events that accompanied the collapse of the Liberian state and the ensuing violence and upheaval—with all the reports of bizarre behavior, including torture, cannibalism, and transvestitism, and sheer greed for the resources of the forests, including diamonds and timber—were inexplicable except under the general rubric of the "heart of darkness" that Joseph Conrad used to describe the African continent and its primitive law of the jungle.[4] Richburg said as much when, after describing the ethnic slaughters he witnessed, he bluntly declared: "Fully evolved human beings in the twentieth century don't do things like that. Not for any reason, not tribe, not religion, not territory. These must be cavemen."[5]

Similar sentiments were echoed by Robert Kaplan, whose highly influential essay for *The Atlantic Monthly*, "The Coming Anarchy," published in early 1994,[6] argued that environmental scarcity, cultural and ethnic clashes, geographical destiny, and transformations in warfare would increasingly drive an impenetrable wedge between West Africa and the rest of the world. In a version of the article published in a subsequent anthology bearing the same title as his seminal piece, Kaplan concluded that what happened in the West African sub-region during the 1990s—"the withering away of central governments, the rise of tribal and regional domains, the unchecked spread of disease, and the growing pervasiveness of war"[7]—were a microcosm of the conflicts to come in underdeveloped parts of the globe.

The very humanitarian crises that once more brought Liberia to the attention of the public in developed countries in the early summer of 2003—especially in the United States where a seemingly relentless media campaign informed the public that "history argues in favor of American involvement,"[8] that "can save lives, stabilize a region and prove America's commitment to Africa is real,"[9] and prove that "the United States is still willing to use its strength for international causes outside its own narrowly defined self-interest"[10]—were, however, only the symptoms of a much deeper failure. The exploration of the complex roots of the collapse of the Liberian state and the forces that drove the civil war—or wars, depending on whether one considers the 1997 election as the conclusion of a war or a mere pause in the conflict that erupted anew in 2000.

Even veteran commentators on Africa like Bill Berkeley who categorically reject "new age primitivism" as an explanation for the violent passions and brutal horrors of the conflict have admitted that: "These catastrophes are not as senseless as they seem. They are not inevitable products of primordial, immutable hatreds. There is method in the madness."[11] The premise of the present book is that by reviewing the history of the West-African country, delving into its political foundations, and examining it social structures, the "method to the madness" of Liberia can be found. Specifically, the book's central argument is that the roots of the Liberian conflict—and a good deal of the horrible brutality with which it was fought—are directly traceable to the ideological origins of the West-African state as well as the exclusionary national vision and divisive strategies that the Americo-Liberian oligarchy employed in order to perpetuate its control for most of the country's history. If this analysis is correct, then it necessarily follows that the remedies for recent crises cannot themselves be imposed from the outside, regardless of the good intentions of any international actors. *Praeterita futura praedicant*, as the classicist would say, the past delineates the path of the future.

In any event, this inquiry, if it is to be of any usefulness, must approach its subject with a certain amount of detachment, a characteristic lacking in much of the impassioned political advocacy—to say nothing of wishful thinking—that has been passed off as analysis of the Liberian conflict in the course of the last two decades. What is needed—and what is attempted in the pages that follow—is what the one of the great figures in twentieth century international relations scholarship, Hans Morgenthau, called *"unbendigte Sachlichkeit,"* the objectivity to grasp its reality without confusing the different spheres of life by overbearing moralizing, a tendency very much inherent in contemporary notions of "political correctness." In this regard, Morgenthau's frank counsel is salutary:

> For my part, I certainly prefer the brutality inherent in this approach to the thoughtless sentimentality that neglects its own interests out of sheer, silly emotionality and leaves no room for objective thinking.[12]

From the discovery of the real roots of the conflict can arise the consideration of the lessons that the tragic episode holds not only for the Liberian nation, but also for entire international community as it confronts the chaos of state failure. Liberia may have been the most recent example of the chaos of a failed state, but alas, it is unlikely to be the last. In this last respect, a study of the factors that led to the outbreak of open hostilities as well as a review of both the civil war and the continuing political and military developments may prove to have more than historical utility.

ENDNOTES

1. See the Appendix for a summary definition and taxonomy of the "failed state."
2. Keith B. Richburg, *Out of America: A Black Man Confronts Africa*, rev. ed. (San Diego/ New York/London: Harcourt, 1998), 134.
3. See, *inter alia*, Douglas Farah, "The Tyrant We're Too Willing to Live With," *Washington Post* (August 3, 2003).
4. See Joseph Conrad, *Heart of Darkness* (1902; New York: Penguin Books, 1995).
5. Richburg, *Out of America*, 91.
6. Robert D. Kaplan, "The Coming Anarchy: How Scarcity, Crime, Overpopulation and Disease are Rapidly Destroying the Social Fabric of Our Planet," *The Atlantic Monthly* 273/2 (February 1994): 44–76.
7. Robert D. Kaplan, *The Coming Anarchy: Shattering the Dreams of the Post Cold War* (New York: Vintage Books, 2000), 9.
8. Editorial "The U.S. Role in Liberia," *Chicago Tribune* (July 23, 2003).
9. Editorial "America's Role in Liberia," *New York Times* (July 24, 2003).
10. Editorial "Liberia Denied," *Washington Post* (July 22, 2003).
11. Bill Berkeley, *The Graves Are Not Yet Full: Race, Tribe and Power in the Heart of Africa* (New York: Basic Books, 2001), 10.
12. Quoted in Hans Frei, *Hans J. Morgenthau: An Intellectual Biography* (Baton Rouge, Louisiana: Louisiana State University Press, 2001), 122.

ONE

FINDING LIBERIA

O N January 31, 1820,[1] the frigate *Elizabeth* set sail from its berth at the edge of Rector Street in New York with eighty-nine passengers bound for the west coast of Africa. With three officials and eighty-six settlers, the party constituted the first of what its sponsors at the American Society for Colonizing the Free People of Color in the United States, otherwise known as the American Colonization Society (ACS), hoped would be waves of black emigrants leaving America to found a new commonwealth on their ancestral continent.

THE AMERICAN COLONIZATION SOCIETY

Like most initiatives dealing with relations between the races throughout American history, the ACS was founded at the confluence of motives and interests that, if they were not outright contradictory, were certainly rather divergent. The moving force behind the establishment of the ACS was the Reverend Robert Finley, a Presbyterian minister who directed a well-regarded church academy in Basking Ridge, New Jersey. Finley felt compelled to act by the increasing numbers of free blacks he witnessed settling, not only near his central New Jersey home, but also in New York, Philadelphia, and other population centers in the North. In New York City alone, even with the influx of immigration in the years after the United States won its independence from the British Crown, the number of black residents in relation to the total population rose from less than 5 percent in 1790 to almost 10 percent by 1810. Finley was moved by the lack of education and poverty of the free blacks and was convinced that, even if these disadvantages were remedied, their general social standing in American society would still not improve. As he later confided in an associate: "When I consider what many others have effected for the benefit of their suffering fellow creatures at an earlier age than mine, I am humbled and mortified to think how little I have done."[2]

Taking up the idea of colonization of free blacks in Africa as both a benevolent cause and a divinely ordained mission for Christians, Finley began organizing a number of colloquia at Princeton College and Princeton Theological Seminary, both located near his home, during 1816. He also initiated a vast correspondence to elicit support from his already-established network of personal, academic, and religious contacts. In a letter to one such individual, Finley outlined his three principal objectives:

> The state of free blacks has very much oppressed my mind. Their numbers increase greatly, and their wretchedness too as appears to me. Every thing connected with their condition, including their color, is against them; nor is there much prospect that their state can ever be ameliorated, while they continue among us...Our fathers brought them here, and we are bound, if possible, to repair the injuries inflicted by our fathers. Could they be sent back to Africa, a three-fold benefit would arise. We should be cleared of them; we should send to Africa a population partially civilized and Christianized for its benefits; our blacks themselves would be in a better situation.[3]

With the assistance of his brother-in-law, Elias Caldwell, a prominent Washington attorney and secretary of the Supreme Court of the United States, Finley convened a meeting in the national capital on

December 21, 1816. Some two dozen prominent men, representing the entire geographical and political spectrum of the young republic, attended this first meeting at the Davis Hotel, including Bushrod Washington, nephew of the first president and an Associate Justice of the U.S. Supreme Court; Henry Clay, Speaker of the U.S. House of Representatives; William Crawford, U.S. Secretary of the Treasury; General Andrew Jackson, future president of the United States; John Randolph and Robert Goldsborough, U.S. Senators from Virginia and Maryland, respectively; Congressman Daniel Webster of New Hampshire; Virginia plantation owners Richard Bland Lee and Edmund Lee, uncles of the future Confederate General Robert E. Lee; Colonel Henry Rutgers, a hero of the War of Independence and wealthy New York industrialist and philanthropist after whom the New Jersey state university was later named; the Reverend William Meade, future Episcopal Bishop of Virginia; and Richard Rush, son of Declaration of Independence signer Dr. Benjamin Rush, who became U.S. Attorney-General and interim Secretary of State the following year under President James Monroe.

At this first meeting, the curious mix of motivations brought to the table by the attendees quickly became evident. Clergymen like Finley saw colonization as both a way to expiate for the evils of slavery and a means to spread the Christian faith. Merchants like Rutgers saw in it the possibilities for acquiring new markets abroad. Abolitionists like Rush saw it as the first step towards the emancipation of slaves. Southerners like the Lee brothers saw it as way of defusing a potential problem with free blacks instigating revolts among their enslaved brethren. True to his reputation as the architect of the great legislative compromises of America's Silver Age, Henry Clay, who chaired the meeting, tried to conciliate the differing opinions by summing up the encounter with a rhetorical question: "Can there be a nobler cause than that which, while it proposes to rid our own country of a useless and pernicious, if not a dangerous, portion, of its population, contemplates the spreading of the arts of civilized life, and the possibility of redemption from ignorance and barbarism of a benighted portion of the globe?"[4] Evidently, it did not occur to the Speaker to ask how a group of "useless and pernicious" people could, at the same time, be reasonably expected to spread "the arts of civilized life" to the African continent.

In any event, the Washington meeting ended with a resolution to form the ACS to plan and implement the colonization strategy. The ACS, and its eventual auxiliary organizations, repatriated freeborn blacks, manumitted slaves, and—in cooperation with the United States government—African slaves recaptured from intercepted slaving vessels, until the American Civil War. After the civil war, the ACS would shift its activities to supporting missionary and educational programs before ceasing to operate in 1904. The society would not be dissolved until 1963, when its papers were donated to the Library of Congress and its remaining properties in Liberia passed to the Liberian government. Despite having defended himself against criticism for sending some of his personal slaves for sale in Louisiana by asserting the right of every slaveholder to sell his property, Bushrod Washington, an accomplished lawyer who served thirty-one years on the Supreme Court,[5] was elected first president of the ACS. This contradiction, typical of the *mésalliance* of aims present in the ACS, prompted the eminent German-American historian Herman Eduard von Holst to indict the whole scheme for hypocrisy—if not duplicity—in his monumental *Constitutional and Political History of the United States*:

> The slave states knew exactly what they wished and laughed in their sleeve at seeing the philanthropists of the North fall so readily in the trap. A bait thrown out by the founders of the Society was the gaining of Africa to the Christian religion and Western civilization by means of the settlement of the Negroes there. But they seized every occasion to brand free colored persons as the refuse of the population, whose departure could not be too dearly bought at any price ... With every year not only did this show itself more plainly, but it was also roundly stated that the Society's aim was, in fact, the purification of the land from the rest of the free colored population in order to give security to slavery ... Such a piece of Don Quixoterie has never been indulged in more bitter earnest, and especially by such men. It would not have been possible if political thought had not already been perverted by the baleful influence of slavery.[6]

Nevertheless, the following year, with a $100,000 subsidy from the United States government—an early example of special interest pork-barrel appropriations, the money was ostensibly voted by Congress for the relief and resettlement of Africans rescued from trans-Atlantic slavers rather than for the emigration of free blacks—the ACS dispatched an exploratory mission of two to meet with British colonization societies in London as well as to explore possibilities near the British colony of

Freetown, which had been founded in 1792 as a settlement for some 1,200 former slaves who had received their freedom after having supported the Crown during the American Revolutionary War as well as some sundry criminals deported from Great Britain. The mission was led by Samuel Mills, a prominent member of the American Bible Society, who died at sea while returning from Africa—an eerie presage of the toll in human lives that the Liberian enterprise would ultimately extract. The report of the mission by its sole survivor, Ebenezer Burgess, a professor at Burlington College, Vermont, recommended the establishment of a colony near the British possessions in Sierra Leone, arguing both the convenience of having nearby a settlement that had been founded with similar motives three decades earlier and the perceived opportunities for stopping the slave trade and substituting legitimate commerce. Tellingly, Burgess ignored the experience of the Freetown colony that was originally settled by a private concern, the Sierra Leone Company, founded in 1791, whose methods are were the subject of a damning observation from the African-American sociologist Charles Spurgeon Johnson:

> And so a Sierra Leone Company was formed with the help of an almost hysterical philanthropy. The Blacks from America, the West Indies, Nova Scotia, and Canada were herded together for repatriation. With grim humorlessness, they added to the company sixty unreclaimable White prostitutes, fully confident that the new life and surroundings would change them into faithful and fertile spouses for the returned sons of Africa.[7]

In any event, after less than two decades, the Sierra Leone Company failed due to the high costs of maintaining and defending the colony, which then became a Crown possession.

INAUSPICIOUS BEGINNINGS

As a result of Burgess's enthusiastic report, the scheme took on its own momentum and the *Elizabeth* set sail to plant the new colony. After a voyage of some six weeks, the party reached Sherbro Island in the Gallinas, an archipelago near the present-day Liberian border with Sierra Leone and now belonging to the latter. The party intended the landfall as a mere port of convenience while it searched for a more permanent territory on the West African mainland. However, within a few months, all three officials and twenty-two of the eighty-six settlers had succumbed to either yellow fever or malaria. The remaining settlers, led by the Reverend Daniel Coker decamped to the British colony of Free-town to wait for reinforcements. A former slave who had purchased his freedom and been ordained a minister in the African Methodist Episco-pal Church, Coker had accompanied the expedition as a missionary sent by the Bethel African Methodist Episcopal Church in Baltimore,

This first setback did not deter the ACS, which quickly dispatched a new trio of officials and thirty-three other settlers on the brig *Nautilus*.[8] This group was the first to actually undertake an exploration of the coast of what was to become Liberia. This voyage, however, cost the new ACS agent, Joseph Andrus, his life. In late 1821, the ACS dispatched its third agent in less than a year, Dr. Eli Ayres, who explored the coast with the as-sistance of the U.S.S. *Alligator*, which was cruising the West African coast as part of the American cooperation with the antislavery blockade by His Majesty's Navy. On December 15, 1821, having selected a small island off Cape Mesurado known to the natives as Doukor, Ayres met with chiefs of the Dei and Bassa peoples to negotiate its purchase. The prolonged discussions were hastened to their conclusion on Christmas Eve when Lieutenant Robert Stockton, captain of the *Alligator*, put a pistol to the head of one of the more recalcitrant chieftains. The chiefs agreed to cede land in exchange for six muskets, one barrel of gunpowder, six iron bars, ten iron pots, one box of nails, one box of beads, one box of pipes, two casks of tobacco, a dozen knives, forks, and spoons, six pieces of blue taft, four hats, three coats, three pairs of shoes, twenty mirrors, three handker-chiefs, three pieces of calico, three canes, four umbrellas, one box of soap, and one barrel of rum.[9] Johnson noted that:

> In fact, just two things were certain about this deal: The agents of the colonists believed that they had bought a strip of the Grain Coast and had the deed to it in the paper on which the chiefs had scratched a mark; the chiefs did not know that they were selling their country on which they had lived from the earliest memory of the tribe but, by the rules of Blackstone, they had so bound themselves to the bargain by acceptance of part payment. And so they separated, each side satis-fied that it had concluded a neat transaction.[10]

Nonetheless, the so-called "Doukor Contract" is considered the foundation of Monrovia, the settlement that eventually rose there after the ACS acquired lands on the adjoining mainland through further agreements concluded over the following weeks. Four months later, "Liberia" was established when the survivors of the *Elizabeth* and *Nautilus* expeditions were transferred to the new settlement.

THE LAND OF LIBERTY

From this inauspicious beginning, the colony grew into present-day Liberia, which encompasses 37,190 square miles (96,320 square kilometers), an area slightly larger than that of the state of Tennessee. The coastline of 360 miles (579 kilometers), running in a southeasterly direction, is straight, interrupted by eight rivers—none of which are navigable more than twenty miles (thirty-two kilometers) from the coast—and no natural harbors. The terrain consists of a coastal plain that stretches about twenty-five miles (forty kilometers) inland, where it meets a forty-to-sixty mile wide band of rolling hills that rise as high as 600 feet (183 meters). Three promontories—Cape Mount, Cape Mesurado, and Cape Palmas—break the coastal plain. North of the hills, a plateau that averages between 600 and 900 feet (183 to 274 meters) in elevation covers about half of the national territory. The plateau is broken in several places by mountain ranges that rise as high as 2,000 feet (610 meters). On the northern fringes of the plateau is a small area of highlands peaking at 5,000 feet (1,524 meters).

Although historically a tropical rainforest ran from the coastal plain into the highlands, settlement and logging, legal and illegal, has wiped much of it out. Despite the depravations suffered by the rainforest, average annual rainfall is still among the highest in the world, ranging from eighty inches (two meters) in the interior to over two hundred inches (five meters) along the coast. The heavy rainfall, coming as it does in a concentrated wet season followed by a prolonged dry season, together with geological conditions does not predispose the country to agriculture. In fact, less than 2 percent of the Liberia's surface territory is considered ideal for agriculture.

Little is known of the human history of the region before the establishment of the Liberia colony. It was thought that there were approximately 100,000 to 150,000 inhabitants in the subregion at the time, divided into three ethnolinguistic groups: the Mel and the Mande in the west and northwest of present-day Liberia and the Kwa in the east and southeast. The Mel-speaking inhabitants of Liberia are divided into two ethnic groups, the Gola and the Kissi, both concentrated in the northwest of the country. The Mande-speaking peoples, who largest ethnolinguistic group in the region, are divided into eight ethnic groups in Liberia: the Vai, Mandingo (or Malinké), Mende, Gbande, Loma, Kpelle, Mano (or Mah), and Gio (or Dan). There are six ethnic groups in the Kwa family in Liberia: the Dei, Kuwaa (or Belle), Bassa, Kru, Krahn, and Grebo. Historically, the coastal Kwa peoples knew some seafaring and were often recruited to assist European traders and sailors cruising in local waters. Some Mel- and Mande-speaking peoples, including the Mandingo and the Vai, had contacts with Europeans dating back to the seventeenth century, their chieftains trading African slaves for Western commodities.

THE EARLY YEARS

Following the establishment of Monrovia in 1822, the ACS dispatched a new party of settlers to the colony each year until its independence in 1847, and even thereafter intermittently sent new emigrants from the United States. Between the sailing of the *Elizabeth* expedition in 1820 and the first census of the colony, undertaken in 1843, some 4,571 settlers were sent to West Africa by the ACS. However, the census showed that only 2,388 people lived in the colony. Of these, however, only 1,819 were so-called "repatriates," freeborn blacks or slaves who had obtained their freedom unconditionally and decided to migrate to the colony. These repatriates, however, represented only 40 percent of those the ACS had sent to settle the colony. Some 529 individuals, representing some 12 percent of the emigrants dispatched to the colony, ended up abandoning the enterprising and returning to the United States or migrating to other destinations. As appalling as it may seem to modern sensibilities, it is nonetheless true that some of the returning *émigrés* had found the entire Liberian colonization enterprise so disappointing they even embraced their former slavery to get away from it. A particularly poignant example came during its 1858–1859 session, when the North Carolina state legislature passed a "Bill for the Relief of Emily Hooper of Liberia" that provided

> That Emily Hooper, a negro, and a citizen of Liberia, be and she is hereby permitted, voluntarily, to return to the state of slavery, as the slave of her former owner, Miss Sally Mallet of Chapel Hill.[11]

The Charlotte *Western Democrat*, in its January 11, 1859, edition, observed that Hooper was the daughter of one of the officials of the Liberian government and although she "ranked among the 'big fish' of the free Negro Colony, is sick of freedom and prefers living with her mistress in the Old North State than to being fleeced by abolition friends (?) in Liberia."[12]

The rest of the attrition, some 2,223 individuals, representing nearly 50 percent of the emigrants, died, with about half of these deaths caused by malaria. The so-called "recatives," African slaves whose captors had been intercepted by British, French, or American naval vessels, and who were freed by being deposited at the colony made up the balance of the population. It should be noted that while, under the provisions of the Webster-Ashburton Treaty of 1842, the United States and Britain both committed themselves to maintaining a naval squadron of at least eighty guns off the coast of West Africa to intercept slave ships, the British took more enthusiastically to the task than their American cousins. Between the treaty signing and the U.S. Civil War, the Royal Navy's West Africa Squadron captured 595 slavers, while the U.S. Navy's African Squadron stopped only twenty-four. Nonetheless, a tour of duty off Liberia became something of a right of passage for American naval officers. For example, Commodore Matthew Calbraith Perry, who commanded the African Squadron during the 1840s, went on to open Japan to the West in the following decade. [13]

From 1831, an affiliate of the ACS, the Maryland State Colonization Society (MSCS), organized the separate sending of settlers, mostly repatriates, to its "Colony of Maryland in Africa," later the "State of Maryland in Africa," near Cape Palmas in the southeast of present-day Liberia. The MSCS was the brainchild of a Baltimore merchant, John Latrobe, who envisioned it being the gateway to trade with the southern coast of Africa, the commerce to be monopolized by American traders associated with the society, to whom the settlers would represent a labor pool. One of Latrobe's main investors was none other than the lawyer Francis Scott Key, author of *The Star-Spangled Banner*. In all, the MSCS settled some 1,454 people in its Maryland colony, which was subsequently annexed by Liberia in 1857 and integrated into the country as one of its counties, before the organization ceased its activities at the time of the U.S. Civil War.

The relatively small numbers of black emigrants from the United States and repatriates settled in the Liberian colony account for the pres-

ent-day ethnic composition of the country. Out of an estimated population of 3.3 million, 2.5 percent are descended from settlers dispatched
by the ACS and the MSCS, 2.5 percent are descendants of captured
Africans who were intercepted during their trans-Atlantic crossing by
U.S. and other naval vessels and released to the colony, and 95 percent
are descendants from the original inhabitants of the region.[14] The last
systematic census of Liberia, the one undertaken in 1984, divided the
then population of 2.1 million into seventeen identifiable groups, giving
their numbers both in absolute terms and in proportion to the overall
population:

Bandi.	59,322	2.8%
Bassa	291,106	13.9%
Gio/Dan	164,823	7.8%
Dei.	7,604	0.4%
Gola.	83,148	4.0%
Grebo	188,275	9.0%
"Immigrants/Congo-Recaptives"	45,957	2.2%
Kissi	84,661	4.0%
Kpelle	408,176	19.4%
Kru	154,100	7.3%
Kuwaa/Belle	10,708	0.5%
Loma.	118,716	5.6%
Mandingo/Malinke.	107,186	5.1%
Mano/Mah	149,277	7.1%
Mende.	16,462	0.8%
Vai.	74,950	3.6%
Wee/Krahn	79,352	3.8%

That census also listed "other Liberian tribes" (24,269 or 1.2 percent)
and "other African tribes" (33,526 or 1.6 percent).[15]

Even before the first settler expedition was dispatched, the Board of
Managers of the ACS adopted, in 1820, a document it called the "Constitution for the Government of the African Settlement," latter known
as the "Constitution of 1820," to provide the framework for the government of the eventual colony. The irony of a legally unincorporated
voluntary association of individuals—for that was what the ACS was,
having failed, despite its prominent patrons, to obtain a U.S. congressional charter—creating the binding constitutional legislation for an over-

seas territory that it had not yet acquired has not escaped jurists.[16] This anomalous status was reflected in the Constitution of 1820, which was basically a contract between humanitarian organization in the United States and a community of individuals in a foreign territory, neither of which had any formal ties to the American government. In fact, the scheme of the Constitution of 1820 proved unworkable for the first resident agent of the ACS, Eli Ayres, who was forced out after barely a year in office after the settlers refused to comply with his orders and ransacked a warehouse owned by the sponsoring society.

The ACS sent a one-man fact-finding mission to sort out the troubles in the newly founded colony. This visit resulted in the replacement of Ayres as resident agent in late 1822 by Jehudi Ashmun, who served in that capacity until 1828. A graduate of the University of Vermont with aspirations to go abroad as a Christian missionary, Ashmun viewed his service in Liberia as the fulfillment of a vocation to the ministry. During Ashmun's tenure, the ACS promulgated for the colony a "Plan for Civil Government of Liberia," also known as the "Constitution of 1825." This document created the post of vice-agent, to be filled by a settler appointed by the resident agent as his deputy and chosen from three nominees proposed by the settler community. This vice-agent and two other individuals nominated by the settlers were to constitute the Colonial Council, an advisory board to the resident agent. The Constitution of 1825 also established the office of justice of the peace and various committees, all of which were to be staffed by settlers. The document, however, left all matters of defense and international relations vested in the hands of the ACS. Likewise, appointments to various offices—including those of clerk of the court, constable, secretary of the colony, and public instructors—were left entirely in the discretion of the agent. Annexed to the Constitution of 1825 was a "Digest of the Laws" for the colony that, among other provisions, stipulated that each settler owed two days a week of public labor and legislated against various offenses, including drunkenness and failing to observe the Sabbath.

Ashmun was followed by a succession of agents, none of whom lasted more than a year or two in office. However, his successors continued Ashmun's policy of establishing outlying settlements and trading posts along the coastline as well as upcountry. While Monrovia always occupied a preeminent position, it was not until 1839 that the various settlements were formally united into a single "commonwealth," under one legal regime, through the Constitution of 1839. This document provided for the appointment of a "governor of the colony of Monrovia and president of Liberia" by the ACS. It also established a commonwealth legislature to be made up of the governors of the outlying colonies of Sinoe, Bassa, and Montserrado, as well as five delegates from each of the colonial settlements, elected by their colonial councils. Judicial authority was vested in a Supreme Court of Liberia, consisting of the president sitting with the governors of the colonies.

While the Constitution of 1839 was an improvement over its predecessors with regard to democratic participation, it still left many settlers dissatisfied. However, the most pressing issue for the Liberian commonwealth was not so much the nature of its government as it was a question of its status under the then-prevailing notions of international law. British colonial authorities questioned the right of the Liberian commonwealth, still legally the colony of what was essentially a private corporation, to assert any claims of legal jurisdiction over trade in any part of the region. As a result, during the governorship of Joseph Jenkins Roberts (1842–1848), a serious incident arose which led to the eventual assertion of Liberian independence.

In April 1845, the schooner *Little Ben*, a coastal trading vessel owned by the Freetown-based firm of Cortland and Davidson, was seized by Liberian officials after it refused to pay customs duties at Bassa Cove. Angered by the seizure, the governor of the Freetown colony dispatched a naval vessel, H.M.S. *Lily*, to the Liberian port on a punitive raid. In its retaliation, the *Lily* seized a merchant ship then docked at Bassa Cove, the *John Seys*, which was owned by the future Liberian president Stephen Allen Benson, and towed her back to Sierra Leone. When Benson refused to pay for his ship's capture and storage, the British authorities sold the vessel and her cargo.

In the aftermath of the incident, the British secretary of state for foreign affairs sought clarification from the United States government of its official position on the Liberian commonwealth. In his reply, the American secretary of state, James Buchanan, future president of the United States, asserted that as Liberia was *not* a U.S. colony and, consequently, the American government would not intervene in any disputes between the settlers and Her Britannic Majesty's government. As a consequence of this official position, the British government informed its naval units that while they were to "avoid involving themselves in contentions with the local authorities of the Liberian settlements," they should nonetheless not fail in their duty to "afford efficient protection to British trade against improper assumption of power" by those local authorities.[17]

The episode prefigured a *leitmotiv* that would recur throughout the history of Liberia. Since the ACS was legally a "private person," it followed that the Liberian commonwealth that the society was the proprietor of was likewise a "private person." Under the international law of the time, private entities could not exercise the prerogatives of sovereignty such as regulating trade and collecting taxes. The British government, observing the incorporation of the ACS in the American state of Maryland as well as the American interests in the organization, officially sounded out the government of the United States as to its specific relationship to the Liberian enterprise. The official response from Washington was an unambiguous denial of any responsibility.

INDEPENDENCE

Faced with this state of affairs—nonrecognition of the commonwealth by foreign states and the refusal of the United States government to officially commit itself in any way—the Board of Managers of the ACS adopted resolution in January 1846 calling on the commonwealth to assume full responsibility for its own governance and defense. On July 5, 1847, a constitutional convention convened in Monrovia, with twelve delegates representing the three counties of the commonwealth. On July 26, the delegates proclaimed the independence of the Republic of Liberia with phraseology reminiscent of the American declaration of 1776:

> We, the representatives of the people of the commonwealth of Liberia, in convention assembled, invested with the authority of forming a new government, relying upon the aid and protection of the Great Arbiter of human events, do hereby in the name and on behalf of the people of this commonwealth, publish and declare the said commonwealth a free, sovereign, and independent station, by the name and title of the Republic of Liberia.
>
> While announcing to the nations of the world the new position that the people of this Republic have felt themselves called upon to assume, courtesy to their opinion seems to demand a brief accompanying statement of the causes which induced them, first to expatriate

themselves from the land of their nativity and to form settlements on this barbarous coast, and now to organize their government by the assumption of sovereign and independent character.

The grievances they adduced, however, differed from those that the signers of the Philadelphia document raised, by the inclusion of the significant issue of racial discrimination:

> We, the people of the Republic of Liberia, were originally inhabitants of the United States of North America.
> In some parts of that country we were debarred by law from all rights and privileges of man—in other parts, public sentiment, more powerful than law, frowned us down.
> We were excluded from all participation in the government.
> We were taxed without our consent.
> We were compelled to contribute to the resources of a country which gave us no protection.
> We were made a separate and distinct class, and against us every avenue of improvement was effectively closed. Strangers from other lands, of a color different from ours, were preferred before us.
> We uttered our complaints, but they were unattended to, or only met by alleging the peculiar institutions of the country.

The signers of the Liberian declaration of independence concluded that "all hope of a favorable change in our country thus wholly extinguished in our bosoms, we looked with anxiety for some asylum" and found that "the western coast of Africa was the place selected by American benevolence and philanthropy for our future home," where they would repay the blessings they received by converting the heathen and combating the slave trade:

> The native African bowing down with us before the altar of the living God, declares that from us, feeble as we are, the light of Christianity has gone forth, while upon the curse of curses, the slave trade, a deadly blight has fallen, as far as our influence extends.

The newly independent republic adopted a flag that was likewise modeled on that of the United States, with the alternating six red stripes and five white stripes representing the eleven signers of its declaration of independence and a blue canton, representing the African continent, charged with a single white star, representing the new nation. The constitutional assembly was clearly influenced in its deliberations by the constitution of the United States that was relatively well known to many of the settlers. The constitutional charter adopted, based on a draft by Harvard law professor Simon Greenleaf that had been forwarded to the convention by the ACS, provided for an American-style national government with three theoretically "separate but equal" branches. Legislative power was vested in a bicameral Congress. A Supreme Court, to be filled by presidential appointment, was vested with judicial power and would hear appeals from unspecified local courts. In contrast to the American model, however, the president was vested with expansive executive power: all public officials, other than the members of Congress, were presidential appointees; and, with the exception of the judges of the Supreme Court, all those officials served at the pleasure of the chief executive. The only effective check on the strong presidency was the short term of office for its incumbent: two years, as opposed to the four envisioned in the American constitution. As Amos Sawyer, himself a former Liberian head of state, has observed: "It is curious that the settlers, who ... had desired greater participation in decision making, would now design a highly centralized constitution that provided few opportunities for participation in decision-making roles."[18]

The fact that power was centralized in Monrovia and no provisions were made for local government sparked opposition in the outlying colonial settlements—neither the first nor the last time in Liberia's history that the provinces would feel resentment for political domination from a centralized authority. In fact, during the constitutional convention, delegates from Bassa advocated that the ACS be allowed to continue playing a role in Liberian affairs, believing the U.S.-based philanthropic organization would serve as a check on the political schemes of Monrovia's politically connected merchant class.[19] Again, this failed initiative was to become the precedent for future provincial movements in Liberian politics to appeal for outside intervention in the country's internal affairs as a counterweight to domestic opponents they perceived as acting against their interests.

When their attempts to shape the draft constitution were rebuffed by the Monrovia delegation, some of its opponents in the Bassa region urged voters to reject the charter. Others tried to obstruct the ratification vote by more direct means. In some settlements, they forcibly closed polling places, while in others prospective voters were harassed into boycotting the referendum. Once more, Liberia's first hesitant steps towards democratic self-government set the tone for many a future political undertaking.

In the end, Liberia constituted itself as independent state under the Constitution of 1847, albeit by a less than clear-cut margin. Of the 600 men in the commonwealth twenty-one years old or older and, hence, eligible to vote, only 269 cast ballots, with 211 voting in favor of the draft constitution (and, consequently, of independence) and 58 voting against. One observer has speculated that if all those who had opposed the constitution had actually cast their ballots, the vote would have been much closer.[20]

Ironically—and ominously for the future—there appears in the historical record no dissension to the fact that, having just vindicated their independence on the basis of the discrimination they were subjected to in the United States, Liberia's founding fathers turned around and established a constitutional order on the basis of same sort of inequality and discrimination. Both the statement in the declaration of independence—"We, the people of the Republic of Liberia, were originally inhabitants of the United States of North America"—and the motto of the new republic—"The Love of Liberty Brought Us Here"—proclaimed that the state was established by and for Americo-Liberian settlers. Article V of the constitution linked the right of suffrage to property qualifications and then proceeded to condition the right to own property to citizens, further specifying that "none but persons of Negro descent shall be eligible for citizenship in this Republic." Members of indigenous ethnic groups were, even more ironically, "officially designated 'aborigines'" rather than "Negroes"—denied the right to own property and, by extension, to participate in the political process.

The last ACS-appointed governor, Joseph Jenkins Roberts, was elected as the first president of new country.[21] Roberts was a born Norfolk, Virginia, in 1809, the first of seven children of a freed couple of mixed raced ancestry, James and Amelia Roberts. After his father's death, Roberts and his family joined an ACS expedition that set off for Monrovia in early 1829 on the *Harriet*. Another emigrant on board was James Spriggs Payne, destined to be the future Liberian state's fourth president. Once settled in their new home, the Roberts family took up commerce, trading in palm products, wood, and ivory. The success of their initial enterprise enabled Roberts and his brothers to expand their business into a flourishing coastal trade and become pillars of the local establishment.

In 1833, at the age of twenty-four, Roberts was appointed high sheriff of the colony, the official responsible for leading expeditions of the settler militia to collect taxes from local tribesmen who lived near Monrovia. In 1839, he was appointed deputy to the ACS governor of the commonwealth, Thomas Buchanan, a cousin of U.S. President James Buchanan. When the latter died two years later, the ACS Board of Managers appointed Roberts as Liberia's first nonwhite leader,[22] presiding over the commonwealth's transition to political independence.

Most of Robert's first term in office was spent trying to obtain recognition of Liberia's statehood by the principal powers of the time, whose own scramble for footholds on the African continent represented the greatest potential threat to the new republic. While the July 26, 1847, declaration of independence provided a legal basis for asserting Liberia's self-government and territorial sovereignty, Roberts realized that the juridical writ was worthless unless it was accepted as legitimate by other states in accord with customary international law. Consequently, in 1848, the president traveled to Europe in search of diplomatic recognition, meeting with both Queen Victoria and the Emperor Napoleon III. Great Britain was the first country to recognize Liberia's independence, concluding a treaty of friendship with the new republic that pledged to accept the Liberian government's legal authority to tax and regulate commerce within borders, although the agreement failed to specify what those borders were—an omission that became a source of tension later. British recognition of the fledgling state was motivated by the government's political interest in placating the powerful antislavery lobby that had historically been friendly to the Liberian enterprise as well as its economic interest in having Liberia's assistance in stemming a trans-Atlantic slave trade that was at odds with Britain's commercial interests in West Africa.[23] In fact, the following year, the British government presented Liberia with its first naval vessel, a four-gun cutter, *The Quail*, with which to patrol its coastline against slave traders.

French recognition followed that of Britain, while recognition from the governments of the German port cities of Hamburg, Bremen, and Lubeck, as well as those of Portugal, Brazil, Sardinia, and Austria, came the following year. Perhaps more importantly, however, despite a flurry of communications, Roberts was unable to obtain U.S. recognition from the administration of President James Polk—a non-recognition that lasted through the four successive administrations until Abraham Lincoln conceded diplomatic recognition in 1862.[24]

Part of the reason for Liberia's failure to obtain diplomatic recognition from the United States came out during the congressional debates following Lincoln's proposal, made to the thirty-seventh Congress in 1861, to establish relations with both Liberia and the other black-ruled state, Haiti. Senator Garrett Davis, Unionist of Kentucky, warned his colleagues:

> If, after such a measure should take effect, the Republic of Haiti or the Republic of Liberia were to send their ministers plenipotentiary
>
> or their *chargés d'affaires* to our government, they would have to be received by the President and all the functionaries of the government upon the same terms of equality with such representatives from the other powers. If a full-blooded Black were sent in that capacity from either of the two countries, by the laws of nations, he could demand that he be received precisely on the same terms of equality with the White representatives from the powers on the earth composed by White people.[25]

Willard Saulsbury Sr., a Democratic member of the House of Representatives from Delaware, was even more pointed, thundering:

> How fine it will look after emancipating the slaves in this district, to welcome here at the White House an African, full-blooded, all gilded and belaced, dressed in court style, with wig and sword and tights and shoebuckles and ribbons and spangles and many other adornments which African vanity will suggest ... If this bill should pass the Houses of Congress and become law, I predict that in twelve months some black will walk upon the floor of the Senate and carry his family into that which is apart for foreign ministers. If that is agreeable to the taste and feelings of the people of this country, it is not to mine![26]

Roberts was reelected president three times, serving a total of eight years during Liberia's formative period, before losing the 1855 presidential election to Stephen Allen Benson, the merchant whose vessel had been seized by the H.M.S. *Lily* in the conflict that helped galvanize Liberian independence. After leaving office, Roberts served as a major general of the nascent Liberian army as well as his country's diplomatic representative in London and Paris. He was also instrumental in the foundation of Liberia College, which became in 1962, the University of Liberia. While the Liberian Congress chartered it in 1851, the College only opened its doors in 1862, with Roberts as its first president.

CONSOLIDATING THE STATE

During his four terms in office, Benson continued his predecessor's policy of securing diplomatic recognition for the Liberian state, successfully establishing ties with Belgium (1858), the United States (1862), Italy (1862), Norway and Sweden (1863), and Haiti (1864). At home, his most significant accomplishment was the 1857 absorption of the MSCS colony of Maryland and its integration into the Liberia state as one of its counties.

Benson also presided over the first major conflict between the Liberian central government and the native peoples of the interior of the country, the Sinoe War of 1855. The conflict began with the trade blockade that the Kru peoples of Butaw imposed on trade destined for the Liberian settlements in Sinoe from other peoples in the interior who were eager to break Butaw's longstanding stranglehold on trade with the coast. The dispute had been simmering for several years when Roberts tried to apply pressure by ordering an embargo against Butaw and its allies in 1853. Meanwhile a parallel tension was building up between the Kru peoples and the settlement at Greenville.

The conflict broke out in late 1855 when Krus from Blue Barre seized three deckhands from a visiting British vessel anchored at Greenville. The three men, all from the interior, were accused of breaking the Blue Barre villagers' control over employment with Westerners. Fighting erupted that quickly spread to other settlements. Benson responded by leading the Liberian militia on a three-month campaign through the Kru lands in 1856, exacting a heavy toll in lives and property. When Butaw and its allies surrendered, Benson imposed harsh terms, including trade concessions and a heavy fine of $1,500 that contributed to starvation of the rebel populations. In addition, the people of Blue Barre were dispossessed of their land.

Benson's successor was Daniel Bashiel Warner, who served as president from 1864 to 1868. Warner had served as secretary of state under President Roberts, but had resigned when his advocacy of protectionist measures such as strict ports-of-entry controls and licensing require- ments for trade with the interior conflicted with the free trade policies of the president. Warner's presidency saw the development of partisan politics in Liberia with his protectionist True Whig Party (TWP) being supported by black settlers and opposed by the free trade Republican Party grouped around former President Roberts and supported by the merchant class, many of whom were of mixed-raced descent.

Warner was also concerned with the "aboriginal problem" of how to integrate the native peoples of the interior into Liberian society, al- though his proposal of intermarriage offended the social mores of the dominant settler class. He dispatched an expedition under Benjamin J.K. Anderson that extended the central government's authority and opened a trade route from the coast to the Mandingo savannah via St. Paul, Bopolu, and Musardhu.

Warner was succeeded by James Spriggs Payne, a member of the Republican Party, who served an uneventful two-year term from 1868 to 1870. Payne is best remembered for his role in the settler conflict with the Grebo tribal confederation that took place just before he assumed the presidency. Payne, president-elect at the time was dispatched to Harper by his predecessor to inquire into the matter. The Grebo main- tained that their 1834 treaty with the colony was invalid since the Libe- rian government had since appropriate more land than had been ceded by the agreement. Payne decided that the Grebo were subjects of the Liberian state and that their lands were essentially in the domain of the central government. This ruling was to lead to the Grebo War that would plague Payne's successors.

In late 1869, Edwin James Roye, reputedly one of the richest men in Liberia, was elected president on the True Whig ticket. A freeborn black, he was born in Newark, Ohio, in 1815, and educated at Ohio University. He emigrated to Liberia in 1844 and soon established him- self as one of Monrovia's most prominent merchants, owning trading vessels, a printing press, and other commercial enterprises. After serv- ing in the Liberian House of Representatives and Senate, he was ap- pointed Chief Justice of the Supreme Court in 1865.

When Roye took office in the spring of 1870, the country was in a profound economic crisis that, although precipitated by the govern- ment's liquidity problem, was of long-standing origin. For want of a national bank, a German firm, Woermann & Company, had been for a number of year the chief financial institution in the country, receiving deposits and issuing payment authorizations. Roye proposed the negotiation of an international loan to finance the establishment of a sound currency at par value with specie as well as the construction of national infrastructure. The loan proposal proved controversial and debates surrounding its pursuit overshadowed most of Roye's presidency. In the 1871 elections, former president Roberts was elected to succeed Roye at the end of the latter's term in 1872.

Meanwhile, when the two commissioners Roye appointed to negotiate with British financiers reported the terms of the agreement in late 1871, Monrovia erupted in turmoil. Because the Liberian government did not enjoy an international credit rating at the time and the only security it could offer was future customs revenues, the best terms that the loan commissioners could obtain was a £100,000 loan, discounted by thirty percent and bearing a seven percent interest rate, payable in fifteen years.

The terms outraged the merchants of Monrovia, who were already opposed to Roye, and led to several days of rioting. An assembly of citizens deputed a delegation to meet with the president and demand his resignation. When he refused, a second delegation forced his agreement with threats to try him for treason should he fail to yield his office. Apparently Roye agreed to resign, but delayed doing so, choosing instead to declare a state of emergency. The president tried to call on militia units from upriver settlements to defend him. When help failed to materialize, he tried to take refuge with the American minister-consul, a free black from New Orleans, J. Milton Turner, but was rebuffed. Roye then attempted to flee the country on the English mail steamer then in the port of Monrovia, but was recognized at the dock and stopped by a mob. Roye was declared deposed on October 28, 1871. Vice President James Smith formed an interim government pending the scheduled inauguration of just elected J.J. Roberts in January 1872. Roye, along with his secretaries of state and of the treasury were arrested. When loan commissioner H.W. Johnson returned in early November, he was likewise arrested. His colleague, loan commissioner W. Spencer Anderson, upon hearing of the events in Monrovia, decided that prudence was the better part of valor: he fled with some $24,000 from the loan that was in his possession.

Once Roberts was installed again in the executive mansion, a series

of treason trials were held for prominent members of the Roye government. The U.S. minister-consul's surviving dispatches describe a tense
atmosphere of political trials that eerily resembles more recent events in
Liberian history:

> Such was the unpopularity of the ex-president that it was with great
> difficulty that he procured legal counsel. This latter fact is true as
> relates to all the prisoners, especially the ex-officers some of whom
> reached conviction without legal counsel. The ex-attorney-general,
> having been acquitted of treason, undertook the defense of the ex-
> president, but was called away in the midst of the trial, by a summons
> from the Senate to be present at the trial of impeachment of himself.
> Being unable to obtain a stay of proceedings in either court, and hav-
> ing the expressed opinion of the presiding officer of the Senate to
> the effect that his impeachment would prove equivalent to his ex-
> pulsion from the legal fraternity, the ex-attorney-general decided to
> remain before the Senate and superintendent of his own trial. Thus,
> the ex-president was left during the remainder of his case without
> counsel.[27]

Convicted of treason on February 10, 1872, Roye managed to escape
from prison. Upon being discovered the following morning as he tried
to reach an English ship harbored in the port of Monrovia, he dove into
the water and tried to swim for it before drowning in the attempt. Ironically, such were the state of Liberia's finances, that the new government
was forced to accept the loan as negotiated by Roye's commissioners.

Joseph Roberts served two terms as president (1872–1876) before
James Payne returned to serve a second term (1876–1878). Payne was
succeeded by Anthony Gardiner (1878–1883), whose election consolidated the political dominance that the TWP was to enjoy for just over
a century.

Meanwhile, the tensions between settlers in the Cape Palmas area
and the Kwa-speaking tribes of the Grebo confederation came to a
head. The Grebo conflict was a complex affair, rendered all the more
so because of the long history of contacts that the tribesmen had had
with Europeans. The Episcopal Church in Cape Palmas had opened,
in 1850, a secondary school at its Mount Vaughan mission, an institution through which many Grebo leaders passed. In fact, by the time
hostilities broke out in the 1870s, the Episcopal missions had trained

more than fifty Grebo teachers and lay missionaries who, in turn, were educating a third generation of educated and Christianized Grebo. In fact, the Episcopal Church played a not insignificant role in convincing the two principal rival groups among the Grebo, the Nyomowe and the Kudemowe, to lay aside their traditional hostility—a factor the settlers had long exploited—and form, in late 1873, the "Grebo Reunited Confederation," ostensibly to foster "the progress of civilization and Christianity" among their peoples.[28] Consequently, unlike indigenous peoples elsewhere in Africa, the Grebo had a cadre of leaders who had obtained a Western education and were prepared to demand a place within Liberian society—or threaten to secede if they were not granted it.

When they attempted to get their grievances over land appropriations redressed by the central government in Monrovia, the Grebo confederation repudiated its treaties with the settlers and mobilized between five and seven thousand men in mid-1875. In response the Liberian government assembled a better armed, but outnumbered and undisciplined, force of some one thousand militiamen at Cape Palmas. The government forces tried to dislodge the Grebo with a surprise assault on their garrison at Hoffman Station on October 10, 1875. The government forces, however, met with heavy resistance and forced to retreat back to Harper. Taken aback by the magnitude of its defeat, the Liberian government—by no means for the last time in the country's history—appealed to the United States naval forces in the region for assistance, citing as its pretense the danger to the lives and property of American missionaries in Maryland county. When no response was forthcoming, former president Roberts was pressed into adding his considerable prestige to the appeal.

Consequently the U.S.S. *Alaska* was dispatched to Liberian waters in early 1876. By that time, the Grebo confederation was in control of all of Maryland county, except for Harper, where the remnant of the Liberian militia was besieged. The presence of the American force with its implied threat convinced the Grebo chieftains, who had already made their point with a military victory, to settle with the government. The Grebo acknowledged the sovereignty of the Liberian state. In turn, the government in Monrovia pledged to grant full citizenship to all eligible Grebo tribesmen. The irony of the entire episode was that it was not a conflict fought for a separatist cause, but one that the Grebo undertook only because they had not been successful in obtaining inclusion in the Liberian polity. Regrettably for future history, the central government learned neither that lesson nor the one that its inability to assert its supremacy within national territory without U.S. assistance should have taught it.

Despite the internal difficulties, the principal challenge of the period, which saw increasing European involvement in Africa, was the definition of Liberia's borders with its neighbors and its consequent occasional run-ins with the European powers. In 1879, a German vessel, the *Carlos*, ran aground on the treacherous coast off Nana Kru. The ship was looted and several of her crew were abused by local Kru tribesmen. The German warship *Victoria*, cruising nearby, responded by shelling Nana Kru and several nearby settlements before sailing into Monrovia, where her captain demanded the payment of £900 in damages to the owners and crew of the *Carlos*. Under threat of naval bombardment, the Liberian government had to hurriedly raise a loan from local businessmen in order to pay reparations to the Germans.

In the mean time, the Liberian government was embroiled in a dispute with British colonial authorities in Freetown over the boundaries of their respective territories—the diplomatic recognition of Liberia by the British Crown in 1848 not having specified the territorial expanse of the country's sovereignty. Liberia had long claimed a coastline extending from the San Pedro River in the east to the Jong (or Sherbro) and Sulima Rivers in the west and taking in the Gallinas, where the first settlers had made landfall. British colonial officials, however, only accepted Liberian jurisdiction as far west as the Mano River—and then only on the condition that the Liberian government effectively occupied and controlled the area in question. The dispute simmered for a number of years, especially as British merchants ran into Liberian officials attempting to enforce their writ in the disputed area.

In early 1882, Sir Arthur Edward Havelock, the new colonial governor of the Freetown colony, sailed into Monrovia with four armed vessels and demanded Liberian acceptance of the British position and the payment of monetary compensation for losses incurred by British merchants within the disputed territories. The British position would cost Liberia some sixty miles (ninety-seven kilometers) of coast west of the Mano River as well as the Gallinas. Failing in its appeal to the United States, Liberia was forced to accept the British terms, an action that so upset the ailing President Gardiner that he resigned, to be succeeded by his vice president, Alfred Russell (1883–1884).

The first Liberian-born president, Hilary Johnson, took office in 1884 and served until 1892. Realizing the implications of the 1885 Congress of

Berlin that had carved Africa up between competing European countries, Johnson moved to prevent further European incursions into territory claimed by Liberia by preventatively exercising the "effective occupation" stipulated by the international conference. In 1885, Johnson announced the establishment of a port of entry at Cavalla on the Kru coastal territory. This incursion was met with resistance and, by 1887, violence had broken out and the central government was hard pressed to maintain the semblance of order, much less open a port. Neither able to fight another war so quickly after the fiasco of the Grebo War nor to meet the "effective occupation" standard of the international law then in effect, the Liberian government appealed once more for U.S. assistance, this time to keep France from occupying the power vacuum.

When the United States again refused to intervene, President Johnson sought a treaty with the British authority, ostensibly to settle some technical questions remaining from the earlier western border dispute with the Sierra Leonean colony, but in actuality to obtain British legal recognition of the eastern border of Liberia along the San Pedro River. When the British colonial authorities in Freetown saw through this ruse, the Liberian government tried to grant trade and mining privileges to British firms in the hope that such commercial involvement would attract British protection. Both strategies, consequently, failed.

Only in 1892 did France agree to settle its territorial dispute with Liberia. According to the agreement negotiated by the Liberian consul in Paris, the Belgian Count de Stein,[29] the government in Monrovia ceded to France all territory east of the Cavalla River, receiving in return 25,000 francs and French recognition of Liberia's sovereignty west of the Cavalla. France was also given the right to pursue into Liberia any runaways from the Ivory Coast who might seek sanctuary in Liberia. Interestingly, France also reserved the right to unilaterally repudiate the treaty—as well as its recognition of Liberian sovereignty—in the event that Liberia failed to exercise "effective occupation" of its territory.

Joseph James Cheeseman succeeded Johnson as president in 1892. He was faced almost immediately with another Grebo uprising as the Kudemowe communities of Rocktown and Cavalla declared their independence from Liberia in early 1893 and besieged Liberian settlers in Harper. Cheeseman personally led an expedition of some two hundred militiamen and Nyomowe auxiliaries. Despite the firepower of a new gunboat, the *Gorronammah*, outfitted through an advance from the German firm of Woermann & Company, it took the president most of the year to carry out a pacification campaign. As a result, he proposed the establishment of the first standing army for Liberia.

Cheeseman died as he started his third term in office in 1896 and was succeeded by his vice president, William David Coleman, who served out the remainder of the term before being elected president on his own right. Coleman brought with him into office big ideas of opening up the interior of the country, hoping both to open new trade routes and to assert the central government's authority over tribal chieftains. Coleman's interest in the interior was due largely to his personal history: raised in the upriver settlement of Clay-Ashland, he was the first Liberian head of state to have had an intimate knowledge of the tribal societies. He was also well aware of the inherent instability of the interior regions that presented European imperialists with a potential pretense to annex the area.

Coleman's strategy was essentially military: establish the standing army his predecessor had proposed, deploy its units at garrisons in the interior, and impose the authority of the Liberian central government on the tribes by force. He also proposed making each ethnic group an administrative unit under the direction of the commander of the military unit stationed in its territory, although the commander was to act in consultation with a local dignitary, presumably the incumbent tribal chieftain, to be designated the unit's "general superintendent." The superintendent would oversee the internal matters and receive a stipend from the central government for his services.

The implementation of Coleman's plans was disrupted by the series of regional conflicts that became known as the Sofa Wars, which took their name from the Mandingo horsemen, the *Sofa*, who were at the heart of the upheaval. By the mid-1880s, the French colonial forces in neighboring Guinea had driven back the forces of the chieftain Samory Touré back from the coast, forcing their retreat into the interior. Cut off from his goldmines, the warlord took to slave raiding in order to finance his military campaigns against the French, a practice that was taken up by his various allies among Malinké, Loma, and Mano chieftains. As Samory Touré was pushed back, and especially after his capture by the French in 1898, his *Sofa* units began to break up into separate bands under individual warlords who hired out their services. In Liberia, these mercenaries were particularly active in Gola territory where they were called in by rivals contesting the authority of chieftains recognized by the government in Monrovia. Coleman was forced to mount repeated expeditions to support one loyal chief or another. Not for the last time in its history, Liberia was caught up in local events that were but manifestations of wider conflicts.

President Coleman was forced to resign in 1900 after legislators and prominent citizens united in blaming him for the continuing conflict in Gola country and demanded an immediate change. Vice President Garretson Wilmot Gibson then completed Coleman's unexpired term as president before being elected to a full term, serving until 1904. Gibson, who had been a teacher and missionary before entering politics, adopted a more pacific strategy with regard to the interior. He proposed to assign teachers to all the major chiefs to instruct them on Liberian law. The chiefs were then to be commissioned as government agents responsible for local affairs and the collection of taxes. They would be paid a salary for their services. Gibson also proposed assigning a clerk to each chief, who would report regularly to the secretary of the interior on the chief's administration.

Gibson was succeeded by Arthur Barclay, who served as president until 1912 and, even in retirement, continued to dominate the Liberian political class until his death in 1938. A protégé of Liberia's founding president, Barclay served as personal secretary to Roberts during the latter's final term as head of state (1874–1876) and then ascended to a number of cabinet positions. Barclay entered the presidency facing the same threat from the European powers, principally Britain and France, to intervene if the Liberian government failed to assert "effective occupation" of its interior. The solution that Barclay envisioned was to utilize the existing ruling families of the various ethnic groups, thereby controlling the interior through a system of indirect rule. The central government would recognize the preexisting tribal power structures and guarantee local rulers their control over their subjects in exchange for their collaboration with Monrovia.

The "Barclay Plan," unveiled in 1904, divided Liberia's interior territories into districts drawn with preexisting ethnic and cultural lines in mind. Each district was to be headed by a district commissioner appointed by the president and reporting back to him through the secretary of the interior. Within each district, the chiefs were to be chosen according to traditional customs, but subject to presidential approval through the district commissioner. As long as its exercise did not conflict with either the authority or the policies of the central government, the district commissioners were to uphold power of the chiefs over their peoples. The district commissioners also heard appeals from traditional courts presided over by the chiefs, with their decisions being, in turn, subject to appeal to the judiciary or to the president when he toured the country and held councils to adjudicate local matters.

The district commissioners were to supervise educational, health, agricultural, and commercial matters within their respective districts. The chiefs were charged with maintaining the general welfare of their communities, resolving local disputes and encouraging agriculture. They were also responsible for collecting the taxes imposed by the national government, including the "hut tax," an unpopular flat tax of $1 per annum leveled against each inhabitable native dwelling in the country, receiving a ten percent commission on the monies they collected. The "civilized" domiciles of Americo-Liberians and others who dwelt in Westernized housing were exempted from tax, which was eventually raised to a rate of $6 per annum. The "hut tax" was "widely viewed as one of the areas of repressive government during the first republic, for the manner in which agents of the state went about collecting... terrorizing the inhabitants in order to secure not only the taxes but to requisition food and other local products."[30]

The chiefs were also obliged to provide their subjects as needed for labor on public works as well as to provide the district commissioners with supplies for their upkeep. This last stipulation was to prove highly unpopular as the quota to be provided—set by Barclay at 125 hampers of rice and two containers of palm oil each month from each chief—was usually in excess of the needs of the district commissioner and his household. In times of scarcity, the free provision to the district commissioner of precious resources that he then turned around and sold at inflated prices to the very communities that supplied it caused all manner of resentment.

While the administrative system that Barclay set up was adjusted by each of his predecessors to suit his needs and interests, it remained essentially unaltered until Liberia's first head of state hailing from a native ethnic group, Samuel Doe, seized power in 1980. Although the "indirect rule" system is in desuetude nowadays, certain of the characteristic elements of continue to influence the Liberian polity.

INVESTMENTS, LOANS, AND INTERNATIONALIZATION

Barclay's presidency was also marked by Liberia's quest for foreign direct investment and the consequences of this pursuit. In 1869, a group of Liberian businessmen established the Mining Company of Liberia and obtained a government concession to exploit the country's potential mineral resources. Nothing came of the endeavor because the consortium failed to raise sufficient capital. Nonetheless, in 1881, the concession, renamed the Union Mining Company, was given an even broader charter to engage in railroad construction and trade as well as mining. Again, the controlling syndicate failed to generate the necessary capital to begin operations. In 1901, in the hope of raising capital on the international market, the Liberian Congress voted to transfer Union Mining's concession to a British consortium, West African Gold Concessions Limited. This company, renamed the Liberia Development Company (LDC) in 1904, was run by a former British colonial officer, Sir Harry Hamilton Johnston. Sir Harry was noted for his explorations in West Africa, especially in the Niger Delta, and was the author of a monumental 1,200-page, two-volume reference work entitled *Liberia*, that was not only a history and ethnology, but also a survey of the country's flora, fauna, and geology.[31] LDC quickly bought up the concession granted to the moribund Liberia Rubber Company, renaming it the Monrovia Rubber Company.

The memorandum of understanding signed by the Barclay administration with LDC gave the company a broad charter for commercial activities. LDC received exclusive rights to minerals in Maryland and Montserrado counties as well as nonexclusive rights to open a bank and issue paper currency. LDC was granted the right to import goods duty free; to build bridges, roads, canals, harbors, warehouses, gas and electric works, and telegraph and telephone networks; and to engage in just about any activity that "may tend to the development or improvement of the territories of the Republic and to the benefit of the company."[32] The company undertook to build two roads—from White Plains to Careysburg and from Millsburg to Bopolu—with the government guaranteeing the £10,000 cost of construction until the LDC recouped the amount through tolls. The bank was to have the minimum capitalization of £60,000, the government agreeing to pay a four percent interest on the investment for ten years. The bank was to advance the government £25,000 so that it could retire outstanding debts owed to German firms, the loan being secured by future customs revenues. LDC was allowed to assign its agents to Liberian customs to assure the collection of these revenues. The one-sided deal that LDC drove with the Barclay administration was to prove to be the model for future foreign investors in Liberia.

Even the sums advanced by LDC were insufficient to satisfy the current needs and past-due creditors of the government in Monrovia. In 1906, the Baron Emil d'Erlanger, head of a family of financiers with operations in Paris and Berlin as well as London, agreed to lend the Liberian government £100,000 through his British firm, d'Erlanger Brothers of London. However, given persistent instability in Liberia as well as its uncertain status vis-à-vis the colonial powers, d'Erlanger conditioned the loan on it being payable through LDC—a primitive precursor of some of the more recent credit schemes that successive Liberian regimes have been involved in. The government, while responsible for the entire amount of the loan at a 6 percent rate of interest, would only directly receive £30,000 to meet its current budgetary needs and to pay off its past-due obligations. LDC would receive £7,000 to meet some of the commitments it had undertaken on behalf of the Liberian government. The remaining two-thirds of the loan, some £63,000, would be given to LDC for capital financing, although the sum would be considered a loan from the Liberian government to the company. To obtain d'Erlanger's money, Barclay agreed to the nomination by the British government of two Britons to take charge of the Liberian customs service, one as chief inspector, the other as financial officer.

When the LDC concession ceased operations less than two years later amid acrimonious accusations of misappropriation of funds on the part of the company and extortion on the part of the government, Barclay found himself challenged by domestic political opposition as well as vulnerable to pressure from the British government, which demanded reforms as well as the appointment of a Briton to oversee Liberia's public finances. Barclay sent a delegation to the United States to appeal for both financial aid and a guarantee of his country's independence in the event of a British move to take it over. Once more, the official response from Washington was to rebuff the attempt to embroil the American government in Liberian affairs, U.S. Secretary of State Elihu Root telling the delegation that the sought-after guarantee was "impractical." However, the U.S. government did agree to dispatch a commission to study the situation,[33] whose recommendation was, underneath the diplomatic language, to effectively substitute British domination with American domination.

This was the state of affairs when Daniel Edward Howard became president of Liberia in 1912. Howard came to the presidency through the machinery of the True Whig Party: his father, Thomas, had served as chairman of the TWP, and he himself had been its secretary. The Republican Party not having survived the death of President Roberts in 1876, the TWP had emerged as the dominant organization in Liberian politics with enormous patronage. The last systematic accounting of the Liberia's finances, carried out in 1910, showed that the national government's total debt stood at $1,298,570, 70 percent of which was owed to foreign creditors. With the encouragement of American administration of President William Howard Taft, who was unwilling to involve the U.S. government directly in Liberia's fiscal and political difficulties, President Howard negotiated a loan from a consortium of American bankers—including J.P. Morgan & Company, Kuhn Loeb & Company, the National City Bank of New York, and the First National Bank of New York—and European institutions—including Robert Fleming & Company, the Banque de Paris, and M.M. Warburg & Company.

The loan, at 5 percent interest and redeemable within forty years, amounted to $1.7 million. The sum was considered astronomical in a country where the official annual salary of the head of state was $2,500 and that of a schoolteacher was estimated to be between $100 and $300.[34] The idea was that the loan would enable the government to consolidate its indebtedness and settle all outstanding claims, with the eventual balance of the proceeds being used to meet its current budget and to build up infrastructure. Once again, the customs duties were pledged in payment for the loan, along with other tax revenues. A four-man board of receivership was constituted with an American chairman and British, French, and German members. The first claim on the assigned revenues would be the payment of the salaries and expenses of the four receivers; the second would be the approximately $100,000 needed annually to service the loan. Any eventual residuals would be turned over to the central government in Monrovia, although its budgets were subject to review by the receivers.[35] Part of the loan was also to be used to fund a new permanent military force, the Liberian Frontier Force (LFF), which was to be trained by black officers retired from the U.S. Army.

While the Monrovia-based elites hailed the loan, happy to be rid—even if temporarily—of creditors and pleased by what they perceived as a breakthrough in the closer relations they had long sought with the United States, the agreement was less enthusiastically received in other areas of the country. In particularly, the presence of the international receivers grated against the proud sensibilities of some of the more rural settlers, leading to a several unpleasant incidents directed at foreigners. In some respects, this caught the Monrovia-based foreign envoys off guard as they were led to believe that the "rescue" of the central government would be well-received by the populace as a whole. In one incident, rioters protesting the terms of the loan destroyed some commercial premises owned by German nationals. The German government responded by sending the warship *Panther* to Monrovia with an ultimatum. The Liberian government subsequently had to pay $5,602 in compensation.[36]

The relief that the 1912 loan package provided was short-lived. In the absence of sound management, the Howard administration soon found the state floundering on the edge of economic disaster again. Even after it resorted to cutting the salaries of public employees in half, giving them the other half of their former pay in nontransferable "statements of indebtedness" that were essentially coupons useful only for the payment of taxes or the purchase of public land. Even with draconian measures, the government soon fell months in arrears to its own employees. Things worsened when the Liberian government decided to join the Allies during the First World War and declared war on Germany. The declaration of war was almost gratuitously self-destructive as German U-boats quickly cut off trade to the West African nation and German firms, an increasingly important part of the local economy, left. From 1914 to 1918, Liberian revenues were cut almost in half, not only leaving no residuals for the government, but also threatening the loan service. In fact, during most of the war, the government was forced to enter into an arrangement with the Bank of British West Africa for monthly advances of $9,000 just to meet its bare minimum expenditures.

President Howard attempted to resolve the crisis by securing a $5 million loan from the United States under the provisions of the Second Liberty Loan Act, with the idea that the amount would enable Liberia to retire the 1912 loan and set its financial house in order with American technical assistance. That he sought such a loan under an American program meant to advance credits to facilitate the prosecution of World War I by its military allies was not only a manifestation of Howard's desperation, but also of the almost delusional relationship that the Americo-Liberian ruling class imagined itself to enjoy with the United States. The then-American president that Howard petitioned, it should be recalled, was the same Woodrow Wilson, who had D.W. Griffith's *Birth of a Nation* (originally entitled *The Clansman*) screened in the White House on

February 15, 1915—the first film ever shown in the executive mansion—and described it as "a splendid production." After long negotiations, the Wilson administration agreed to the loan, but only after exacting the most stringent conditions from the Liberian government, including control for an eventual American receiver-general over all revenues and the appointment of several dozen Americans, to be designated by the U.S. government, to supervisory positions over the administration of the Liberian interior and the LFF. In any event, the loan agreement was never carried out because, while it passed the U.S. House of Representatives, failed in the U.S. Senate, where it was debated on the floor before being sent back to die in the Finance Committee. The opposition to the loan was led by Senator William Edgar Borah, Republican of Idaho, who won his colleagues over with his argument that the loan would entangle America in the affairs of the African nation:

> I had rather go down to the Treasury of the United States and take out the $5,000,000 and hand it to the President of Liberia than to turn it over in this way. Then, if the Liberian people could not administer it, it would be their own fault; but I am not in favor of taking over Liberia and bringing it under our protection and control ... I would rather give them the money outright then get messed up in African affairs which will cost us many millions to get away from.[37]

The same Senate also rejected a State Department recommendation of an advance of $12,000 to enable the Liberian delegation to travel to the peace conference at Versailles. As a result of its failure to raise a loan, the Liberian government had to make do with stopgap measures until the Firestone Tire and Rubber Company came on to the scene two years later.

THE COMING OF FIRESTONE

Charles Dunbar Burgess King, Howard's secretary of state, succeeded as Liberia's president in 1920 and was immediately confronted with the country's precarious financial position. With the country's possible liquidation at the hands of its European and American creditors a very real possibility after the U.S. Senate's rejection of the bailout loan, the survival of Liberia became a *cause célèbre* among African diaspora in the Americas. The United Negro Improvement Association (UNIA), an organization dedicated to heightening a sense of black dignity and culture that was founded by the Jamaican-born pan-Africanist Marcus Garvey, proposed to King that it would raise the more than $2 million that Liberia needed to retire its international debt in exchange for a land grant for agricultural and commercial development. Garvey believed that Liberia, then the only independent black-ruled African state other than the mysterious Ethiopian empire that few in the pan-African movement had discovered yet, was the foothold he needed to pursue his vision of liberating the entire African continent. He proposed to move UNIA's headquarters to the land that would be granted to it under the proposed deal and resettle some 20,000 African-American families from the United States there.

Desperate for any solution, President King agreed to deal and appointed his son-in-law, who also happened to be mayor of Monrovia, as the government's official liaison with UNIA in 1920. Within a few years, several hundred black families from America had been sent to Liberia and established in upriver settlements and some agricultural and industrial equipment shipped. However, the promised loan failed to materialize, and the Liberian government grew steadily disenchanted with UNIA and its leader whose self-proclaimed status as "provisional president of Africa" not only struck at the authority of the government in Monrovia, but also antagonized the British and French colonial administrations that President King was trying to fend off. UNIA's opponents in the United States, including the National Association for the Advancement of Colored People (NAACP), also lobbied to undermine its position. The deathblow to the movement in Liberia came with King's inauguration in 1924 when the official U.S. delegate, W.E.B. DuBois suggested to the president that he look favorably at the deal being offered by the Firestone Tire and Rubber Company. Shortly thereafter, UNIA officials in Liberia were arrested and deported and the Garvey's doctrines were proscribed as subversive.[38]

In the wake of the post-World War I economic expansion—one that was literally driven by America's expanding automobile industry—the United States became the world's leading consumer of rubber. However, the British Empire controlled more than three-quarters of the rubber produced globally, making American industry dependent upon an increasingly monopolistic British pricing schemes. In response, aided by a Congressional research subsidy, American businesses sought alternative supply sources. In its quest, the Firestone Rubber and Tire Company of Akron, Ohio, sent a delegation to Liberia in early 1923. Liberia not only had known sources of wild rubber, but also a modest 2,000-acre commercial rubber plantation at Mount Barclay that had been established and subsequently abandoned by the failed LDC.

The Firestone delegation negotiated a series of three agreements with the Liberian government. The first accord granted Firestone a ninety-nine year lease on the Mount Barclay plantation for a $1 an acre rent for the first year and, a flat $6,000 per year rent thereafter.

The second accord gave the firm the right to lease up to one million acres of land, mostly near Harbel, about thirty miles (forty-eight kilometers) north of Monrovia, for ninety-nine years for the annual rent of six cents for each acre actually developed, with a $1,200 per annum minimum and subject to the condition that at least 20,000 acres would be developed within five years. The government was also to receive a 1 percent tax on the value of the rubber exported, calculated on the basis of the prevailing price of the commodity on the New York markets. The agreement also gave the company broad rights to construct, at its own expense, such roads, canals, railroads, and other infrastructure needed to develop its leasehold, even outside the lands granted to it, without any additional rental payment.

The third agreement, never actually implemented, permitted Firestone to build and manage a harbor in Monrovia, obliging the government to reimburse the company up to $300,000 for the construction costs with the balance of the cost, with 7 percent interest, to be collected by the company through docking fees it would charge other users.

As part of its agreements with Firestone, the Liberian government received under provisions of the famous "Clause K"[39] a loan of $5 million from the Finance Corporation of America, a wholly owned subsidiary of Firestone, for purposes of retiring its foreign and domestic debts and funding public services and works, including education and the Liberian Frontier Force. One of the beneficiaries of this funding was Liberia's first radio station, which began broadcasting in 1927. The loan was payable over forty years with revenues to be collected from Liberian customs, postal services, and internal taxes. The revenues were to be administered under the supervision of a financial advisor to be nominated by the president of the United States—needless to say, at the suggestion of the Firestone Company—and formally appointed by the president of Liberia.

The Firestone agreements, at least apparently, proved to be a boon to the Liberian economy as some 10,000 Liberians found employment by 1930, even though the company only developed one-third of the land in its concession area, a larger plantation near Harbel and a smaller one at Cavalla, about thirty miles (forty-eight kilometers) north of Harper in the southeast of the country. The company profited handsomely from its initial $28 million investment, so much so that in 1962, it agreed to pay the government a thirty-five percent royalty on the profits of its Liberian properties. In 1976, the company formally gave up its rights to the 700,000 acres not used and agreed to increase its annual rent to fifty cents an acre. It also agreed to pay for the education through junior high school of the dependents of its Liberian employees. Firestone withdrew from Liberia in 1988 when it transferred its remaining holdings to a Japanese firm.

The presence of Firestone and the other rubber companies that eventually followed Firestone's lead into Liberia[40] served as the principal catalyst for development of Liberia's infrastructure. Firestone provided the impetus for the development of the country's transportation network. Major arteries such as the road between Monrovia and Saniquellie, near Liberia's borders with Guinea and Côte d'Ivoire, were built by the company to meet the needs of its plantations to communicate with the interior. The port of Monrovia and country's international airport were likewise developed as a result of the commercial interests. The hospitals that Firestone operated for its employees and their dependents at Duside and Cavalla were, until the 1960s, the only major medical centers in Liberia. The rubber company also provided elementary schools for the children of its dependents.[41]

On the darker side of the development of the rubber industry was the system of labor recruitment that, although long used in Liberia, only came to the world's attention during this period. Under the agreements with Firestone, the government's Bureau of Labor, an agency of the Department of the Interior, undertook to recruit workers for the rubber plantations and the associated construction works. By an accord with the government, the American tire company's Liberian subsidiary was to pay each unskilled worker a daily wage of twenty-four cents. In addition, the firm was to pay a commission of one cent to the government, one half-cent to the district commissioner of the worker's home district, and one half-cent to the worker's chief for each day of labor provided by the worker. While no significant allegations of mistreatment were brought against the company, the system certainly gave the government and the native chiefs incentives to insure that workers stayed at their jobs.

Similar labor practices in the exportation of workers to the Spanish colony on the island of Fernando Po (now part of Equatorial Guinea), with far less felicitous results, led to the establishment by the League of Nations of an International Commission of Inquiry in 1929. This incident, which will be discussed in the following chapter, led to the resignation, in 1930, of President King and Vice President Allen Yancy.

EDWIN J. BARCLAY

A cousin of former president Arthur Barclay, Secretary of State Edwin James Barclay assumed the presidency after the twin resignations and served until 1944. During his tenure, Barclay had to contend with secessionist agitation among the Kru of Sinoe County, the global economic depression, international pressure to reduce Liberia to a protectorate, and the beginning of the Second World War.

The Kru tribesmen had long served as intermediaries in the slave trade, the suppression of which disrupted social patterns and caused resentment. The central government's attempts to break another long-standing practice—that of exacting tolls for passage through the traditional Kru lands—likewise fueled the tensions. Barclay's response, not only to launch a military campaign against rebellious communities, but to also establish new garrisons of the LFF throughout Kru territory, left deep scars.

The decline in revenues as a result of the worldwide economic depression made Liberian service on its $5 million international debt nearly impossible. By 1932, payments on the 1926 loan consumed nearly two-thirds of the government's revenues. When Firestone refused to renegotiate the terms of the loan in 1932, Barclay declared a unilateral moratorium on payments. He also launched a nationalist economic policy based on the belief that indigenous industries—the spinning wheel was even reintroduced—would be the key to the development of the country.

The response of the international powers, however, was different. A series of League of Nations commissions as well as the diplomatic pressures applied by the American, British, French, and German governments sought to bring the Liberian administration under various forms of international supervision that would have effectively transformed the country into a colonial protectorate. In order to resist this pressure, Barclay embarked on a series of administrative reforms that brought the interior of the country under tighter centralized control. Barclay also had several stringent sedition laws passed which, in their application, fueled the resentment of the educated classes among the ethnic groups of the Liberian interior.

With the outbreak in Europe of World War II, Barclay availed himself of the opportunity to cut ties with the colonial powers of the old continent and to strengthen those with the United States. The Liberian government decreed that British currency would no longer be legal tender within its territory and that only Liberian coins and United States currency would be accepted. In 1942, Barclay negotiated Liberia's nominal entrance into the war on the Allied side in exchange for American assistance with infrastructure construction. The Defense Areas Agreement of that year granted the U.S. the right to build, maintain, and defend military installations in Liberia. The Mutual Aid Agreement of 1943 permitted the U.S. to begin work on Liberia's first deep water port. En route home from a wartime conference with British Prime Minister Winston Churchill at Casablanca, U.S. President Franklin Delano Roosevelt stopped in Liberia on January 26–27, 1943, to pay an informal visit to Barclay, becoming the first American chief executive to visit the West African nation.

Barclay's presidential legacy is a mixed one. While he preserved Liberian sovereignty, he did so at the cost of imposing a centralized presidential regime that contained within itself the seed of future discord. However, perhaps this statesman is best understood, as Amos Sawyer has argued, within context:

> The forced resignation of the King administration in the face of the contract labor scandal struck a blow to presidential authority. The League of Nations' attempts to establish a mandate, under which Liberia was to become a protectorate of a European imperial power, created a grave crisis for the Liberian elite. Developing concomitantly with the pressure to reduce Liberia to a colonial protectorate were internal demands for secession, particularly along the Kru Coast. Faced with these internal and external pressures, President Edwin Barclay sought to reestablish presidential authority. For him, however, the establishment of presidential authority was not an end in itself; he sought to use that authority as an instrument to preserve the integrity of the state.[42]

In fairness to Barclay, it should be noted that, as a check on the presidency, he did push through a constitutional amendment limiting presidential tenure to one term of eight years, whereas the term was previously set at four years with no limitation on reelection (the original two-year term stipulated in the Constitution of 1847 was amended in 1908 to four years).

WILLIAM V.S. TUBMAN

Barclay retired from the presidency at the end of his term of office in 1944, having endorsed William Vacanarat Shadrach Tubman as his successor. Tubman was, in some respects, an outsider to the political establishment in Monrovia. All of Liberia's presidents since 1896 had come from Montserrado County. In fact, with the exception of President Coleman, all had hailed from Monrovia itself. Despite the personal and political differences that distinguished these leaders, they nonetheless came from the same elite circle. Tubman, in contrast, hailed from Harper in Maryland County, where his father had been a prominent Methodist minister before being elected to the Liberian Senate as an ally of the future vice president, Allen Yancy. After attending Cape Palmas Seminary, a secondary institution for the training of lay preachers for the Methodist Church, Tubman read law under the direction of several prominent local practitioners before serving in several county-level administrative posts. Tubman entered national politics in 1923, when he was elected to the Senate with the backing of Yancy, and became a protégé of President Charles King. He was dropped from the True Whig slate in 1931 because of his association with the resigned administration—he had once served as Yancy's lawyer in a labor contract matter—but won back his Senate seat in a by-election in 1934. President Edwin Barclay appointed Tubman as an associate justice of the Liberian Supreme Court in 1937.

Having come to power as a relative "outsider," Tubman undertook to ease the Monrovia elite from their monopoly on the machinery state. His motives, however, were not entirely altruistic: his ambition was to establish a personal power base that was independent of the institutional constraints that acted as a limited check on his predecessors. To this end, Tubman had to enlarge the circle of those involved in the political process, in the hope that the newcomers would create a personal constituency. By constitution amendment, women received the right to vote in 1945. He encouraged the participation of "country people" from the Liberian interior in politics and extended suffrage to indigenous peoples through a 1946 statute. Tubman also appointed men of indigenous descent into positions of power, including Momolu Dukuly, a Mandingo, who served as secretary of state from 1954 to 1960. In 1964, he presided over legal reforms that granted the provinces of the interior the status of "county" on par with the coastal regions. Despite Tubman's efforts, however, while the general welfare of the indigenous majority improved during his tenure, they still faced discrimination from the Americo-Liberian elite.

In his quest to build a personal power base, Tubman also availed himself of the prerogatives that the centralization carried out by his predecessors concentrated in the presidential office. He consequently used the civil service, expanded with the post-World War II economic prosperity, as part of his patronage network. One journalist described Tubman's highly personalized style of rule in the following manner:

> He was the president of Liberia for twenty-eight years, and belonged to what is today a rare category of political boss who rules his country like a squire his manor: they know everyone, decide everything ... Tubman received around sixty people daily. He made appointments to all official positions in the country himself, decided who should receive a concession, which missionaries were to be allowed in. He sent his own people everywhere, and his private police reported to him everything that was happening in this village, or in that one. Not much happened ... Now and then, a group passed before the gates to the government palace carrying a large banner reading "A gigantic manifestation of gratitude for the progress that has taken place in the country thanks to the Incomparable Administration of the President of Liberia — Dr. W.V.S. Tubman."[43]

Having used his influence to repeal Barclay's one-term limit on the presidential incumbent, returning to the previous system of unlimited four-year-terms, and disqualified a new party supported by indigenous intelligentsia, Tubman ran unopposed for reelection in 1951. In the wake of his second inauguration in 1952, a coalition of disenchanted elements from Monrovia elite and indigenous peoples formed an Independent True Whig Party around former president Edwin Barclay to oppose the TWP controlled by the president in the 1955 legislative elections. Although Tubman prevailed over his opponents and was returned to office every four years until his death in 1971, he did so by banning indigenous attempts to register a political party in 1951 and fighting off a challenge by dissident members of the TWP who tried to form an Independent True Whig Party around former president Edwin Barclay in 1953. Thereafter, Liberia was essentially a one-party state. The limited opposition that he did encounter led Tubman to institute a complex network of overlapping security services, including a criminal investigation division of the national police force, a Special Security Service, a National Bureau of Investigation, an Executive Action Bureau, and a National Intelligence and Security Service. These agencies spread fear when they killed Samuel Daniel Coleman, son of former president Coleman and chairman of the Independent Whigs in 1955. In the 1960s, they provided "evidence" for a series of prosecutions of Tubman's opponents, culminating in the 1968 treason trial of Ambassador Henry Boima Fahnbulleh, Sr., who was convicted and sentenced to twenty years at hard labor (he was granted clemency by Tubman's successor in 1971).

Another achievement of the Tubman presidency was the expansion of Liberia's economic sector, with the president's "open door" policy to business. The retirement of the Firestone loan in 1951, the introduction of iron mining by the Liberian-American Mining Company in 1953, and, perhaps most importantly, the enactment of the 1948 Maritime Code which continues to generate revenues for the Liberian state through the registration of foreign-owned ships that are allowed to fly the Liberian flag—and enjoy tax and other economic benefits—contributed to steady economic growth from the mid-1950s through the mid-1960s.

The establishment of the "open registries" program of the fictitious "Liberian Merchant Marine" deserves special mention for its significance not only to the Liberian government to which it contributes nowadays the relatively not-so-negligible sum of over $17,000,000 annually,[44] but also to the international system of commerce. Under the aegis of the International Trust Company of Liberia (and, since January 1, 2000, the Liberian International Shipping and Corporation Registry), a ship owner forms a corporation with a Liberian charter for which he registers the vessel with the payment of minimal application and administrative fees and nominal tonnage taxes. The corporation and its vessel are consequently tax-free outside Liberia since they are legally under Liberian jurisdiction. The entire process could be carried out in Liberia through the office of the Commissioner of Maritime Affairs in Monrovia, or abroad through deputy commissioners based in New York and

Reston, Virginia. The first vessel to participate in this tax dodge scheme was the tanker *World Peace*, owned by Greek shipping magnate Stavros Niachos and chartered to Gulf Oil, which was registered in March 1949. Nowadays, the ship registry operates offices in Vienna, Virginia; New York; London; Zurich; Piraeus, Greece; Hong Kong; and Tokyo; as well as its bombed-out quarters in Monrovia. Business can be transacted even via the internet, complete with downloadable legal forms. In the last quarter of 2002 alone, even as the Liberian government was reeling from rebel attacks, it registered 112 new "Liberian" ships—mainly tankers, cargo vessels, and drilling rigs—to sail the world's oceans.[45] As a result of this facilitation of a "flag of convenience," the "Liberian" merchant marine is second in size only to that of Panama.[46]

Tubman's long tenure in the presidency is difficult to assess. He owed his longevity was a combination of factors, including a long-term vision, his dynamic personality, the network of personal loyalties he built, the manipulation of the political process, and even brute force. On the other hand, his open-door policy enabled Tubman to be able to boast at his 1952 inauguration that he was "happy to confirm that Liberia's internal and external debts had been fully liquidated and Liberia [was]... master of her fiscal affairs."[47] Recognizing the lack of a cadre of civil servants, Tubman used the newfound wealth to increase Liberia's educational budget from the $83,000 he inherited from Edwin Barclay to over $2 million in 1959 as well as to send numerous students to schools abroad, incorporating them into his administration upon their return.[48] Perhaps the most balanced verdict on the president was the one J. Gus Liebenow, who was until his death in 1993 perhaps America's leading scholar of Liberia, rendered shortly before Tubman's death:

> For all his authority, however, Tubman is not a dictator. He has served rather as the managing director of an experiment in controlled change, and he has not been able at any particular moment to stray away from the interests of the Americo-Liberian group that constitutes his main base of political power. Nevertheless, to the possible detriment of his own program of long-range reform, he has become the Indispensable Man. Tribal challengers have not lingered long on the scene, and few Americo-Liberians have been able to build substantial bases of support among the tribal people ... The frequency of Tubman's extended health leaves and his age compel the leadership of the Liberian state to ask the long-avoided question: "After Tubman, what?"[49]

WILLIAM R. TOLBERT, JR.

When Tubman finally died in 1971, his vice president, William Richard Tolbert Jr. succeeded to the presidency amid a period of economic stagnation and increasing discontent over the authoritarian excesses of the last years of the Tubman's tenure. Less charismatic than his predecessor, Tolbert faced an almost impossible task in fulfilling his inaugural pledge to broaden the base of popular participation in government and overcome the historical divisions in Liberian society. While educational opportunities improved during the period—elementary school enrollment went from 31 percent of the population in 1960 to 60 percent in 1980, while secondary school enrollment rose from 2 percent to 20 percent during the same period—the drop in the market prices for Liberia's two principal exports, rubber and iron ore, coupled with the increase in the price of its chief import, oil, wrecked havoc with the economy. Between 1970 and 1979, Liberia's foreign debt rose from $158 million to over $600 million.

The economic stagnation added to domestic tensions and resentment over the wealth of the presidential family. President Tolbert, while still vice president, had cofounded a fishing venture with his University of Michigan-educated brother, Stephen Allen Tolbert, a fishing venture that expanded into the first Liberian-owned multimillion- dollar conglomerate, the Mesurado Group of Companies, that included fishing, frozen foods, detergent, feed, window manufacturing, household soap, agriculture, and other enterprises. Stephen Tolbert, appointed finance minister by his brother in 1972, did not hesitate to use his public office to advance the interests of his conglomerate, prompting the veteran civil rights advocate Albert Porte to pen his broadside *Liberianization or Gobbling Business?*, a book that galvanized the nascent reform movement among Liberia's university teachers and students.[50]

While things simmered at home, Tolbert enjoyed acclaim abroad for his ambitious engagements in international affairs. He reached out to states that his predecessor had avoided, including the Soviet Union and the People's Republic of China, with whom he established diplomatic relations in 1972 and 1978, respectively. While increasing Liberia's involvement with the Organization of African Unity and other African organizations, including the Economic Community of West African States (ECOWAS), which Liberia joined in 1975, he also reached out to South Africa, receiving Prime Minister B.J. Vorster who came to Monrovia in a secret visit that same year. In June 1979, at an estimated cost of $200 million, Tolbert hosted the sixteenth summit of the Organization of African Unity, during which the Liberian president was elected chairman of the OAU.

Overseas, Tolbert was fêted as a model Christian leader and was even elected head of the Baptist World Alliance, an umbrella group for organizations belonging to the denomination. In 1974, the Council of Churches of the City of New York conferred on him its "Family of Man" Gold Medal Award, a recognition that Tolbert held as second in importance only to his chairmanship of the OAU. U.S. President Jimmy Carter visited Tolbert in Monrovia on April 3, 1978, becoming only the second American leader to come to Liberia and the first to do so on an official state visit (Roosevelt's stopover was defined as an "informal call"). Tolbert left a lasting impression on Carter who, twenty-five years later, continues to consider the Liberia of the time as "a symbol of stability and economic progress in West Africa" and to hail its leader as "an enlightened Christian gentleman."[51] Subsequent events were to reveal that many Liberians did not share the American president's optimistic appraisal.

ENDNOTES

1. This is the date given by Amos Sawyer, *The Emergence of Autocracy in Liberia: Tragedy and Challenge* (San Francisco: Institute for Contemporary Studies, 1992), 97; the date of February 4, 1820, is given by Charles S. Johnson, *Bitter Canaan: The Story of the Negro Republic*, edited with introduction by John Stanfield (1987; New Brunswick, New Jersey/ London: Transaction Publishers, 1992), 11.

2. Quoted in Philip John Staudenraus, *The African Colonization Movement, 1816–1875* (New York: Columbia University Press, 1961), 17.

3. Quoted in Werner T. Wickstrom, "The American Colonization Society and Liberia: An Historical Study in Religious Motivation and Achievement, 1817–1867" (Ph.D. diss., Hartford Seminary, 1958), 22.

4. Quoted in Archibald Alexander, *A History of Colonization on the Western Coast of Africa* (1846; New York: Negro Universities Press, 1969), 81–82.

5. See William H. Rehnquist, *The Supreme Court*, rev. ed. (2001; New York: Vintage Books, 2002), 26.

6. Quoted in Johnson, *Bitter Canaan*, 20.

7. *Ibid.*, 18.

8. Regretfully, like all-too-many agencies involved in African relief since, the ACS refused to allow the execution of its pre-conceived plans to be upset by realities on the ground. Rather, it ascribed the increasing mortality rates to everything but the soundness of its original project. As the bad news filtered back over the years, the directors of the ACS employed all sorts of excuses: the conditions in West Africa were no worse than those in the United States, the sick had become such because they had failed to take precautions, etc. See Antonio McDaniel, *Swing Low, Sweet Chariot: The Mortality Cost of Colonizing Liberia in the Nineteenth Century* (Chicago: University of Chicago Press, 1995).

9. See J. Gus Liebenow, *Liberia: The Quest for a Democracy* (Bloomington, Indiana: Indiana University Press, 1987), 19.

10. Johnson, *Bitter Canaan*, 44.

11. Quoted in John Hope Franklin, *The Free Negro in North Carolina, 1790–1860*, rev. ed. (Chapel Hill: University of North Carolina Press, 1995), 219. I am grateful to Ron Clouse for calling to my attention the cases of the freedmen who returned to slavery by securing passage of private bills.

12. *Ibid*.

13. See Hugh Thomas, *The Slave Trade: The Story of the Atlantic Slave Trade*, 1440–1870 (New York: Simon & Schuster, 1997), 661–662, 727–728

14. The data are the estimates, updated to July 2003, contained in *The World Factbook 2003* published by the U.S. Central Intelligence Agency; see www.cia.goc/cia/publications/factbook/geos/li.html.

15. See D. Elwood Dunn, Amos J. Beyan, and Carl Patrick Burrows, *Historical Dictionary of Liberia*, 2nd ed. (Lanham, Maryland/London: Scarecrow Press, 2001), 261.

16. Only in 1831 when, despite repeated petitions, the ACS continued to fail in its attempt to obtain a congressional charter, did its officers apply for and receive a charter of incorporation from the state of Maryland.

17. The documentation of these diplomatic communications can be found in the first volume of the two-volume work of Charles Henry Huberich, *The Political and Legislative History of Liberia, 1847–1844* (New York: Central Book Company, 1947).

18. Sawyer, *The Emergence of Autocracy in Liberia,* 94.

19. See Huberich, *The Political and Legislative History of Liberia,* vol. 1, 822–832.

20. See *ibid*., 845–846

21. The precise date that Roberts ceased to function as "Governor of Monrovia and President of the Liberian Commonwealth" and began to govern as "President of the Republic of Liberia" is uncertain. Most Liberian scholars have opted to simply give his presidency the generic inaugural date of "1848"; see Sawyer, *The Emergence of Autocracy in Liberia*, 315. Sawyer, a respected U.S.-educated scholar who served himself as Liberia's head of state as president of the Interim Government of National Unity from November 23, 1990, until August 18, 1993, is as good of a source as any on the matter of Liberian presidential succession.

22. Johnson observed about Roberts that "his sharp, chiseled figures, brown hair, blond mustache, and gray eyes marked him as Black largely by courtesy" (*Bitter Canaan*, 74)

23. See David M. Foley, "British Policy in Liberia, 1862–1912" (Ph.D. diss., University of London, 1965).

24. On March 11, 1863, Lincoln appointed John J. Henry of Delaware as "United States Commissioner and Consul-General in Liberia." Henry, however, refused to accept the appointment. Abraham Hanson was appointed on June 8, 1863, and arrived on post on February 23, 1864. Hanson died in Monrovia two years later. Hanson's successors, all businessmen with commercial interests in the region, carried the title of "Minister Resident and Consul General" until the appointment of Charles E. Mitchell on January 20, 1931, as "Envoy Extraordinary and Minister Plenipotentiary." This upgrade in the mission's rank had less to do with Liberia's status within American diplomacy as the diplomatic title of "minister resident" was hardly applicable to Mitchell who never even presented his credentials to the Liberiam government. On March 18, 1949, Edward R. Dudley, then U.S. Envoy Extraordinary and Minister Plenipotentiary was promoted to be the first U.S. Ambassador Extraordinary and Plenipotentiary in Liberia. Only with the appointment of Elbert G. Mathews on August 12, 1959, did the post of chief of mission in Liberia become an appointment for a career diplomat within the American diplomacy. In addition, throughtout the nineteenth and well into the twentieth century, almost all of the U.S. envoys sent to Liberia were African-Americans, the position being considered—along with that of envoy to Haiti—by the State Department a "negro post."

25. Quoted in Johnson, *Bitter Canaan*, 83.

26. *Ibid*.

27. Quoted in Sawyer, *The Emergence of Autocracy in Liberia*, 349.

28. Jane Jackson Martin, "The Dual Legacy: Government Authority and Mission Influence among the Grebo of Eastern Liberia, 1834–1910" (Ph.D. diss., Boston Universoty, 1968), 264.

29. Until the 1930s, all of Liberia's permanent diplomatic representatives abroad were non-Liberians.

30. Dunn *et al., Historical Dictionary of Liberia*, 170.

31. See Harry Hamilton Johnston, *Liberia*, 2 vols. (New York: Dodd, Mead & Company, 1906)

32. Quoted in Foley, "British Policy in Liberia, 1862–1912," 137.

33. The commission was chaired by Roland Post Faulkner, an official of the U.S. Immigration Commission. The two other members were George Sale, superintendent of schools of the American Baptist Home Mission Society, and Emmet Scott, former secretary of the noted African-American scholar Booker T. Washington. The composition of the commission has been echoed down throughout the history of U.S-Liberian relations: a mixture of bureaucratic, religious, and African-American interests.

34. Raw (and fragmentary) economic data are complied in Sawyer, *The Emergence of Autocracy in Liberia*, 351–353.

35. It should be noted, however, that the receivers exercised this power only once, in 1913, when it revised down the revenue estimates in the budget passed by the Liberian Congress; see Raymond Leslie Buell, *The Native Problem in Africa*, vol 2 (1928; Hamden, Connecticut: Archon Books, 1965), 806.

36. See *ibid*., 807.

37. Quoted in Johnson, *Bitter Canaan*, 109.

38. Notwithstanding the expulsion of UNIA, small numbers of individual adherents to Garvey's ideology continued to come and settle in Liberia until the 1950s, believing that it was the place where they could build an African civilization.

39. Although the provision is known as "Clause K," the designation under which it was debated at the time, the relevant text is actually to be found at clause J of the fourth article of the agreement.

40. B. F. Goodrich received a concession in 1964. The Liberian Agriculture Company and the Salala Rubber Company were established in 1959.

41. Although an 1912 law made elementary schooling obligatory in Liberia, the country's persistent financial difficulties left it unable to make provision for its implementation.

42. Sawyer, *The Emergence of Autocracy in Liberia*, 275

43. Ryszard Kapuscinki, *The Shadow of the Sun*, trans. Klara Glowczewska (New York/Toronto: Alfred A. Knopf, 2001), 242.

44. Economist Intelligence Unit, *Guinea, Sierra Leone, Liberia Country Report* (September 2002): 56.

45. See *Flagship: News from the Liberian Registry* 9 (June 2003): 3.

46. See Toby Shelley, "Union Queries Role of Flags of Convenience," *Financial Times* (December 12, 2002).

47. Quoted in Thomas Patrick Melady, *Profiles of African Leaders* (New York: Macmillan, 1961), 104.

48. See *ibid*., 105.

49. J. Gus Liebenow, *Liberia: The Evolution of Privilege* (Ithaca, New York: Cornell Univserity Press, 1969,) 219.

50. See Albert Porte, *Liberianization or Gobbing Business?* (Crozierville, Liberia: Porte, 1974).

51. Jimmy Carter, "There's Hope in Liberia's History," *New York Times* (July 13, 2003).

TWO

A COMPLEX TAPESTRY

J OURNALISM, ESPECIALLY IN THE AGE of the sound-byte and news-as-entertainment, necessarily simplifies not only the manner facts are reported, but also what events actually receive any attention. However, simplification always carries the risk of distortion and the consequent misperceptions of reality. While in most cases this process operates at an almost subconsciously, without willful intent, it can happen that the resulting misinformation about realities coincides with the interests of one or another side in an ongoing situation of conflict. This has certainly been the case with coverage of the Liberian conflicts of recent years when journalists and other commentators have referred to the West African nation as "founded in 1847 by offspring of American slaves,"[1] "a homeland for freed American slaves,"[2] or other similar terms. The impression left is that Liberian society is relatively homogenous, when the truth is quite the opposite, as has been seen. In fact, the very idea of the colonization, enshrined in the Liberian Declaration of Independence that defined the new state as "an asylum for free people of color" who "were originally inhabitants of the United States of North America," is intensely divisive, excluding from the founding vision of the political community the overwhelming majority of the population, who were, in fact, legally excluded until the reforms enacted under President William Tubman beginning in 1946. Consequently, in reporting as historical fact what is essentially a divisive ideological vision, the media unwittingly compromised its claim to journalistic objectivity.

SETTLERS AND CONGOS

Social divisions, in fact, have characterized the complex tapestry of Liberian society from the very beginning. As noted in the previous chapter, the population of the early Liberia colony divided itself into two classes of settlers. The first group consisted of free blacks as well as mulattoes and other persons of mixed descent who alone were considered citizens under the provisions of the Liberian Commonwealth Constitution of 1839 which limited the rights and privileges of citizenship "to all colored persons emigrating from the United States of America, or any District or Territory thereof, which the approbation, or under the sanction of the American Colonization Society, or of any Society auxiliary to the same, or of any State Colonization Society of the United States, which shall have adopted the Constitution of the American Colonization Society, shall be entitled to all the privileges of citizens of Liberia." For the brief period up to 1827, these settlers from America constituted the bulk of the emigrants to the new colony.

The Americo-Liberian settlers, as they came to be known, were themselves subdivided between mulattoes and full-blooded blacks, the division being not only one of ethnic heritage, but also of politics: the mulattoes tended to support the free-trade Republic Party, while the blacks tended toward the protectionist True Whig Party. Of Liberia's early leaders, Presidents Roberts and Payne were mulattoes, while Presidents Benson, Warner, and Roye were blacks. After Payne's second term, all subsequent Liberian leaders were black, as the distinction receded and mulattoes and blacks integrated into a single settler aristocracy.

In the two decades from 1827 until independence, however, the majority of those who arrived in the colony consisted of the so-called recaptured Africans ("recaptives") who had been taken into slavery after slave trading had been officially abolished by the British Empire (1807) and the United States (1808). Slaves ships that were intercepted were rerouted to either the British colony at Freetown or to Liberia, where their human cargo was released. Since these individuals were often taken from more distant parts of the western and southwestern coastlines, they were generally unable to return home and were settled in the colonial settlements. In Liberia, the recaptives were often called "Congos" because of the presumption that they came from the Congo River basin area. While the early recaptives were absorbed directly into the settler community, in 1834, a new agricultural settlement, New Georgia, was established exclusively for them near Monrovia.

The trend towards a cleavage between voluntary settlers from America and the recaptives who became, effectively, involuntary settlers in the colony, was reinforced with the capture, in 1846, of the trans-Atlantic slave ship *Pons*, whose 756 captives were deposited in Monrovia. Over the next fourteen years, until the American Civil War, the U.S. Navy dropped some five thousand recaptured Africans in Liberia, a number that seemed overwhelming to the settlers and threatened their sense of cultural homogeneity.[3] To deal with this challenge, the Legislative Council of the Liberian Commonwealth passed the Apprenticeship Act of 1846, which stipulated that each recaptive was to be assigned to a settler. Adult male recaptives were to be assigned to merchants or craftsmen to learn their trades. Adult female recaptives were to be assigned to settler women to learn domestic skills. When these "apprentices" completed their training, they were settled in towns like New Georgia that adjoined those occupied by the settlers from America and soon became known as "Congo towns."

Recaptive children were also assigned to families to be trained, although their hosts were obliged by law to see to it that they attended school at least one month each year. The children were to live with their assigned settler families, who were paid an allowance for their upkeep, until the reached the age of twenty-one, in the case of boys, and eighteen, in the case of girls. In many cases, in addition to the incentive of receiving the monetary allowance, the host families saw the system as one that provided them with free labor in exchange for room and board. In an eerie recall of symbols of status in the antebellum American South, one Liberian statesman has admitted that "it was usually a proud boast and an indication of status for New World settler families to have recaptives working in their fields or households."[4]

Despite abuses, the apprenticeship system served over time as a vehicle for cultural assimilation as many recaptives adopted the language, names, religion, and culture of their settler guardians. Eventually, after finding themselves a place in the working classes of Liberian society, most recaptives were admitted to citizenship. In fact, until the 1940s, settlers and Congos were the only social groups admitted to Liberian citizenship. Although some social, economic, and political discrimination continued well into the middle of the twentieth century, by and large, descendants of the recaptives had become almost entirely assimilated into the overall settler society. In recent years, although the distinction between Americo-Liberian settlers and Congos is still noted, its social significance has been much diminished.

KNITTING THE SOCIAL FABRIC

Just as the ACS was motivated by a variety of interests, so too binding the settlers together during the difficult early years of the Liberian enterprise was a unifying vision that was a curious mixture of religion and political ideology, a vision that continued to exercise its influence throughout the country's history. Stephen Ellis described the outward manifestations of this vision:

> During the heyday of the rule of the settler-dominated True Whig Party, which governed Liberia for all but six years between 1870 and 1980, elite families were intensely proud of their Christian heritage and the American-style institutions of government and culture which marked them out from the despised "country people" or "tribal people," the name generally applied to Liberians of non-American origin. As late as the 1960s, Liberian politicians dressed for formal occasions in top hats and tail-coats. Elite Liberians did not speak African languages. Office workers sweltered in three-piece suits, collars and ties. Young Liberian sophisticates danced to Tamla Motown at discos and parties and despised African music. The sons and daughters of the wealthy, educated in the United States and Britain, referred to other West Africans disdainfully as "coasters."[5]

The settlers viewed themselves as pioneers in establishing an African beachhead for civilization and the Christian religion, the two goods being perceived as intrinsically linked as the Declaration of Independence boasted: "The native African bowing down with us before the altar of the living God, declares that from us, feeble as we are, the light of Christianity has gone forth, while upon that curse of curses, the slave trade, a deadly blight has fallen, as far as our influence extends." Ryszard Kapuściński chronicled the practical implications of this ideology as it unfolded in both the settlers' conduct and in their relations with indigenous ethnic communities:

> The two groups [of settlers and native peoples] usually lived far from each other, and their contacts are infrequent and sporadic. The new masters keep to the coast and to the settlements they have built there ... It would not be until one hundred years after the creation of Liberia that its president ... ventured for the first time into the country's interior. The newcomers from America, unable to set themselves apart from the locals by skin color or physical type, try to underline their difference and superiority in some other way. In the frightfully hot and humid climate, men walk about in morning coats and spencers, sport derbies and white gloves. Ladies usually stay at home, or if they do go out into the street ... they do so in stiff crinolines, heavy wigs, and hats decorated with artificial flowers. The houses the members of these high, exclusive echelons live in are faithful reproductions of the manors and palaces built by white plantation owners of in the American South. The religious world of the Americo-Liberians is similarly closed and inaccessible to the native Africans. They are ardent Baptists and Methodists. They build their simple churches in the new land, and spend all their free time within, singing pious hymns and listening to topical sermons. With time, these temples will come to serve also as venues for social gatherings, as exclusive private clubs.[6]

During their long domination of Liberian politics, the Americo-Liberian settlers (and their assimilated Congo neighbors) found it impossible to separate their religious and political doctrines. In his 1904 inaugural address, President Arthur Barclay even declared explicitly: "Every convert from heathenism to the Christian faith in this country is also a political recruit."[7]

Consequently, from the establishment, in 1823, of Monrovia's first house of worship, the Providence Baptist Church, by the Reverend Lott Carey, a former slave in Virginia who had purchased his freedom and studied for the ministry, religion has played prominent role in Liberian society, albeit not without problems. By the 1830s, missionaries from the Episcopal, Methodist, Presbyterian, and Roman Catholic churches were being sent to establish mission stations to propagate their respective faiths. While missionary work in Liberia was directed primarily at making converts, "education, especially literacy in English, was perceived as an indispensable instrument of Christian conversion and the Western style of life as requisite outward evidence of conversion."[8]

Not surprisingly, the Christian clergy supplied a disproportionate number of Liberia's political leaders. The Reverend Carey served briefly as the interim colonial agent in 1828 and was subsequently elected vice-agent. During the nineteenth century every settler who served as colonial agent, commonwealth governor, or president of the republic was either an ordained Christian minister or a high-ranking officers of one of the Christian denominations. This trend has persisted to the present day with the recently resigned President Charles Ghankay Taylor, a Baptist lay minister, who was given to addressing mass revival meetings alongside internationally renowned evangelical preachers.[9]

This close association of church and state is not without detriment to the traditional role of churches within civil society to call attention to injustice and other moral faults in the body politic. In many respects, their longstanding ties with the country's power structure and their relationship to the national ideology have, to a greater or lesser extent, compromised the independence of the various Christian denominations in Liberia. President William Tolbert's last deputy, for example, Bennie Dee Warner, was simultaneously vice president of Liberia and bishop of the country's United Methodist Church. Even the current Roman Catholic archbishop of Monrovia, Michael Kpakala Francis, the recipient of the 1999 Robert F. Kennedy Human Rights Award and other marks of international acclaim, tempers his advocacy according to the changing political currents. While Francis, the son of a Lebanese merchant and his Liberian wife, likes to compare himself to St. Thomas à Becket, the twelfth century archbishop of Canterbury whose resistance to King Henry II cost him his life,[10] a more apt model might be that offered by Charles-Maurice de Talleyrand-Perigord, the wily bishop who not only survived the vicissitudes of the French Revolution, the Napoleonic Wars, the Bourbon Restoration, and the July Monarchy, but prospered because of his uncanny ability to defect to the winning side in each transition by recasting himself as the sworn enemy of the fallen regime. In

2001, Francis happily accepted an *ersatz* national award from President
Taylor, having previously served the regime on several government
commissions, including one that voted the Liberian leader a doctorate
from the University of Liberia. Earlier in his career, the archbishop was
decorated with the Order of the Star of Liberia by the last True Whig
president, William Tolbert. Interestingly, during the incursions into
Monrovia by the rebel forces of the Liberians United for Reconciliation and Democracy (LURD) in 2002, during which several Catholic
missionaries were kidnapped, the prelate found it convenient to be
abroad touring Canada and Mexico as well as the United States, where
he maintains a *pied-à-terre* in New Jersey as well as several "charitable"
corporations and bank accounts, some dating to the TWP era.[11]

Liberian historian Amos Jones Beyan has agrued convincingly that
Christianity in Liberia allowed itself to be perverted into an ideological
tool that the entrenched rulers of any given period used to oppress the
masses:

> [Christianity] enabled [Liberian leaders] to easily veil their political
> and other mistakes. No wonder Christian thoughts and values were
> encouraged, or, in some cases, made compulsory in Liberia ... While
> this helped to secure the leverage and leadership of the individuals
> in question, it made Liberia's elite unable to treat critically the vari-
> ous social problems of that country ... [Thus Christianity should be
> counted] among the obstacles to the meaningful development of that
> country.[12]

Paul Gifford recounted how this faith-as-ideological-tool worked
during the rule of Samuel Doe:

> Doe could use Christian phraseology at will—almost as well as Tub-
> man and Tolbert before him. So could his ministers ... when it suited
> them. And it seemed to be one of Vice President Moniba's functions
> to receive visiting evangelists, to give them his blessing—even to re-
> cite the sinner's prayer with them. This function was of considerable
> value to the regime, for the evangelists would invariably speak of
> Liberia's "God-fearing leaders" in their crusades, usually to sustained
> applause. Meanwhile society did not change for the better. Quite the
> reverse.[13]

The Christian denominations were instrumental in establishing education institutions in Liberia. The Methodists established the Liberia Conference Seminary, later renamed the College of West Africa, in 1839. This was followed by the Alexander Academy School, founded in 1849, by the Presbyterians, and destined to be the alma mater of many of nineteenth century Liberia's most prominent public figures. The following year, the Episcopal Church opened a secondary school at its Mount Vaughan Mission, near Cape Palmas. The establishment of the post-secondary Hoffman Institute, founded in 1862, followed. However, in keeping with the vision of "civilizing and Christianizing"—not necessarily in that order—the country, the curricula of these institutions revealed a greater preoccupation with classical liberal arts than with meeting any practical educational needs of a West African society. The College of West Africa, for example, had a curriculum consisting of algebra, Bible history, English literature, French, geometry, Greek, history, Latin, music, physics, political science, psychology, rhetoric, zoology, and a course called "General Knowledge in Quotation."[14] It was only at the beginning of the twentieth century with the realization that Liberia needed to develop economic self-reliance that more practical training was incorporated into the curriculum of the schools.

Alongside the churches, fraternal organizations, many of them importations from the United States or imitations of associations among the white population of America, played an important part in the maintenance of the social fabric of society in Liberia. Among the organizations established were the Ancient Free and Accepted Masons of the Republic of Liberia, founded in 1867, and the Grand United Order of Odd Fellows, founded in 1888. Membership in these organizations was an important status symbol and their historical role in Liberian polity has yet to adequately studied. Among the grand masters of Liberian freemasonry were Presidents Joseph Jenkins Roberts, William David Coleman, Charles D.B. King, and William V.S. Tubman.

Perhaps even more important than their substance is the form that the various institutions of Liberian civil society—churches, schools, and associations—lent in a settler culture that was driven by almost compulsive drive to give the perception of being "civilized," not only for the sake of self-reaffirmation, but for that of vindication before the court of international public opinion. While this was especially true in the age when notions of the "white man's burden" and the *mission civilisatrice*" were employed to justify colonial imperialism, its essential truth remains undiminished in the era of globalization when the gap between the haves and have-nots is all the more stark.

OUTREACH TO NATIVES

From the earliest days of the colonization enterprise, relations between the Americo-Liberian settlers (and the recaptives who had been absorbed into settler society) and the native peoples of what would be Liberia were characterized by the particular local version of the *mission civilisatrice*. The ACS stressed from the beginning that one of its goals was to have the settlers "aid the natives in procuring instruction in the elements of knowledge in agriculture, and the arts of civilized life, and the doctrines and precepts of our Holy Religion."[15] To this end, as early as 1825, the ACS encouraged an apprenticeship scheme, similar to the one employed for the recaptives, whereby children from indigenous ethnic communities were placed with settler families to be taught reading, writing, and arithmetic, in addition to some trade or skill, before being returned to their native communities at the age of twenty-one for boys or eighteen for girls. This practice continued throughout the nineteenth century, even after Liberia achieved independence, with as many as 2,500 children being placed as "apprentices" at any given time.

However, despite this initiative, with the exception of instances when indigenous peoples resisted the establishment of the Liberian state's authority, such as was the case with the Grebo upheavals in the 1870s, they were generally ignored by the central government in Monrovia. Although the Liberian Congress passed the Interior Department Act creating a government agency to deal with the affairs of the territories and peoples of country's interior provinces during its 1869–1870 legislative session, it was not until over two decades later that a secretary of the interior was appointed in 1892. By that time, the Liberian government was faced with the task of establishing "effective occupation" of the territories it claimed or risk losing them to European colonial powers. Despite the racial discrimination they had suffered in America before emigrating the Americo-Liberian settlers' "views of Africa and Africans were essentially those of nineteenth century whites in the United States. The bonds of culture were stronger than the bonds of race, and the settlers clung tenaciously to the subtle differences that set them apart from the tribal 'savages' in their midst."[16]

As noted in the previous chapter, in 1904, President Arthur Barclay incorporated the preexisting ruling families of the different ethnic groups, organizing the interior into a system of indirect rule whereby resident district commissioners appointed from Monrovia would uphold the authority of traditional tribal chieftains in exchange for the chiefs implementing such policies as ordained by the central government. Barclay's successor, Daniel E. Howard, refined the system in 1913, creating the position of commissioner-at-large, a sort of traveling inspector reporting to the secretary of the interior, as well as introducing government attachés to supervise the proceedings of the *Poro* (for men) and *Sande* (for women) societies that play an integral part in the initiation rituals and general social ordering of the indigenous peoples of Liberia. In 1914, the Howard administration introduced new legislation that amalgamated the traditional clans, around which indigenous communities were organized, into territorial chiefdoms, each headed by a paramount chief who ostensibly was to be elected, but who was actually appointed by the government in Monrovia. This process, a break with the traditions associated with the clan chiefs, undermined the legitimacy of the paramount chiefs who came to be seen as representatives of the regime among their people rather than their people's representative to the national authorities.

With the establishment of the Liberian Frontier Force (LFF), the district commissioners—many of whom were less successful relatives or clients of members of the coastal political elites who hoped to utilize their appointments as an entry to higher positions in the civil service back on the coast—acquired the muscle to enforce their writ in the areas they governed. In 1921, amid Liberia's financial crisis, the government empowered the commissioners to tax residents of their districts to obtain their salaries and those of the members of their staff. These taxes came in addition to the rations of food and other supplies that the commissioners were already authorized to collect from the local chiefs. The local villages were also obliged to supply any additional provisions and services that the commissioner deemed necessary for official reasons, such as the visit of government officials from Monrovia.

In addition to the collection of the different taxes and other imposts, the district commissioners could employ their LFF detachments to conscript villagers to carry out public works, including road construction and the maintenance of district headquarters. This prerogative to compel involuntary labor was open to a number of abuses. As Graham Greene related in the chronicle of his travels through the Liberian in-

terior in 1935, *Journey Without Maps*,[17] many district commissioners
pressed people into service as porters for private individuals, augment-
ing their official salaries with the sums that travelers paid to them (and
which they presumably did not pass on to the indigenous porters) to
impress able-bodied men to carry them in their hammocks as well as
their supplies while they toured the interior. For those who failed to
submit to the abuse were dealt with harshly, as one African-American
visitor reported:

> The incentives were punishments which took ingenious turns—
> "smoked in the kitchen" and "No. 1 basket," for example. In the
> first instance, a refractory native was put up on the roof of one of
> the windowless native huts and fire built under him. The discomfort
> of slow suffocation inevitably changed the victim's attitude toward
> work. The "No. 1 basket" was a favorite punishment for natives and
> was likewise sport for the soldiers who oversaw the gangs. A double
> woven container with curled edges, about two feet in diameter and
> fifteen inches deep, with a concave bottom, constituted the basket.
> Normally, when filled, it required four men to carry it. For the recal-
> citrant laborer the basket was filled with dirt and stones and placed
> on the man's head, and given a spin. Or a man might be ordered to
> walk or turn around with it upon his head. It could break the neck or
> otherwise injure the spine, and there were many fatalities.[18]

The system of indirect rule was adapted even as, with the introduction of the plantation economy in the 1920s and 1930s and the post-
World War II development of the mining industry, significant numbers
of members of indigenous ethnic groups migrated from their traditional lands in Liberia's interior to coastal areas. These migrants settled into
townships that were incorporated around traditional tribal lineage with
property rights held on a communal basis, rather than on the basis of
personal private ownership as was the case in settler communities. Ex-
amples of these township communities can still be found in Monrovia
and other urban centers, in districts such as New Kru Town and Vai
Town, which were governed by governors and councils nominated according to the customs prevalent in the home communities and then
appointed to office by the central government. These township officials,
many of whom have since the 1960s eschewed titles such as "chief" in
favor of "modern" designations like "justice of the peace," reported to

the Department of the Interior, rather to the local urban jurisdiction. The perpetuation of this system has led, on occasion, to rather unfavorable comparisons by visiting South African officials to the notorious segregated townships of the apartheid era.

The hierarchical structures imposed upon the indigenous peoples of the interior by successive Liberian governments had different effects, depending on the preexisting institutional structures. As a general rule, the Mande- and Mel-speaking peoples, who had traditionally been organized according to a rigid hierarchical pattern, adapted to the new structures with greater facility than the Kwa-speaking peoples, who belonged to societies that had been more egalitarian.[19] Consequently, resistance to the authority of the new governmental structures often led to violent uprisings, such as those that took place on the Kru Coast in 1915 and 1916. In 1918, an alliance of Gola villages in central Liberia put up such a staunch resistance to demands for taxes and labor that the government in Monrovia had to arm their traditional rivals, the Loma, to put them down. The LFF fought a running battle to assert the central government's authority over the Kpelle from 1919 to 1921. President Edwin Barclay organized expeditions under the command of Colonel Elwood Davis, an African-American officer who received a commission in the LFF, to stamp out secret societies among the Kpelle. In his travelogue, Graham Greene chronicled a meeting with Davis, whom he described as the "Dictator of Grand Bassa," who boasted of having "court-martialed and shot fifty members of the Leopard Society in a village near Grand Bassa."[20]

Perhaps most infamously, the LFF was deployed among the Krahn throughout the 1920s in a violent campaign of "pacification" that was, no doubt, remembered by Master Sergeant Samuel Kanyon Doe, an ethnic Krahn, when he lined up the predominantly Americo-Liberian cabinet of the assassinated President William R. Tolbert, Jr., on a Monrovia beach and executed them in 1980.

Although President Tubman ameliorated the situation in 1946, when he moved to give the franchise to members of indigenous communities who owned a hut and paid taxes upon it, he continued to govern the interior as a *de facto* protectorate until well into the 1960s. Tubman, in fact, expressed fears that the "civilized" portion of the Liberian population was in danger of being overwhelmed by "a large semi-civilized population."[21] To this end, the president undertook several trips to the United States as well as Haiti, Jamaica, and other places in the West

Indies in order to encourage emigration to Liberia by "more advanced" black individuals.

Given Tubman's dim view of the development of the tribes of the Liberian interior, it is not surprising that the *Code of Laws* he promulgated in 1956 invested neither the tribal groups nor individual tribal members with title to the lands they occupied. Indigenous communities were granted the *use* of *public land*. When "a tribe shall become sufficiently advanced in civilization," it was permitted to "petition the government for a division of tribal land into family holdings."[22] Needless to say, in addition to penalizing the individual, the law gave no specific criteria for determining when any given group achieved the state of being "sufficiently advanced in civilization."

While the legal system discriminated against indigenous communities with regard to land holdings, it encouraged, in the name of increasing a "civilized" settler presence in the interior, politically connected members of the Americo-Liberian elite to acquire vast estates—some as large as 20,000 acres—for the paltry rent of fifty cents per acre. As if to add salt to the wounds, these plantation owners, many of whom were absentees, were exempted from the taxes and other imposts collected by the district commissioners.

DEVILS AND *JUJU*

Although the central government was ultimately successful in asserting its dominion over the chieftaincies of the indigenous communities of the country's interior, it never achieved much in its campaign to bring the mysterious *Poro* (for men) and *Sande* (for women) societies that are associated with the "bush devils" who preside over the "bush schools" that play an important role in the transmission of traditional lore and initiation of indigenous Liberians. These institutions are especially strong among the Vai, Gola, Dei, Mende, Bandi, Loma, Kpelle, and Ma ethnic groups. One of the most astute contemporary scholars of Liberia, Stephen Ellis, has summarized these institutions in the following manner:

> The most widespread system of traditional religious belief associated with the use of masks, extending over all the northwest of the country, is the complex of religious societies or sodalities known as Poro (for men) and Sande (for women). Poro and Sande are corporations,

controlled in each town by local councils of elders whose identity and whose rituals may not be divulged to outsiders. Some Poro members are also initiates of other, more exclusive societies often associated with some particular skill, such as the ability to cure snake bites ... In functional terms, the practice of secrecy enables senior officials of the Poro and Sande to exercise their authority more effectively, as it generally does in all hierarchies. Within the Poro society are high grades whose ritual and membership may not be divulged to people of a lower grade, thus constituting a structure of authority in what were otherwise, at least in the recent past, communities with a weak concentration of power in matters of civic government.[23]

Although today not all members of indigenous communities where the Poro and Sande societies are present are initiated, such individuals remain the exception to the rule. Even practicing Christians are initiated, despite the *prima facie* contradiction between Christian beliefs and the cult of the bush devil. Nowadays in the Liberian interior, it is not uncommon to enter a church on any given Sunday and come across Catholic priests or other Christian clergy who bear the marks of Poro initiation. Others even engage in ritual sacrifices associated with cult of the societies. In 1995, for example, the Reverend Jimmie Digbie, then general superintendent of the Assembly of God mission in Liberia, was indicted by a grand jury for attempting to kidnap a five-year-old girl for sacrifice in order to win reelection to his ecclesiastical position at his denomination's upcoming convention.

Authority in local Poro chapters is exercised by a priest known as a *zo* (plural, *zoes*). The *zoes* are themselves organized in a hierarchical structure, admission to the higher grades requiring increasingly heavier sacrifices, including, especially in past times, human sacrifice.[24] The latter was especially true with regard to the more exclusive complementary societies that had political overtones, such as the human leopard societies that were prevalent in Liberia, Sierra Leone, and Guinea in the early decades of the twentieth century, where membership was restricted to the most senior members of a community. Charles Spurgeon Johnson, an African-American who was professor of sociology at Fisk University and who visited Liberia in the 1930s as part of the League of Nations commission investigating charges of slavery brought against the Liberian government, reported that:

This strange, ferocious society had killed and consumed hundreds of individuals, raided towns, and even, on occasion, had brought human flesh to the market for sale. At first, in the effort to check the outrages, [Liberian President Edwin] Barclay tried sounding out natives to locate the mainsprings of the movement, but when these investigators had tasted the flesh, they too became addicts. Finally, Barclay had the whole society rounded up, and some 600 were brought in, all of which could not be executed, naturally. Barclay picked the sixteen ringleaders and ordered them shot; some others he put in prison virtually for life. [25]

Despite these attempts, the indigenous societies could not be stamped out. If anything, the increasing attempts by central government to co-opt the tribal chieftains within the system of indirect rule correspondingly strengthened the influence of the *zoes* within their communities. This ironically, led to the situation where even members of the ostensibly Christian Americo-Liberian settler class became devotees of bush devils, albeit for reasons of superstitious belief in supernatural powers of *juju*, West African voodoo, rather than the traditional social initiation aspects important in indigenous societies. President Charles King is believed to have been the first Liberian president who was a Poro initiate and was rumored to have been a member of the exclusive Alligator Society (crocodiles are called "alligators" in Liberian English). When, in 1930, the League of Nations sent a commission to investigate his government's complicity in the contract labor scandal that would eventually cost him his presidency, King and several members of his cabinet are said to have sacrificed a goat. Graham Greene reported that: "After the sacrifice, which should traditionally have been a human one, a boatload of young Krus had been drowned close to the beach at Monrovia, and it was generally felt that the alligator was dissatisfied with the goat."[26] Greene also noted the reason that the governing elites put up only "the feeblest resistance" to the sacrificial cults was "because they *believed*."[27] This observation was confirmed by two more recent scholars, who concluded that:

When the African American settlers and their Americo-Liberian descendents who dominated the government instituted indirect rule in the early 1900s in order to control the "country" people, traditional authorities lost power; control of public life shifted to officials appointed by the state. In turn, in order to boost their own power, those state-appointed officials used the powers and privileges of traditional secret society in new ways. Practices, such as human sacrifice, became privatized, and political elites hired free-lance "heartmen" (who removed the hearts of their victims, to be eaten ritually) to gain spiritual power and to intimidate enemies. In short, Liberia's Americo-Liberian rulers, who portrayed themselves as Western-oriented and far more "civilized" than "native" Liberians, co-opted elements of traditional society to enhance their own power.[28]

President Tubman, as part of his campaign to bring all aspects of Liberian life under his authority, had a law passed in 1952 creating the post of assistant secretary of the interior charged with overseeing "matters pertaining to the Poro, Sande, and other societies in tribal areas."[29] Tubman's successor, William Tolbert, was not only president of the World Baptist Alliance, but also an initiated *zo*, the first Liberian head of state to have been a priest in the indigenous cult. Samuel Doe forced a council of leading *zoes* to acknowledge him as their leader and, as tragically revealed at the time of his death, wore all sorts of amulets.

During the 1989–1997 Liberian civil war, Charles Taylor assiduously cultivated the support of the *zoes* and eventually was proclaimed the *dakhpannah*, or supreme *zo* of Liberia. One prominent *zo* living on the slopes of sacred Mount Gibi in Margibi County, a certain dwarf named Singbe, accepted a commission as a "general" in Taylor's National Patriotic Front of Liberia (NPFL). Singbe was alleged to be able to confer invulnerability to bullets and struck terror among fighters of all factions. Alas, Singbe's powers failed him when he was ambushed in 1992 by the rival United Liberian Movement for Democracy (ULIMO) militia and killed in a hail of bullets. While Taylor may have been the master of the art, all sides during the conflict employed the power of traditional beliefs and symbols in an attempt both to reinforce the morale of supporters and to strike fear in opponents. Consequently, one saw such phenomena as fighters smearing their faces with white clay (a Poro ritual known as *leh*) and male fighters going into battle dressed in women's clothes (transvestitism is considered a powerful charm).[30] The U.S. State Department reported that during the war, "Fighters—whether AFL, LPC or one of the ULIMO sub-factions—also targeted their enemies, fighters and civilians alike, removed their victims' body parts and ate them in front of civilians."[31]

Even after the 1997 peace, similar allegations of ritual cannibalism continued to beset the government of President Charles Taylor, who is believed by many Monrovians to participate in the human sacrifices that his uncle, Jensen Taylor, is generally suspected of organizing. Whatever the truth of these accusations, they reveal the continuing belief in contemporary Liberian society of the power of spiritual forces that can be propitiated through traditional cultic practices.

CONTRACT LABORERS

Perhaps no issue in Liberian history is as sensitive as that of the contract laborers. With the notable exception of Amos Sawyer, the American-educated academic who briefly served as Liberia's president at the head of the Interim Government of National Unity (IGNU) in the early 1990s, Liberian writers have either ignored the issue or passed over with barely a cursory mention, if they acknowledge it at all.[32] However, few issues are as emblematic of the complexities and contradictions of Liberia that point to the root causes of present-day tensions and rivalries among the various groups who make up contemporary Liberian society.

While the slave trade was suppressed and the gradual abolition of the institution of slavery during the nineteenth century by Great Britain (1833), France (1848), and the United States (1865), the need for gang-style labor for the labor-intensive production of commodities such as sugar and cotton remained. This need for manual labor increased with the introduction of plantation agriculture in the new colonies acquired by the European powers during the nineteenth century. The British developed the system of contract labor whereby, for example, between 1841 and 1867, some 32,000 Africans were taken from Sierra Leone to work in British colonies in the Caribbean. Likewise the French colonial officials in Senegal developed the institution of the "*engagement à temps*" through which Africans were indentured for up to fourteen years to provide labor in French possessions in the Caribbean and in the Indian Ocean. In 1853, the Liberian government recognized this practice by issuing administrative norms to regulate it.

In 1887, the Liberian government itself entered this traffic in persons by signing a deal with an agent of the Viscount Ferdinand de Lesseps, builder of the Suez Canal, whose French firm that was attempting at the time to build a canal in Panama. Under the agreement, the firm was allowed to recruit up to 5,000 men from the indigenous ethnic groups in the Liberian interior. Each laborer recruited was to be paid $10 a month at the end of fourteen months of work. He was to be advanced $2.50 before departure and to be given clothing, food, and lodging, as well as monthly allowance of two Colombian pesos for personal expenses. In the event that a laborer died before the completion of his contract, the wages he had earned to date were payable to the Liberian government for transmission to his survivors. For its assistance in facilitating the transaction, the government received a $2 commission for each worker as well as passport and other administrative fees. Despite deaths—the mortality rates from disease ran as high as 10 percent per annum[33]—and complaints of mistreatment, the Liberian government allowed another group of workers to be recruited in 1897.

In 1903, facing the nation's chronic fiscal crisis, the Liberian Congress enacted a law to raise government revenue through contract labor, which was highly demanded for the plantations established in the German colony of Cameroon and the Spanish colony on the island of Fernando Po (now part of Equatorial Guinea). According to the legislation, in order to recruit workers, a firm was required to obtain a license from the government for $250 plus a deposit of $150. The government was to receive a commission of $5 for each laborer recruited in addition to passport and other administrative fees. The laborers themselves, who had to be at least twenty-one years old, were to be paid between 24 and 36 cents per day. Despite the law, conditions for the laborers were less than desirable, to put it charitably. In fact, the Liberian government was rather embarrassed when, in 1913, the British government protested the slavelike conditions of *Liberian* workers on Fernando Po in a diplomatic note dispatched to the governments in Madrid and Monrovia.

As a result of the British complaint, Liberia signed a convention with Spain in 1914 to regulate its contract labor arrangements with the colonial regime on Fernando Po. Recruiting was centralized in the person of an agent, appointed by the Spanish governor of Fernando Po, who worked in Monrovia under the resident Spanish consul. Workers could enlist for up to maximum of two years of labor on the island's plantations. The agreed-upon wages were to be paid half in monthly installments of local currency and half in pounds sterling upon the worker's return to Monrovia. Liberia posted a consular official on Fernando Po who was authorized to ensure the rights of workers. The deal permitted the Liberian government one source of revenue that was not subject to the international receivership imposed over its finances.

The system, however, proved to be too subject to abuse. Local chiefs and district commissioners received either a commission or some other incentive to recruit laborers and to keep them from breaking their contracts. And, assuming they returned from their sojourns abroad, contract laborers faced a host of abusive fees: an obligatory "gift" to the local governor of his ethnic township in Monrovia; a one shilling tax payable to the township municipal fund; a "health department" tax of three and one-half shillings; a head tax leveled by the national government; a tax to his village headman; customs duties on any goods brought home with him; and other sundry charges.[34] Once he paid off the debts accrued by his family for food and clothing during his absence, many a returning laborer found that he had nothing to show for his work. So great was the strain imposed by the system that on a several occasions Kru and Grebo chiefs made appeals for the United States, the "international community," and even the defunct ACS to intervene.

As the force of international disapproval kept the Liberian government from directly supplying labor, the business was transferred to individual Liberian politicians, theoretically acting in their private capacities. Consequently, in 1928, the *Sindicato Agricola de Guinea*, representing the Spanish plantation owners on Fernando Po, signed a two-year contract with a Liberian firm headed by former vice president Samuel Alfred Ross Jr., then serving in President Charles D. B. King's cabinet as postmaster-general. Other partners in the firm included Vice President Allen Yancy and E.G.W. King, the president's brother. The Spanish syndicate agreed to pay its Liberian counterparts £9 for each laborer recruited as well as a £1,000 bonus for every 1,500 workers—with some two million hectares (4,942,100 acres) being cultivated, Fernando Po's plantation owners needed some 40,000 laborers. The syndicate would also pay the transportation costs. The Liberian recruiters were responsible, under the agreement, for the payment of all taxes and fees, which amounted to $6.50 per laborer. At the then prevailing exchange rate, this left the recruiters with a handsome profit of approximately $38 per laborer exported to the Spanish colony. The laborers themselves were to be paid one pound ten shillings each month, one-half of which was payable monthly in Spanish pesetas while one-half was to be paid in pounds sterling or U.S. dollars upon the worker's return to Liberia.

While the conditions of the laborers under the 1928 deal have not been shown to have been any worse—or better—than those of others under similar circumstances, their case became an international *cause célèbre* when President King rigged the 1927 elections, claiming to have won an astonishing total of 229,527 votes from an electorate that numbered less than 15,000 men. The defeated candidate, Thomas J.R. Faulkner, an immigrant from North Carolina, angrily contested the election results and published an indictment of the King administration, including the labor contract, in the United States. The concern that Faulkner's account engendered in America and Europe led the League of Nations into launching an official investigation of the affair. The final report of the investigative commission[35] was a devastating exposé of enslavement, forced labor, and other abuses by Liberian officials of every echelon. The abuses documented revealed a mendacity that was not beneath cheating returning tribesmen of their rightful wages. The three-member commission—chaired by Dr. Albert Christy, a British physician who had worked in Africa, included Professor Charles Spurgeon Johnson, the distinguished African-American scholar,[36] and former Liberian president Arthur Barclay—interviewed illiterate workers whose pay stub showed they were owed $700, but who were given $25. It also uncovered evidence that, while President King kept the local chief, Jeh, detained in Monrovia, Vice President Yancy had personally led a group of LFF soldiers on a raid along Wedabo Beach, on the Kru-Grebo Coast, that captured 316 men and boys who were exported to Fernando Po. The commission summarized its findings in somber judgment:

> Although all laborers to Fernando Po have not been forced, it is quite clear that force has been relied upon for numbers; that the blind eagerness for private profit has carried has carried the traffic to a point scarcely distinguishable from slavery; and that only by help of the instruments and offices of Government could the traffic have reached such tragic effectiveness. A great deal could be said of the danger, everywhere evident, to the wholesome economic development of the country, the deserted villages, neglected farms, "hungry time." At least an important element of the native population, which is without doubt the strength of the country, cannot look but with restless, harried dissatisfaction upon the general abuses of the machinery by which they are ruled.[37]

The international commission's report was a major embarrassment for the Liberian elite that prided itself on the nation's proclaimed *raison d'être* of being, in the words of its Declaration of Independence, "an asylum from the most grinding oppression" of forced servitude and labor. Consequently, a number of "citizens' caucuses" forced both President King and Vice President Yancy to resign from office. Their removal, however, seems to have assuaged the ire of the governing classes, which then turned against the indigenous communities whose leaders had provided the damning evidence to the international commission. King's successors and the local officials they appointed, in a concerted effort to reassert the central government's authority, engaged in a campaign of harsh recrimination against independent indigenous leaders on the Kru Coast alone, some nine chiefs were hanged. New legislation in 1932 created new districts in the hinterland and amalgamated the districts into provinces to be administered by provincial commissioners appointed from Monrovia. For their part, such indigenous leaders who survived the "pacification" campaigns acquired a new sense of the existence of an outside world that could be appealed to against the depravations of the national government.

The ultimate consequence of this conflict between the settler-dominated national government in Monrovia and indigenous peoples in the interior, however, was not to be fully appreciated until decades later when Liberia was plunged into the dark cycle of civil war following the overthrow of the constitutional government of President William Tolbert. The appointment of chiefs by the central government had already been a source of tension. The revelation that some of them misused their authority to personally profit as well as to aid their Americo-Liberian patrons profit from the export of their subjects undermined such authority as they still enjoyed among their people. The unintended result of the government's policy of emasculating the authority of the chiefs even further through the bureaucratization of the administration of the interior destroyed the remaining credibility of these tribal figures. While the authority of the central government was momentarily strengthened, over the long run the effect was an increasing number of indigenous youth who were alienated from both the national life and traditional tribal structures. With the social fabric weakened by the lack of mediating figures and institutions, the seeds of future conflict were sown deep into the soil of the Liberian interior.

ENDNOTES

1. Howard W. French, "When Liberians Looked to America in Vain," *The New York Times* (July 13, 2003).
2. Jefferson Morley, "Should U.S. Troops Go to Liberia?" *The Washington Post* (July 21, 2003).
3. See Tom W. Shick, "A Quantitative Analysis of Liberian Colonization from 1820 to 1843 with Special Reference to Mortality," *Journal of African History* 12/1 (1971): 45–59.
4. Amos Sawyer, *The Emergence of Autocracy in Liberia: Tragedy and Challenge* (San Francisco: Institute for Contemporary Studies, 1992), 116.
5. Stephen Ellis, *The Mask of Anarchy: The Destruction of Liberia and the Religious Dimension of an African Civil War* (New York: New York University Press, 1999), 43.
6. Ryszard Kapuściński, *The Shadow of the Sun*, trans. Klara Glowczewska (New York/ Toronto: Alfred A. Knopf, 2001), 239–240.
7. Cited in Nathaniel R. Richardson, *Liberia's Past and Present* (London: Diplomatic Press, 1959), 122.
8. *Ibid.*, 118.
9. In one presidential proclamation, sealed with the great seal of the Republic of Liberia, and countersigned by Foreign Minister Monie R. Captan, Taylor declared that "God the Holy Spirit spoke through men of God as Dr. Pat Robertson and Bishop John Gimenez, President of the Rock Church International, confirming that the only way to save Liberia is to have a mass gathering of Christians from all over the world pray for Liberia." For the full text of this proclamation, see Robertson's website at <www.patrobertson.com/ pressreleases/liberiaproclamation.asp>.
10. See "Candle in the Dark: Modern Becket in Liberia," *Our Sunday Visitor* (September 28, 2003).
11. The official reason for Archbishop Francis's convenient absence was that he was attending World Youth Day in Toronto, Canada—a pretense that rings a little hollow when one notes that there was no delegation on Liberian youth attending the event. In fairness to the prelate, however, he was not the only shepherd to go abroad while the sheep were being attacked: Bishop Boniface Nyema Dalieh of the Catholic Diocese of Cape Palmas found it equally convenient to visit his niece in Chicago, Illinois, and Bishop-elect Lewis Zeigler of the Catholic Diocese of Gbarnga had to go to Rome to shop for the vestments for his new office. In fairness to the Liberian prelates, the record of their native Sierra Leonean counterpart is not much better. During that country's civil war, while the Italian missionary, Bishop George Biguzzi of the Catholic Diocese of Makeni accompanied his people to refugee camps in Guinea, and the nearly octogenarian Irish missionary, Bishop John O'Riordan of the Catholic Diocese of Kenema, escorted his people into hiding in the forests, the Mende Archbishop Joseph Ganda of the Catholic Archdiocese of Freetown and Bo slipped away to Florida's Gulf Coast, where he remained safely and comfortably until his old friend, President Ahmed Tejan Kabbah, was reinstalled in his presidential palace.
12. Amos J. Beyan, "The American Colonization Society and the Socio-Religious Characterization of Liberia: A Historical Survey, 1822–1900," *Liberian Studies Journal* 10/2 (1984–1985): 5–8
13. Paul Gifford, *Christianity and Politics in Doe's Liberia* (Cambridge: Cambridge University Press, 1993), 305.
14. See Bertha B. Azanga, "The Historical and Philosophical Development of Liberian Education," Liberian Historical Review 1 (1968): 28–37.
15. Quoted in Sawyer, *The Emergence of Autocracy in Liberia*, 186–187.
16. J. Gus Liebenow, Liberia: The Quest for a Democracy (Bloomington, Indiana: Indiana Unviersity Press, 1987). 15.
17. Graham Greene, *Journey Without Maps* (1936; New York: Penguin Books, 1980).

18. Charles S. Johnson *Bitter Canaan: The Story of the Negro Republic*, edited with an introduction by John Stanfield (1987); New Brunswick, New Jersey/London: Transaction Publishers, 1992), 196–197.

19. See Merran Fraenkel, "Social Change on the Kru Coast of Liberia," *Africa* 36/2 (1966): 154–172.

20. Greene, *Journey Without Maps*, 174.

21. Quoted in Sawyer, *The Emergence of Autocracy in Liberia*, 208.

22. *Liberian Code of Laws*, vol. 1 (Ithaca, New York: Cornell University Press, 1957), 272. The specific citation is from chapter 11, sec. 60–61, of the *Code*.

23. Ellis, *The Mask of Anarchy*, 200.

24. See Patrick Joseph Harrington, "Secret Societies and the Church: An Evaluation of the Poro and Sande Secret Society Spcieties and the Missionary among the Mano of Liberia" (Th.D. dissertation, Pontifical Gregorian University, 1975), 17–18.

25. Johnson, *Bitter Canaan*, 169.

26. Greene, *Journey Without Maps*, 174.

27. *Ibid*.

28. Shelly Dick and Wiebe Boer, "The Spirits are Angry: Liberia's Secret cults in the service of the civil war," *Books and Culture* 7/1 (January/February 2001): 26.

29. Kenneth Best, *Cultural Policy in Liberia* (Paris: UNESCO, 1974), 28.

30. See Ellis, *The Mask of Anarchy*, 259–260.

31. United States Departmentof State, *Liberia Country Report on Human Rights Practices for 1996* (January 30, 1997); seewww.state.gov/www/global/human_rights/1996_hrp_report/liberia.html.

32. See Sawyer. *The Emergence of Autocracy in Liberia*, 211–236: also see idem., "Proprietary Authority and local Administration in Liberia," in James S. Wunsch and Dele Olowu (eds.), *The Failure of the Centralized State: Institutions and Self-Governance in Africa* (Boulder, Colorado: Westview Press, 1990), 148–173.

33. See Gary C. Kuhn, "Liberian Contract Labor in Panama, 1887–1897," *Liberian Studies Journal* 6/1 (1975): 43–52.

34. See Raymond Leslie Buell, *The Native Problem in Africa*, vol. 2 (1928; Hamden Connecticut: Archon Books, 1965), 775.

35. *Report of the International Commission of Inquiry into the Esixtence of Slavery and Forced Labor in the Republic of Liberia* (Geneva: League of Nations, 1930).

36. For Johnson's account of his participation in the commission, see *Bitter Canaan*, 175–197.

37. *Report of the International Commission of Inquiry*, 46.

THREE

TOWARDS THE PRECIPICE

B Y THE MID-1970s, even as he was receiving accolades from abroad, President William Tolbert's position in Liberia became increasingly precarious. A civil servant in the Treasury until he succeeded to his father's Montserrado County seat in Liberia's House of Representatives, where he served without distinction until President William V.S. Tubman tapped him to be vice president in 1952, Tolbert remained in his autocratic patron's shadow for nearly two decades until the latter's death in 1971 thrust him into the presidency. While Tolbert entered office with almost no personal constituency—his parents, the children of freed slaves, had come to Liberia from the United States, hence Tolbert was not part of the old settler aristocracy—he nonetheless set for himself the ambitious goal of rationalizing the national administration by taking on and eventually dismantling his predecessor's patronage network. His hope apparently was to carve for himself a base of support consisting of a broad coalition of the newly emergent groups in Liberian society who would most benefit from his "de-Tubmanization" of the country, including educated young professionals and students, entrepreneurs, educated rural dwellers, and the professional military. Ultimately, his downfall was that while his reforms were sufficient to alienate the entrenched interests of the Americo-Liberian ruling elite, they failed to bear fruit fast enough to win over to his side those groups he sought to bring in. Caught in that tension between resistance to innovation and pressures for change, Tolbert vacillated, especially after his brother and chief confidant, Finance Minister Stephen Allen Tolbert, died in a 1975 plane crash.

A number of political movements that were established during this period of ferment, including the Movement for Justice in Africa (MOJA), founded in 1973 by an economics professor at the University of Liberia, Togba Nah Roberts, an ethnic Kru who was born Rudolph Nah Roberts and who later changed his name again to Togba Nah Tipoteh. Armed with a pan-Africanist platform of anticolonialism, MOJA advocated the nationalization of Liberia's major businesses, including the large landholdings of the country's ruling classes, and the punishment of corrupt government officials. MOJA, which drew its support primarily from the educated middle class, also established nonprofit business and agricultural cooperatives as well as other social services under the umbrella of "SUSUKUU" in an effort to reach out to other constituencies. Among MOJA's leaders were two political science professors: Amos Sawyer, the Americo-Liberian dean of the College of Social Sciences and Humanities who later became head of one of the transition governments during the civil war, and Henry Boima Fahnbulleh Jr., an ethnic Vai whose father had been an ambassador before President Tubman charged him with treason.

Another group, the Progressive Alliance of Liberia (PAL) was organized in 1975 by a group of Liberian scholars and students then living in the United States. Led by Gabriel Baccus Mathews, who had quit his post as Liberian vice-consul in the U.S. to dedicate himself to political activism, the group called for rapid political reform, the adoption of socialism, and an activist pan-African foreign policy. Drawing its support within Liberia primarily from the urban poor, PAL's stated immediate objective was the establishment of a "Progressive People's Party" (PPP).

The establishment of these groups only increased the pressure on President Tolbert, whose tentative reform efforts were increasingly frustrated not only by conflicting forces beyond his control, but also by his own personal limits. While he released Tubman's political prisoners—including the jailed and tortured Ambassador Henry Fahnbulleh, Sr.—and encouraged free debate, Tolbert seemed to draw the line when criticism touched his family. In 1974, he permitted the Supreme Court, presided over by James A.A. Pierre, the father-in-law of his finance minister-brother, to fine the almost septuagenarian independent journalist Albert Porte $250,000 for alleged libel when Porte published accounts critical of the shady dealings of the Tolbert-owned Mesurado Group of Companies conglomerate. As one businessman remarked, the contrast between the corruption under the Tolbert administration with that under Tubman was at least the latter tried to spread the benefits of the graft: "When Tubman stole a dollar, he would give ninety cents back to the people in the form of food or minor amenities; as for Tolbert, he would return ten cents."[1]

THE "YEAR OF FERMENT"

Matters came to a head in early 1979 when the government proposed increasing the price of rice, one of the staples of the Liberian diet, from $22 per hundred-pound bag to $30, a sum that represented more than one-third of monthly income for an average Liberian family. The price increase sparked a massive campaign of protests and civil disobedience, culminating in an April 14 demonstration organized by the PAL. Police fired on the marchers, killing at least several dozen[2] and wounding hundreds. This incident marked the start of what Liberians came to call the "Year of Ferment." In the aftermath of the shootings, widespread rioting ensued, leading Tolbert to invoke the mutual defense pact he had signed earlier that year with Guinea's dictator Ahmed Sékou Touré. Consequently, seven hundred Guinean soldiers landed in Monrovia and, after three weeks, succeeded in quelling the riots.

Although order was temporarily restored and tensions abated after the government backed off the rice price increase, the incident left Tolbert weakened. Members of the old oligarchy questioned his ability to govern and were further alienated when the president confirmed the death sentence imposed by the Supreme Court on several leading TWP politicians, including the son of the party chairman, for ritual murder. The political opposition, meanwhile, emboldened by their success, demanded further concessions. In desperation, Tolbert obtained emergency powers from Congress and appointed his son-in-law, Burleigh Holder, as minister of national security. Subsequently, the security services arrested Gabriel Baccus Mathews and thirty-two other PAL leaders, charging them with treason and conspiracy to overthrow the government.

On June 26, Tolbert released the jailed PAL leaders who immediately began organizing a registration campaign for their Progressive People's Party to challenge Tolbert and the TWP in the legislative and presidential elections, scheduled for 1981 and 1983, respectively. Meanwhile, another challenge arose in Amos Sawyer's campaign to be elected mayor of Monrovia, the first instance of anyone seeking political office in Liberia in nearly twenty-five years without the blessing of the TWP. After some indecisive blundering—including an attempt to resurrect the old property qualifications for voter registration in order to disenfranchise Sawyer's middle and working class supporters—Tolbert decided to postpone the election until June 1980.

When the government tried to prevent the registration of the PPP, the threat by the parent group, PAL, to organize further disturbances forced Tolbert, after a period of indecisiveness, to back down and agree to the registration of the opposition party on January 8, 1980. However, when PAL/PPP leader Mathews called for a nationwide general strike on March 8, to force the president to resign before the elections, he was jailed along with thirty-seven other party leaders. Tolbert scheduled a treason trial for the prisoners for April 14. It became clear to observers that events were spinning out of control for the Tolbert administration, faced as it was with contradictory pressure on every side. However, when it came, the *coup de grâce* came from unexpected quarter.

MILITARY TAKEOVER

Unlike many of its African neighbors, Liberia did not have a martial tradition, much less a history of military involvement in politics. For most of the country's history, the only military force was a militia, composed of citizen volunteers who were called up as necessary to put down uprisings and other disturbances caused by friction with indigenous peoples. The Liberian Frontier Force (LFF) was created only in 1908 to assert the country's claims along its borders with the neighboring British and French possessions when the colonial powers threatened to encroach upon Liberian territory if it the government in Monrovia failed to establish "effective occupation" as mandated by the Congress of Berlin. The LFF, a corps that number on average between 600 and 1,500 soldiers in total, was subsequently also given the charge of serving as a national constabulary to assist the district commissioners and other officials in enforcing the national government's writ over the interior by maintaining order among and collecting taxes from the tribes.

Initially founded with the assistance of British officers, the LFF was commanded by black officers from the U.S. Army—who were seconded for the purpose at the request of the Liberian government—from 1912 to 1922, during the period of American receivership. In 1961, U.S. President John F. Kennedy authorized the beginning of a military assistance program to the LFF, which became the Armed Forces of Liberia (AFL), with National Guard and Coast Guard components, in 1962. Like most other national institutions in Liberia, the AFL, numbering some 6,000 men under arms by 1980, had an almost-exclusively Americo-Liberian officer corps and an almost entirely indigenous corps of noncommissioned officers and private soldiers. In the wake of the events of the "Year of Ferment," the increasingly isolated Tolbert government unwittingly made matters worse by removing many officers on the suspicion that they were disloyal, leaving the remaining officers disaffected. The president had also offended many of the rank-and-file of the AFL by calling in foreign troops from Guinea to deal with a domestic situation.

This context was the stage for the *coup d'état* that took place in the early morning hours of April 12, 1980—just two days before the planned trial of Gabriel Baccus Mathews and the other PAL/PPP leaders. Master-Sergeant Samuel Kanyon Doe stormed into Monrovia's Executive Mansion accompanied by two staff sergeants, four sergeants, eight corporals, and two privates. A quasi-illiterate twenty-eight-year-old ethnic Krahn from Grand Gedeh County on Liberia's eastern border with Côte d'Ivoire, Doe seemed an unlikely candidate to lead a military *putsch*: a junior officer with no following whose wife, Nancy, was an illiterate "market woman" who peddled wares on the street outside the Rally Time market, he had no established political or military following. Yet within minutes, the seventeen low-ranking soldiers had brutally disemboweled President Tolbert as he lay in his own bed and butchered twenty-six other occupants of the presidential residence.

The announcement of the government's overthrow was a shock to most Liberians, although many were also relieved that the increasingly repressive rule of the Tolbert regime had been brought to an end. In fact many civilians broke into riotous celebrations of what they perceived to be liberation from over a century of domination by the settler oligarchy. One of the songs that the crowds on Monrovia's streets danced to spoke volumes about their mood: *"Congo woman born rogue / Country woman born soldier."* The festive atmosphere, however, soon led to violence and the looting of the grand mansions and other symbols of the settler establishment, including the Masonic Temple in Monrovia, which was destroyed by drunken soldiers.

The seventeen soldiers who carried out the coup, none of whom had so much as a high school education, declared themselves to be the "People's Redemption Council" (PRC) with Doe, the senior-ranking officer, as the chairman and head of state. The PRC constituted itself as the highest authority in the land in all matters executive, legislative, and judicial, although it left the laws and government ministries of the deposed republic in place so long as they did not conflict with the objectives of "the revolution." The seven also awarded themselves summary military promotions, including: Master Sergeant Doe became five-star General Doe, chairman of the PRC and head of state; Staff Sergeant Thomas Weh Syen became Major General Syen, cochairman of the PRC and deputy head of state; Corporal J. Nicholas Podlier became Brigadier General Podlier, speaker of the PRC; and Sergeant Thomas Gunkama Quiwonkpa became Brigadier General Quiwonkpa, commander of the AFL.

Since all the *putschists* were low ranking noncommissioned officers or private soldiers, the PRC moved to purge more senior officers from the AFL. Consequently, the Liberian coup was even more chaotic than military takeovers in other countries where, typically, military command structures are substituted for civilian authority. In the case of Liberia, the killing or dismissal of senior officers shortly after that of the civilian authorities meant the creation of a leadership vacuum in both the government and the military simultaneously.

Quickly realizing, however, that not only did its members lack the technical skills to manage a government but that the regime needed a broader base of support, the PRC expanded its membership to twenty-eight, inviting leading members of the PAL/PPP, who were freed from prison just two days before their scheduled trial, and those of the MOJA to join the government. Ultimately, four cabinet posts went to the PAL/PPP, including the foreign affairs portfolio assumed by its leader Baccus Mathews, and three went to the MOJA. Younger Americo-Liberians who were not closely identified with the former administration, especially those with technical skills acquired during their education abroad, were encouraged to return home and were given positions of responsibility in state institutions. Among the young technocrats who received an appointment from the PRC was a thirty-two-year-old with an economics degree from Bentley College in Waltham, Massachusetts, Charles McArthur Taylor, who was destined to figure prominently in Liberian politics for the next two decades. The son of a settler father and a Gola mother, Taylor was living in the United States and working as a mechanic in a plastics factory. He happened to be present in Liberia as part of a delegation of the Union of Liberian Associations in the Americas (ULAA) when the coup took place. Answering the new regime's call for volunteers, he was appointed—thanks in part to his relationship by marriage to the newly appointed General Quiwonkpa—managing director of the General Services Agency, the government procurement office. Less than three years later, in 1983, he was appointed deputy minister of commerce.

However, the cadre of young, educated Liberians that Doe assembled to serve the PRC regime soon proved that its members could be as corrupt as the ousted True Whig oligarchy. As Arthur Kulah, who succeeded ousted Vice President Bennie Warner as Liberia's United Methodist bishop, lamented:

> Many of these technocrats were "bought" by the system and became lax in their commitment. Many of them joined the leaders who lived luxuriously. A good number of these Liberian professionals studied on the graduate and post-graduate level in the United States and in Europe. Having traveled abroad and after seeing what progress and development is, they might be expected to transfer these methods and policies for the benefit of the nation. Instead, these technocrats and professionals allowed themselves to be ruled by materialism and their leadership style dictated by greed, making themselves what Liberians call "gravy-seekers"... A culture of lies, deception, and misinformation was developed.[3]

The new regime did not wait long, however, to reveal itself to be far more brutal than the bumbling autocracy of Tolbert's final days. Hundreds of civilians associated with the deposed republican government were arrested and tortured. Just ten days after slaying Tolbert, Doe and his colleagues had thirteen prominent figures from the old regime—including the President *pro tempore* of the Senate, the Speaker of the House of Representatives, the Chief Justice of the Supreme Court, the Chairman of the TWP, and four cabinet members[4]—tried by a special military tribunal for "high treason, rampant corruption, misuse of public office, and violation of human rights," convicted, and publicly executed on a Monrovia beach as cameras broadcast the images.

One extrajudicial killing, however, was to return to haunt Doe. President Tolbert's son, Adolphus Benedict Tolbert, had managed to escape the arrests by taking refuge in the French embassy in Monrovia. The young Tolbert was married to Désirée "Daisy" Delafosse, daughter the late Maurice Delafosse, cofounder with Côte d'Ivoire's President Félix Houphouët-Boigny of that country's ruling *Rassemblement démocratique africain* (RDA) party. When her father died, Houphouët-Boigny had adopted the girl. West Africa's elder statesmen personally appealed to Doe for his son-in-law's life and received a promise of safe passage into exile for Adolphus Tolbert. Consequently, when Doe's men arrested Tolbert after he left his asylum in the French mission, dragging him off to the notorious Belle Yella prison where he was killed, *le Vieux* ("the old one, elder, wise man"), as the Ivorian president was known throughout West Africa, took it as a personal affront and swore vengeance. Doe's problems only multiplied when Houphouët-Boigny married the new widow's foster sister Chantal off to Burkina Faso's leader, Blaise Compaoré, and Daisy Delafosse-Tolbert, now exiled from Liberia, went to live with the new couple in Ouagadougou. Consequently, Doe soon found himself encircled by regional rivals who had very personal scores to settle with him.

REPRESSION

The PRC regime moved quickly to consolidate support among those military and civil service personnel who had not been eliminated during its initial purges. Despite the wretched state of public finances, the new rulers raised military salaries by 150 percent and civil service salaries by 100 percent. In addition, it handled public sector jobs in a manner that put the old True Whig patronage to shame: between 1980 and 1983, the number of people drawing a government salary went from 18,000 to 56,000. Not surprisingly, the Liberian government's international debt increased from the $750 million to over $1.4 billion during the same period.[5]

All hailing from underprivileged backgrounds, the members of the military junta took to the reins of state like children unleashed in the proverbial candy store. Within a matter of days of the 1980 takeover, the entire fleet of fifty Mercedes-Benz sedans purchased the preceding year by the Tolbert government when it hosted the Organization of African Unity summit the previous year had been wrecked by the new proprietors. Wealthy Liberians were arbitrarily detained by individual members of the PRC demanding ransoms from the families of the captives. One unfortunate merchant, having paid off the officer holding him was walking out of prison when he was sighted by another *putschist* and rearrested on a different set of trumped-up charges. By the end of their rule, it was estimated that Doe and his surviving colleagues has looted the national treasury of some $300 million in public funds.[6] What Ugandan President Yoweri Kaguta Museveni has said *à propos* another sergeant-turned-president, Idi Amin, could also be applied to Doe:

> Another problem that beset the Africa state was the low cultural level of the people who took charge of our affairs. You must have heard of people like Idi Amin and Bokassa. If you examine the matter carefully and pose the question, "Who was Idi Amin?" you will find that Idi Amin was a sergeant in the British Army. A sergeant is ordinarily taught to manage thirty people under the supervision of an officer. He is not allowed to manage those thirty people on his own: he must do so under the supervision of someone more cultured and better trained than himself.
>
> But here we had a situation where suddenly people who were simply ignorant and hopelessly out of their depth were propelled into positions of very great power. This is a big problem. The endemic corruption in Africa is partly caused by this low level of culture. Culture first generates knowledge, then it generates ethics. How do you define right and wrong? How do you differentiate between what is acceptable and what is not acceptable in society?[7]

Doe, meanwhile, was also busy building a personal power base. Although the original membership of the PRC consisted primarily of members of Doe's own Krahn ethnic group, it also contained representation from the Kru, Gio, Grebo, and Loma peoples. Shortly after assuming power, Doe began to fill strategic positions with Krahns who owed personal loyalty to him. With a few years, while the Krahns constituted less than 5 percent of the Liberian population, they held a full one-third of positions in central government in addition to the commands of all four of the infantry battalions of the AFL as well as those of the Executive Mansion Guards and the Special Anti-Terrorist Unit. For many Liberians, the "revolution" was little more than a "changing of the guard" with Krahns replacing Americo-Liberians. Patrick Seyon, an ethnic Kru who as vice president of the University of Liberia was arrested and flogged twice a day for two weeks by Doe's agents in 1981, lamented: "Those who found themselves in power after 1980 went along with the world that had been set in place by the freed American slaves ... No one saw that there was something systematic in the level of inequality that existed. They followed right in line."[8]

With his personal position strengthened, the former master sergeant began to ease his former colleagues from power. By 1985, of the original seventeen members of the PRC, six had been executed, one had died in an automobile "accident," one had fled for his life, and four had been involuntarily "retired," including the Brigadier General Thomas Gunkama Quiwonkpa, commanding officer of AFL. Leading political opponents of the Tolbert government who had initially agreed to work with the new regime were also forced out, including Togba Nah Tipoteh, Henry Fahnbulleh Jr., and Gabriel Baccus Mathews.

Human rights came increasingly under attack. Shortly after seizing power, the PRC imposed a ban on political activities and ruthlessly crushed any attempts to violate the prohibition or to otherwise challenge the regime. In 1984, for example, when students at the University of Liberia protested the arrest of their dean, Amos Sawyer, military units sealed off the Monrovia campus and began a five-day spree of looting, rape, torture, and killing. Although Sawyer was ultimately released after three months in prison, he was kept effectively under house arrest until early 1985. Independent newspapers became subject to censorship and other harassment and outspoken journalists found themselves targeted or even killed, as was the case with broadcaster Charles Gbenyon who was bayoneted at the Executive Mansion in 1985 after he refused to surrender an audiocassette in which he had recorded the head of Doe's election commission admitting to plans to rig the planned elections. Rufus M. Darpoh, managing editor of the *Sun Times*, Isaac Bantu of the *Daily Observer*, Arthur Massaquoi and Andrew Robinson of *Foot Prints*, and

Thomas Nimely, then of the *Sun Times* and later a senator for Charles
Taylor's National Patriotic Party, all spent time in jail during this period.
Borrowing a page from South Africa's apartheid regime, Doe even introduced the penalty of "banning" whereby a Liberian citizen who contra-
dicted the head of state could be forbidden all forms of social, economic,
and political contacts with the rest of society and anyone having contact
with him or her would be subject to punishment.

Fearing the popular General Quiwonkpa, Doe launched an attack
aimed at destroying the Quiwonkpa's base of support among his fellow
Gios in Nimba County. The infamous "Nimba Raid" of late 1983–early
1984 was launched on Doe's orders. Krahn-led AFL units were sent
into Nimba County and given free rein to loot and burn villages. Scores
of villagers were slaughtered, including the venerable retired county
superintendent Robert Saye, while hundreds of others, including Quiwonkpa, fled abroad.

In addition to favoring his fellow members of his Krahn ethnic
group, Doe also reached out in particular to the members of the Mandingo tribe. Numbering approximately five percent of the Liberian
population, the Mandingos, also known as the Malinké, are primarily
Muslim. In connection with ethnic cousins, they maintain a traditional
trading route that stretches from Morocco to Côte d'Ivoire and control
the lucrative commerce between Liberia and the interior provinces of
Sierra Leone and Guinea. Doe offered the Mandingo protection in exchange for a portion of the profits. He also built a mosque in Monrovia
and appointed prominent Mandingos and other Muslims, including the
future warlord Alhaji Kromah, to his government.

While the Tolbert administration had bequeathed to its successor
a country teetering on the brink of economic disaster, its mismanagement by the uneducated Doe pushed it over the edge. Liberia's gross
domestic product declined every single year of Doe's rule. And, when
one considers that the gross domestic product shrunk by an average of
4.4 percent during those years while the population grew by an average
of 3.4 percent, the true magnitude of the deterioration in standard of
living is quite unambiguous.

A RETURN TO "CONSTITUTIONAL" GOVERNMENT

Early in his rule, Doe co-opted a group of eminent Liberian scholars
and lawyers to form a National Constitutional Commission under the

chairmanship of Amos Sawyer.[9] The task of the Commission was to prepare a draft constitution that the dictator hope to lend legitimacy to his rule by serving as a framework for the PRC's reinvention of itself as a "democratic" civilian government. Doe did not read the fine print of the draft charter that the Commission presented him with in early 1983 if he had learned to read by then, the matter is unclear. Consequently, the then-thirty-four-year-old dictator was enraged to discover, after a plebiscite ratified the constitution on July 3, 1984, that the wily Sawyer had inserted a clause into the document, copied from the United States Constitution, that set the minimum age for presidential candidates at thirty-five (Sawyer's cleverness, no doubt, contributed to his being jailed in the incident related earlier). Not to be perturbed by such technicalities, Doe issued a decree revising his age to add two years.

The elections, set for October 15, 1985, were never intended by the PRC to be anything other than a *pro forma* ratification of the dictator's rule. The regime's Special Elections Commission banned Gabriel Baccus Mathews's PAL/PPP, which was running as the United People's Party (UPP), and Amos Sawyer's Liberian People's Party (LPP) on the grounds that the opposition groups espoused "strange and foreign ideologies." The banning of the two parties left Doe's National Democratic Party of Liberia (NDPL) with the only legal opposition that presented by the Liberian Action Party (LAP), a minor faction headed by Jackson Fiah Doe (no relation to Samuel Doe), an ethnic Gio who had been adopted raised as part of Americo-Liberian by the distinguished diplomat and jurist Louis Arthur Grimes and who had served in the Senate as a member of the TWP. Not content with banning the opposition, however, the regime sporadically jailed prominent opponents in the lead-up to the 1985 poll. In addition to Amos Sawyer, who was under virtual house arrest, Mathews and several of his UPP colleagues were detained for a week and Ellen Johnson Sirleaf, a former finance minister who had broken with the regime, spent several months in jail.

The elections were farcical. State-owned ELTV gave extensive coverage to the NDPL and its colleagues, while virtually ignoring any opposition. The news editor of the state-owned ELWA radio was sacked after he filed a "defamatory" report on electoral fraud. One week before the voting, Doe declared that: "The real meaning of democracy ... is to give jobs to somebody who can promote you."[10] Consequently, all 56,000 government employees were required to produce evidence that they belonged to the NDPL or face dismissal. Despite these tactics, the regime was so unpopular that exit polls showed the relatively unknown Jackson Doe's LAP leading in both the presidential and legislative elections. As the press began to predict a landslide victory for the LAP, soldiers loyal to Samuel Doe confiscated the ballot boxes and brought them to government conference center where an *ad hoc* committee consisting of fifty of the dictator's Krahn kinsmen from Grand Gedeh County was appointed to count the votes. Not surprisingly, two weeks later the committee certified that Samuel Doe was elected president with a razor-thin majority of 50.9 percent and that the NDPL won 84 percent of the legislative vote. As a precaution against public reaction, Justice minister Jenkins Scott banned all unauthorized gatherings lest the Liberian people's "jubilation might get out of hand."[11]

Less than a fortnight later, Brigadier General Thomas Quiwonkpa, a former member of the PRC, returned from exile in the United States and, operating from a base in neighboring Sierra Leone with the connivance of that country's leader Joseph Momoh, launch an attack on Monrovia with the aim of overthrowing the regime and installing the presumed victor in the elections, Jackson Doe, as president. Quiwonkpa, an ethnic Gio from Nimba County who was appointed commander of the AFL after the 1980 coup, was widely credited with restoring discipline to the army after the PRC takeover had destroyed the military chain of command. Jealous of Quiwonkpa's increasing popularity, Samuel Doe had the AFL commander dismissed in 1983, and he went into exile the following year after the "Nimba Raid" killed a number of his kinsmen. The coup quickly collapsed, however, when Quiwonkpa's soldiers joined with civilians in celebrations of the regime's overthrow before actually capturing Samuel Doe. The delay gave the dictator time to organize a successful counterattack by the Krahn-dominated Executive Mansion Guard and the 1st Infantry Battalion. Quiwonkpa was arrested, castrated, and beaten to death, his dismembered body being displayed openly. Other participants in the plot were summarily executed and the AFL was purged of all Gios. Samuel Doe then unleashed predominantly Krahn military units on a rampage through Nimba County where they massacred an estimated three thousand Gio and Mano civilians and pillaged villages. In Monrovia and Grand Gedeh County, regime loyalists staged smaller *pogroms* that targeted civilians from the Gio and Mano ethnic groups.

His opponents crushed, Samuel Kanyon Doe was inaugurated as Liberia's twenty-first civilian president on January 6, 1986. With Doe's control firmly reestablished, the political opposition quickly withered away. Thirteen of the eighteen opposition politicians who the regime had permitted to be elected to the Liberian Congress broke with their earlier mutual pact not to legitimize the dictator by taking their legislative seats. Some of them, including former Chase Manhattan bank teller Ruth Sando Fahnbulleh Perry, who was to serve as the head of Liberia's transitional government in 1996, even crossed the aisle to join the ruling NDPL—such was the allure of the state patronage that was now in the former master sergeant's gift. Amos Sawyer later reflects sadly on the period:

> While it is true that repression and social malaise were not first introduced into Liberian Society by the military junta government, these conditions became more intensified under military rule. Murder, torture, and imprisonment became normal instruments of national policy. Similarly, graft and corruption were also perceived as normal business practices. The combination of ill-trained military people in search of bounties and ambitious former clients of a decaying patronage system seeking to maintain their privileges had produced the right chemistry for ineptitude, plunder and brutal repression — the trademarks of military rule and tragedy in Liberia.[12]

"CHAIRMAN MOE," AMERICA'S "DEPENDABLE ALLY"

In the immediate aftermath of the overthrow and brutal killing of President William Tolbert, the incumbent chairman of the Organization of African Unity (OAU) who was widely popular among his fellow heads of state, the Doe regime found itself shunned by its neighbors. The Nigerian government refused permission for the plane carrying the new Liberian foreign minister to land in Lagos when Gabriel Baccus Mathews tried to attend the OAU economic summit in 1980. Later that same year, Liberia's defense minister was likewise excluded from the conference of the defense chiefs of the Economic Community of West African States (ECOWAS). At the instigation Côte d'Ivoire's President Félix Houphouët-Boigny whose personal motives were discussed previously, Doe himself was excluded from the annual summit of ECOWAS heads of state, held that year in Lomé, Togo. Nigerian President Shehu Shagari closed his country's embassy in Monrovia. Anti-Doe forces were eventually given sanctuary in Côte d'Ivoire, Sierra Leone, and Burkina Faso. The utter hypocrisy in the self-righteous condemnation of the Liberian ruler by African leaders who themselves either lacked democratic credentials or abused human rights—or both—did not seem to deter any of them.

Ostracized by his neighbors, Doe looked further for diplomatic and other support. In fact, Libya as well as the Soviet Union, Cuba, and other communist bloc countries had been quick to hail the "revolution" proclaimed by the PRC after its takeover. When the United States froze economic aid to Liberia in the wake of the executions of the TWP dignitaries, Doe was encouraged by PRC vice chairman Thomas Weh Syen and some of the leftist intellectuals co-opted by the ruling body to build closer ties with Libya and the Soviet bloc. Consequently, the new regime sent envoys abroad to these countries with feelers.

Driven by strategic calculations conditioned by the Cold War, the U.S. responded to Doe's outreach to the erratic Libyan leader and to members of the Communist bloc by dispatching the assistant secretary of state for African affairs, Richard Moose, to meet with Doe in June 1980. On his return to Washington, Moose recommended the resumption of the suspended aid programs and an increase in both economic and military assistance to Liberia. The calculation paid off as Doe moved to eliminate the radical leftist elements from his government. By the following year, the Liberian dictator had broken diplomatic relations with Libya. He followed that up with the resumption of Liberia's diplomatic relations of the state of Israel, which had been broken at the time of the 1973 Arab-Israeli War, and, in contradiction of OAU policy, paid an official visit to Jerusalem from August 22 to 26, 1983. Liberia's diplomatic representatives were instructed to support U.S. foreign policy at the United Nations, the Non-Aligned Movement, and other international bodies. The Doe regime also cooperated with American efforts to frustrate the overtures that Libyan leader Muammar Qaddafi directed towards sub-Saharan Africa. Doe gave the newly created U.S. Rapid Deployment Force rights to Liberia's sea and airports and allowed the Central Intelligence Agency to use the Roberts International Airport to ship arms to Jonas Savimbi's UNITA forces in Angola. Doe also forged ties with other U.S. allies, including South Korea and the nationalist Chinese government on Taiwan.

In return, for this cooperation, Liberia received an incredible increase in U.S. largesse. American aid to Liberia went from $20 million a year in 1979 to over $90 million in 1986, including $14 million in military assistance. By the time Doe was inaugurated as the civilian head of state of Liberia that year, the U.S. government was responsible for a full third of the Liberian government's revenues.[13] In fact, U.S. economic and military assistance to Liberia between 1981 and 1985 totaled over $500 million—more than the country had received from the America in the more than century and a half that had passed between the Congressional grant of $100,000 to the American Colonization Society and the overthrow of the Americo-Liberia oligarchy.[14] Timely shipments of rice from USAID fed hundreds of thousands of Liberians as well as saved the regime from a repetition of the Rice Riots that had been so cataclysmic for the Tolbert administration. A U.S. Presidential Agricultural Task Force was dispatched to Liberia in late 1982 to assist the country's small and medium farmers. In addition, American private investment in Liberia during Doe's rule is estimated at over $5 billion.[15]

Even before his transformation into a constitutional head of state, Doe was officially welcomed to the White House by President Ronald Reagan on August 17, 1982. During that visit—the same one during which President Reagan famously referred to the Liberian leader as "Chairman Moe"—Doe was assured that "the United States stands by its commitments to Liberia, and looks forward to continued, mutual cooperation."[16] The following year, while visiting the United Nations in New York, Reagan received Doe once again, calling him "a dependable ally, a friend in need" during their private meeting in Reagan's suite in the Waldolf-Astoria Hotel.[17]

American officials even bent over backwards to excuse their wayward ally. Following the fraudulent 1985 elections, the U.S. assistant secretary of state for African affairs, Charles Crocker, in testimony before the U.S. Senate Committee on Foreign Relations Sub-committee on Africa, hailed the polls as "the beginning, however imperfect, of a democratic experience that Liberia and its friends can use as a benchmark for future elections" and "a rare achievement in Africa and elsewhere in the Third World."[18] Crocker, whose eight years at the State Department's Africa bureau make him the longest-serving secretary of state in American history, went on to make the extraordinary assertion that:

> The prospects for national reconciliation were brightened by Doe's claim that he won only a narrow, fifty-one percent election victory virtually unheard of in the rest of Africa where incumbent rulers

normally claim victories of ninety-five to one hundred percent. In claiming only fifty-one percent of the vote, Doe publicly acknowledged that a large segment of society—forty-nine percent—supported other points of view and leadership than his own.[19]

Crocker's Senate testimony, broadcast into Liberia by the BBC and the Voice of America and extensively reprinted by the Liberian press, subsequently made him a controversial figure in West African circles. Perhaps in part to rehabilitate his reputation in these sectors that the former official, now an elder statesman and scholar at Georgetown University, responded to the Liberian crisis of 2003 by calling upon the United States to intervene directly to "promote good governance" in Monrovia.[20]

TOWARDS THE END

The coming of the end of the Cold War altered the variables in America's strategic calculations and the relative significance of Liberia and its dictator diminished in the view of Washington's policy makers. Already the U.S. House of Representatives and Senate has passed, respectively in December 1986 and January 1987, nonbinding resolutions conditioning continued American aid to Liberia to progress on human rights and democratization. American aid to Liberia plummeted from $53.6 million in 1986 to $19.5 million in 1989. In 1990, there was no aid appropriated except for some $10 million in food and other humanitarian assistance.[21]

International institutions, taking their signal from America, tightened their stance vis-à-vis the Doe regime. The International Monetary Fund cut off Liberia's access to drawing rights, citing its default on $900 million in past-due debts in 1986. The following year, the World Bank refused to consider new loans to Monrovia, forcing Doe to slash the salaries of the bloated government bureaucracy.

These measures caused Doe to run afoul of a provision of American legislation known as the Brooke Amendment to the U.S. Foreign Assistance Act of 1961. The Brooke Amendment, which went into effect in 1989, stipulated that aid would not be given to any country that fell six months or more in default on payments of interest or principal of loans made by the U.S. government. Despite a desperate attempt at the eleventh hour to raise funds from private sources in Liberia in order to meet its payments, the regime failed to service its debts. Consequently, the Brooke Amendment was invoked in May 1989 and aid was cut off, beginning with military assistance.

With the revolutions sweeping through Central and Eastern Europe that momentous year, the long Cold War was coming to an end, sweeping into the dustbins of history not only the communist despots of the soon-to-be-former Soviet bloc, but also the strategic importance of Third World strongmen like Doe, who circumstances had constrained American policy makers to accept a marriage of convenience with. But with the circumstances changed, America was prepared to go back to its more historic hands-off relationship with Liberia. While Liberians and perhaps American scholars sympathetic to them are wont to recite clichés about the West African state being "the only country in West Africa which has enjoyed a sustained relationship with the United States"[22] for over a century, the truth of the matter is that it has been a story of unrequited love—as Doe and, sadly, his countrymen would soon learn to their sorrow.

ENDNOTES

1. Quoted in Sanford J. Ungar, "Liberia: A Revolution, or Just Another Coup?," *The Atlantic Monthly* 246/6 (June 1981): 26.
2. The number of those killed in the "Rice Riots" of 1979 has long been disputed. Estimates range from forty to over two hundred; see Adekeye Adebajo, *Liberia's Civil War: Nigeria, ECOMOG, and Regional Security in West Africa* (Boulder, Colorado/London: Lynne Rienner Publishers, 2002), 23; and Sawyer, *The Emergence of Autocracy in Liberia*, 292.
3. Arthur F. Kulah, *Liberia Will Rise Again: Reflections on the Liberian Civil Crisis* (Nashville, Tennessee: Abingdon Press, 1999), 73–74.
4. Vice President Bennie Dee Warner was traveling in the United States with his entire family at the time of the coup and thus escaped the fate that was, no doubt, reserved for him.
5. See D. Elwood Dunn and S. Byron Tarr, *Liberia: A National Polity in Transition* (Metuchen, New Jersey: Scarecrow Press, 1988), 126–127. The first co-author, presently professor of political science at the University of the South, Sewanee, Tennessee, served in President Tolbert's cabinet as minister of state for presidential affairs.
6. For an exhaustive catalogue of the abuses committed by Doe and the PRC during their first years in power, see *Liberia: A Promise* Betrayed (New York: Lawyers Committee on Human Rights, 1986).
7. Yoweri K. Musaveni, *What is Africa's Problem?* ed. Elizabeth Kanyongonya (Minneapolis: University of Minnesota Press, 2000), 170–171.
8. Quoted in Bill Berkeley, "Liberia between Repression and Slaughter," *The Atlantic Monthly* 270/10 (December 1992), 26.
9. See Amos Sawyer, "The Making of the 1984 Liberian Constitution: Major Issues and Dynamic Forces," *Liberian Studies Journal* 12/1 (1987): 1–15.
10. Quoted in J. Gus Liebenow, *Liberia: The Quest for a Democracy* (Bloomington, Indiana: Indiana University Press, 1987), 281.

11. Quoted in *ibid.*, 294.

12. Sawyer, *The Emergence of Autocracy in Liberia*, 296.

13. See Liebenow, *Liberia: The Quest for a Democracy*, 304–306.

14. See William O'Neill, "Liberia: An Avoidable Tragedy," *Current History* 92/574 (May 1993): 213–217.

15. See Paul Gifford, *Christianity and Politics in Doe's Liberia* (Cambridge: Cambridge University Press, 1993), 36–37.

16. The complete text of Reagan's remarks can be found at his presidential library's website at <www.reagan.utexas.edu/resource/speeches/1982/81782d.htm>.

17. Quoted in Gifford, *Christianity and Politics in Doe's Liberia*, 234.

18. Quoted in Liebenow, *Liberia: The Quest for a Democracy*, 293; also Adekeye Adebajo, *Liberia's Civil War*, 35.

19. Quoted in Bill Berkeley, *The Graves Are Not Yet Full: Race, Tribe and Power in the Heart of Africa* (New York: Basic Books, 2001), 66. A profile of Chester Crocker can be found in *ibid.*, 63–101.

20. Chester A. Crocker, "A War America Can Afford to Stop," *New York Times* (August 1, 2003). For the present author's response to that *volte-face*, see "Intervention in Liberia," *New York Times* (August 8, 2003).

21. See O'Neill, "Liberia: An Avoidable Tragedy," 215.

22. Liebenow, *Liberia: The Quest for a Democracy*, 3.

FOUR

THE DARK YEARS

ON CHRISTMAS EVE 1989, some 168 lightly armed men crossed into Liberia's Nimba County from their base in neighboring Côte d'Ivoire. The band quickly reached the Nimba capital of Saniquellie and announced itself as the "National Patriotic Front of Liberia" (NPFL)—a name previously used by General Thomas Quiwonkpa for his partisans during the abortive coup of 1985 and no doubt chosen to for its resonance in the slain military commander's home county—and declared that its express purpose was the overthrow of Samuel Doe. Although few realized it at the time, the invasion signaled the start of a civil war that would engulf the entire region and continue right to the present with low-intensity fighting interspersed with occasional flare-ups as well as periods of relative calm.

THE MANY FACES OF CHARLES TAYLOR

Leading the NPFL force into Saniquellie was a forty-year-old exile, Charles McArthur Taylor, who had been born in the Montserrado settlement of Arthington, on the outskirts of Monrovia, to an Americo-Liberian father and a Gola mother. Coming to the United States in 1972, and working his way through school with a variety of odd jobs—including stints as a security guard and a truck driver—Taylor studied at Chamberlayne Junior College in Newton, Massachusetts, and eventually received a bachelor's degree in economics from Bentley College in Waltham, Massachusetts, in 1977.

However his real passion was student politics and he soon developed a reputation as an outspoken critic of President William Tolbert. After his graduation, Taylor earned a living as a mechanic in a plastics factory while serving as national chairman of the Union of Liberian Associations in the Americas (ULAA), an umbrella organization representing some thirty-five thousand Liberian students and other émigrés living in the United States. During his tenure as chairman, Taylor turned the ULAA from a service organization into a political group. In 1979, during Tolbert's visit to New York, Taylor led a noisy demonstration outside the Liberian mission to the United Nations. Rather than ignore the protesters, the good-natured Tolbert engaged Taylor in a bantering debate that had the unintended consequence of instantly enhancing the ULAA leader's stature and earning him admirers on both sides of the Atlantic. Tolbert then invited Taylor and other ULAA leaders to return to Liberia for further discussions.

Taylor return to Monrovia in early 1980, on the eve of events that would change Liberia as well as his own personal fortunes. When, on April 12, Tolbert was murdered during the military coup headed by Master Sergeant Samuel Doe, months of bloody retribution by indigenous Liberians against Americo-Liberians ensued the overthrow of the long-dominant True Whig oligarchy. However, as previously noted, the new regime needed the technical expertise of educated Liberians, of whom a disproportionate number came from Americo-Liberian backgrounds. Consequently Taylor's American education and his mixed Americo-Liberian and Gola parentage as well as his anti-Tolbert political background—to say nothing of his relationship by marriage to Doe's fellow *putschist*, Thomas Quiwonkpa—played in his favor when, on the very morrow of the coup, he walked into Doe's headquarters and volunteered his services. He was appointed managing director of the General Services Agency, the Liberian government's purchasing department. In early 1983, he was appointed deputy minister of commerce. However, when he was accused of diverting more than $900,000 in public funds to a private account at Citibank, Taylor fled the country and apparently entered the United States sometime in late 1983.

Taylor was arrested by U.S. marshals in Somerville, Massachusetts, on May 24, 1984, on the authority of the extradition treaty that the U.S. had with Liberia. He then spent fifteen months in prison while former U.S. Attorney-General Ramsey Clark tried to fight his extradition. When a federal court ruled that sufficient evidence existed to support the Liberian government's request for his return, Taylor escaped from the Plymouth House of Corrections, where he was being held, in September 1985. According to one report, Taylor convinced a guard to bend the rules at the facility to allow him to pass from the north wing, where he was held, to the east wing, telling the guard he wanted to play cards with a friend. Once there, he used a hacksaw blade to cut through an iron window bar and, using bed sheets tied together, he and four other inmates climbed down from the second floor, scaled a fence, and ran into the nearby woods.[1]

While details concerning his movements over the next four years are sketchy, it seems that Taylor made his way to Accra, Ghana, via Mexico, Spain, and France. Basing himself in the Ghanaian capital, he seems to have traveled throughout the West African region, apparently being jailed briefly in Ghana and Sierra Leone, and possibly Guinea as well. While in Accra, Taylor befriended the ambassador of Burkina Faso, Memunu Ouattara, a cousin of the Burkinabè strongman Blaise Compaoré. Possibly through the Burkinabès, Taylor was introduced to Libyan leader Muammar Qaddafi, who allowed Taylor to train in Libya. Qaddafi's patronage was part of the pattern of behavior whereby, since the early 1970s, he had supported with Libya's considerable oil revenues, in the name of anti-imperialism, insurgencies and coups as well as radical governments in sub-Saharan Africa. In the 1990s, the Libyan regime reinforced this policy, disappointed with the limited support that it had received from Arab countries in its effort to remove the sanctions imposed after the bombing of Pan Am flight 103 over Lockerbie, Scotland.[2]

Originally, Taylor planned to launch his invasion of Liberia from Sierra Leone. Traveling on a Burkinabè passport, Taylor traveled to

Freetown in early 1988 and offered to pay President Joseph Momoh for permission to operate out of bases in Sierra Leone. Instead, Taylor was briefly jailed. As Stephen Ellis later observed: "The notoriously venal Momoh promptly sought from Samuel Doe a higher sum, turning the approach into an auction, an action for which his country was later to pay dearly."[3]

During the civil war he launched, Taylor dropped his quintessentially America-Liberian middle name, "McArthur," in favor of "Ghankay," which means "strong in the face of adversity" in his mother's tribal language of Gola—a clear appeal to ethnic loyalties. In fact, as events unfolded one of the most remarkable aspects of Taylor's political career—and perhaps the key to his survival and success—has been his uncanny ability to discern and adopt the persona that is most likely to win over his audience. Eventually as head of state, his official name and title—as the protocol office of the Liberian Ministry of Foreign Affairs took great pains to emphasize to the diplomatic corps accredited to the government in Monrovia—was "His Excellency, Dahkpannah Dr. Charles Ghankay Taylor, President of the Republic of Liberia."

To Westerners, Taylor takes pains to present himself as "Charlie"—not to be confused with his son "Chucky," who has been accused of murder and various other crimes—a U.S.-educated "baby boomer" who appreciates Bach and Handel (but "not Beethoven"), listens to American pop music ("my favorite singer is Mahalia Jackson"), watches Hollywood flicks (his favorite is supposedly *Dirty Harry*), and plays tennis and basketball to stay in shape. In short, he tries to convince them that he is "one of them." This strategy was not entirely unsuccessful, especially in the early days. Taylor was represented in his fight against extradition by no less a lawyer than former U.S. Attorney-General Ramsey Clark. His supporters included African-American political leaders like the Reverend Jesse Jackson and Democratic Congressman Donald Payne of New Jersey, as well as seasoned political activists like Lester Hyman, a former protégé of the Kennedy family who served as chairman of the Massachusetts Democratic Party before becoming Taylor's Washington-based counsel.[4] Nor was Taylor's support confined to political left: the Reverend Pat Robertson was so charmed that he invested money received from the faithful in a Liberian gold mining concession granted by Taylor, by then president of Liberia.[5]

To his fellow Gola tribesmen and members of ethnic groups that were not only oppressed during the long America-Liberian hegemony, but were also targeted during the Krahn-dominated Doe regime, Taylor is "Ghankay," the avenger who is, as the name implies, "strong in the face of adversity," the natural leader of an ethnic coalition of disgruntled citizens who had seen some three thousand Gio and Mano civilians massacred in Nimba County alone after General Quiwonkpa's failed invasion in November 1985. In fact the choice of the NPFL label for his band was calculated by Taylor to present himself as the successor to the general although there was no evidence of any political ties between the two. By cleverly manipulating the ethnic tensions, Taylor had little difficulty recruiting supporters in the slain military man's home region and when, in the aftermath of the new NPFL invasion, the paranoid Samuel Doe began lashing out at Gio and Mano soldiers and civilians, even more recruits came in to Taylor from the ethnic kin of the slain, eager to wage war against Krahns and Mandingos.

Once he had established his effective control of a significant portion of Liberian territory, in early 1997, Taylor awarded himself the title of "*Dahkpannah*," which literally translates as "Supreme *Zo*." Although some Liberian scholars abroad have tried to downplay the mystical connotations the office of *zo*, perhaps out of self-conscious embarrassment about the extent to which "the supernatural" still figures into modern politics in their homeland,[6] the irreverent Western rendition of the title as "chief witch doctor" is perhaps closer to the claim that Taylor attempts to stake out of his position as the ultimate head of all of Liberia's indigenous cults.[7]

While it is perhaps overly simplistic to claim, as some Liberians have, that each of Taylor's names connotes a certain pattern of behavior,[8] the is something to be said about the uncanny ability that Taylor would show—and continues to show—during the civil conflicts to play various factions against one another and not only to survive, but to prevail, against adverse conditions.

LIBERIA UNRAVELS

The initial band of 168 NPFL fighters that entered Liberia under the command of Charles Taylor would never have succeeded even in that endeavor without the active support of a trio of African states whose distinct interests came together to seek the overthrow of the Samuel Doe.

The NPFL had invaded Liberia from Côte d'Ivoire. As previously noted, the Ivorian President, Félix Houphouët-Boigny never pardoned

Doe for the slaying of Adolphus Tolbert, which left his adopted daughter Daisy a widow, especially since the killing had come after *le Vieux* had personally interceded for his life. The death was thus not only a personal blow to the Ivorian leader's family, but a public disgrace that had cost him, an octogenarian Baoulé chieftain who was a trained physician as well as the grand old man of West African politics, loss of face at the hands of an illiterate, twenty-eight-year-old soldier. The patronage of the Ivorian president, who had served in the French National Assembly and in the cabinet of General Charles de Gaulle before leading his country to independence, opened for Taylor access to French arms suppliers as well as French commercial investment in the areas of Liberia he would eventually control during the civil war.[9]

Burkina Faso's strongman, Blaise Compaoré, who had become head of state following a 1987 coup, had close personal links to both Houphouët-Boigny and his thirst of vengeance against Doe: Compaoré was married to the widow Delafosse-Tolbert's foster sister Chantal, whose father had been one of the Ivorian president's ministers. Furthermore, the exiled widow had come to live with him and his bride in Ouagadougou, becoming a constant reminder of what Doe had perpetrated. Furthermore, landlocked and impoverished Burkina Faso was dependent upon Côte d'Ivoire both for jobs for its migrant workers and for access to the sea, leaving Compaoré particularly susceptible to Houphouët-Boigny's pressures. Consequently, not only had Compaoré been instrumental in introducing Taylor to Libya's Muammar Qaddafi for training and assistance, but he had permitted Taylor and his followers to prepare for their invasion at a camp in Burkina Faso. The Burkinabè leader was to remain one of the main sources of arms for Taylor throughout the Liberian civil war and, as he subsequently admitted, even lent the NPFL the combat support of some seven hundred Burkinabè soldiers at one point in the conflict.[10] And throughout the civil war, Taylor, perhaps mistrustful of his own compatriots, entrusted his personal security a special detachment of Burkinabè bodyguards provided by Compaoré.

Doe had, early in his rule, broken diplomatic ties with Libya, expelling the staff of the Libyan embassy in Monrovia and cooperating with American and Israeli efforts to frustrate Colonel Muammar Qaddafi's policies in sub-Saharan Africa. Consequently, it was not surprising that Qaddafi not only provided training for Taylor and the NPFL, but also funneled arms to them through Burkina Faso.

As subsequent events later proved, Liberian president Doe made the mistake of not taking the NPFL invasion seriously. After all, the AFL had over six thousand men under arms while the rebel band did not even number two hundred. It was five days after the invasion before Doe ordered the AFL to suppress it, sending tanks and artillery into Nimba County. Doe, however, had misjudged the level of resentment against his regime as well as the discipline and loyalty of his troops. The NPFL soon attracted a host of tribesmen to its banner, the number swelling even further as AFL units outraged the population by rampaging through the county, killing civilians and burning homes and villages in an attempt to destroy the rebels. The AFL expedition sent to suppress the rebels was beaten back with heavy losses. By May 1990, NPFL forces had captured Gbarnga, capital of Bong County and crossroad for Liberia's network of communications to the interior. The same month, the NPFL took the port city of Buchanan, Liberia's second largest town. By this time the NPFL's ranks had increased to an estimated ten thousand fighters while the national government's AFL was rapidly disintegrating, barely maintaining itself at the level of two thousand men.

Now fully cognizant of his desperate plight, Doe tried broaden his base of support by releasing political prisoners and lifting the bans on opposition political parties and independent newspapers. However, these moves were motivated more by a desire to garner sympathy from the international community than from any newly found zeal for reform. In January 1990, the United States had briefly sent two military observers to accompany the AFL on its expedition against the NPFL in Nimba County, but the duo was withdrawn after the AFL began committing atrocities. On May 1, Doe sent a delegation to Washington to plead his cause, a move that was countered by Taylor, who sent Tom Woewiyu, a former official of the Doe regime who had defected to the NPFL, to brief U.S. officials on May 14. On June 3, the U.S. deployed 2,500 Marines off the coast of Liberia, but gave them strict orders to limit their duties to safeguarding U.S. installations and the eventual evacuation of the one thousand U.S. citizens remaining in the country. Increasingly isolated—no fewer than seven of his cabinet ministers deserted him—the Liberian dictator even wrote, on June 4, a pathetic six-page appeal from the fortified Executive Mansion where he was bottled up by then, addressing it to U.S. President George H.W. Bush:

My relationship with my country might be likened in some respects to that of a man who loves his wife very much but at times is tempted to be unfaithful...I realize that people have said that I have been driven by power, greed or other unhealthy desires but these have not been my primary motivations. If I have failed in regards at times, I ask for the forgiveness of my people... Our capital is named after your President Monroe. Our flag is a replica of yours. Our laws are patterned after your laws. We in Liberia have always considered ourselves 'stepchildren' of the United States. We implore you to come help your stepchildren who are in danger of losing their lives and their freedom.[11]

Receiving no response to his appeal, the desperate president even orchestrated a letter-writing campaign by his relatives, who bombarded the "letters to the editor" sections of major U.S. newspapers with testimonials such as the one that his brother Chayee Doe, safely in the United States, sent to the editors of the *Washington Post*, in which he affirmed that: "My brother Liberian President Samuel Doe is not an African despot clinging to power, as some in the media would like to believe."[12] After his brother's fall, Chayee Doe became involved in Liberian politics and went on to become one of the leaders of the Liberians United for Reconciliation and Democracy (LURD) that fought in Liberia's second civil war.

However, the appeals fell on deaf ears as, in the "new world order" that emerged after the collapse of the Iron Curtain, Doe had lost his strategic significance and the U.S. administration was hesitant to commit itself to in the absence of a vital national interest. As one senior official at the State Department declared: "The bottom line is, it's not in the United States' interest to get in the middle of this fight ... It is not something we would put U.S. boys on the line for."[13] Iraqi dictator Saddam Hussein's invasion of neighboring Kuwait on August 2 eliminated any possibility of a U.S. military commitment in Africa as America fixed its attention on the Gulf region. Ultimately, the U.S. Marine force was deployed only to evacuate the remaining American citizens and other Western nationals on August 5.

Failing to obtain support from abroad with the exception of some arms shipments from Nigeria, Doe tried to rally support in Monrovia with a number of liberalization measures. Some seventy-five political prisoners were freed. The bans on the independent *Footprints* and

Suntimes newspapers were lifted as was the prohibition on the Catholic Church's ELCM radio station. Not having much to show for these gestures—most Liberians perceived them as insincere and, in any event, too little, too late—Doe became increasingly paranoid of "traitors" whose presence he suspected within Monrovia. A 6:00 P.M. curfew was imposed on the capital. Each morning, Monrovians woke up to find on the streets the bodies of the latest victims of the vigilante squads formed by Doe loyalists. Fearful for their lives, such Mano and Gio tribesmen who remained in Monrovia sought refuge at the United Nations compound on Tubman Boulevard in the Congo Town neighborhood. On May 28, men in AFL uniforms raided the compound, killing a security guard and abducting thirty of the refugees. On June 26 and 30, government forces violently broke up peace marches organized by the Inter-Faith Mediation Committee representing Liberia's Christian churches as well as Islamic representatives.

On July 2, barely six months after invading Liberia, Taylor's NPFL forces took the Monrovia suburb of Paynesville and cut off the capital's water and electrical supplies. The following day, the NPFL began to pound Monrovia with heavy artillery and rocket attacks. As the crumbling regime became increasingly desperate, Doe's Krahn loyalists began lashing out at anyone that they believed to be an enemy. Political and religious leaders left in the city went into hiding as death squads sought them out. On the night between July 30 and July 31, AFL soldiers entered Monrovia's St. Peter's Lutheran Church and massacred six hundred refugees who had taken refuge there, many of them children. Most of the victims were Gio and Mano, although some were Americo-Liberians with ties to those ethnic groups. Among the victims of the massacre was Nelson Taylor, father of NPFL leader Charles Taylor.

As a result of atrocities like the St. Peter's Church massacre, the war took on the dimensions of a full-fledged ethnic conflict. One observer, writer Denis Johnson, described one "check point" manned by orphans who joined up with the NPFL:

Taylor's rebels—boys from the Gio and Mano tribes, most of them between the ages of eleven and fifteen, armed with AK-47s and M-16s—had dedicated themselves to separating out and killing anyone from the Krahn or Mandingo tribe, and those from the president's army or the former government. Thirty-eight miles out, in the town of Klay, refugees encountered the first check-point. "Do you smell that smell?" the rebels asked, speaking of the stench of putrefaction on the breeze. "You'd better know who you are," they said, "or you're going where that smell is coming from." Anyone who didn't speak the right dialect, anybody who looked too prosperous or well fed was shot, beheaded, or set on fire with fuel oil.[14]

By August 1, 1990, over 5,000 Liberians had died in the conflict and some 345,000 had fled their country for shelter in neighboring states: 225,000 in Guinea, 150,000 in Côte d'Ivoire, and 70,000 in Sierra Leone.

Meanwhile a fissure had developed within the ranks of the NPFL. One of Taylor's deputies, Prince Yormie Johnson,[15] abandoned the rebel leader to form his own rebel movement, consisting mainly of fighters from his Gio ethnic group, the Independent National Patriotic Front of Liberia (INPFL). Johnson, who had been junior officer in Doe's AFL before deserting in 1983, had been Taylor's chief training officer. In the highly personalized politics of West Africa, this opening was enough for the Nigerian leader, General Ibrahim Badamasi Babangida, to exploit in a last-ditch attempt to save the embattled Liberian president. Relations between the two military leaders had been close. During Doe's rule, the Nigerian strongman had contributed to the establishment of the Ibrahim Babangida Graduate School of International Studies at the University of Liberia. The Liberian section of the Trans-African Highway—likewise paid for by the Nigerian treasury—was also named after Babangida. Just before the civil war began, Nigeria had paid off Doe's arrears to the African Development Bank in early December 1989 and had invested $25 million in a Liberian iron ore project and $4.5 million in the failing Liberian National Oil Corporation. Some three thousand Nigerian citizens were employed in technical positions by the Doe regime. Furthermore, the overthrow of Doe by Taylor, with his ties to Côte d'Ivoire and Burkina Faso, would also represent a shift in the regional balance of power against Nigeria. Moreover, as one Nigerian political scientist put it, Nigeria was "a restless giant in a volatile subregion in search of a role it had long sought but had never been able to play" and for which "Liberia offered the first opportunity to flex Nigeria's subregional muscle."[16] Furthermore, as Nigerian Nobel laureate Wole Soyinka has noted:

Babangida's love of power was visualized in actual terms: power over Nigeria, over the nation's impressive size, its potential, over the nation's powerful status within the community of nations. The potency of Nigeria, in short, was an augmentation of his own sense of personal power.[17]

Consequently, it was no surprise that Babangida had sent military supplies to Doe early in the uprising. Now noting the dissensions in the ranks of the rebels, Babangida saw an opportunity to seize the opportunity offered. A meeting in the Gambian capital of Banjul of ECOWAS's Standing Mediation Committee (SMC), held August 6–7, attended by the Nigerian leader, agreed to establish the Economic Community of West African States Cease-fire Monitoring Group (ECOMOG). To be made up of military personnel from the five member states of the SMC (The Gambia, Ghana, Mali, Nigeria, and Togo) as well as Guinea and Sierra Leone. ECOMOG's mandate was to supervise the establishment of a cease-fire, after which Doe would resign to make room for an interim government that would organize elections within twelve months. The leaders of the belligerent factions would be excluded from the interim administration, while the head of the transitional authority would, in turn, be excluded from the standing in the eventual elections. The Banjul decision carried the implicit blessing of both the United Nations, represented during the deliberations by Assistant Secretary-General James Jonah, and the Organization of African Unity, represented by Secretary-General Salim Ahmed Salim, who brushed aside legal arguments over the legitimacy of ECOMOG from ECOWAS's francophone members, especially Burkina Faso, Côte d'Ivoire, and Senegal, about the SMC's right to make decisions in name of the entire Community. In fact, the establishment of ECOMOG opened a linguistic fissure within the SMC as its two French-speaking members, Mali and Togo, refused to contribute troops to the intervention. Nonetheless, on August 29, an assembly of Liberian political and other self-appointed interest groups, meeting in Banjul, elected Amos Sawyer, as president of the interim government that ECOMOG would install. Despite Sawyer's sterling credentials, the democratic legitimacy of the Interim Government of National Unity (IGNU)—quickly dubbed the "Imported Government of No Use" by war-weary Liberians—was subject to question since it was constituted, as one Liberian intellectual put it, "by a few dozen people who were invited and could afford to attend."[18] This criticism was and, unfortunately, continues to be valid for the host of succeeding "transitional" arrangements brokered in subsequent "peace agreements."

Ominously, Charles Taylor, who had not been represented in Banjul, denounced the establishment of ECOMOG and pledged to resist the intervention. He saw the peacekeepers as an attempt by his rivals to impose a resolution in the Liberian conflict that would rob him of the fruits of his nearly certain victory just as the NPFL was on the verge of conquering Monrovia. Having already proclaimed himself provisional president on July 28, he now established a twenty-member National Patriotic Reconstruction Assembly Government (NPRAG), headquartered in Gbarnga, in opposition to Sawyer's interim regime and declared himself president of "Greater Liberia."

While the writ of Sawyer's IGNU and its successor, the Liberian National Transition Government (LNTG), established in 1994, would never extend beyond Monrovia—and then only with the backing of the ECOMOG forces—Taylor's NPRAG issued its own currency and administered its own banking system (the Bong Bank) as well as maintained an official newspaper (*The Patriot*), a television and radio network, airfields, and, until 1993, a deepwater port at Buchanan. For a while, the writ of the NPRAG extended into Sierra Leone, where Revolutionary United Front (RUF) leader was "Greater Liberia's governor" for the eastern parts of that country that he had overrun.

THE END OF DOE

On August 24, 1990—coincidentally Liberia's Flag Day—a flotilla bearing the ECOMOG force sailed into Monrovia's Freeport. The contingent consisted of three thousand men—a battalion each being contributed by Ghana, Guinea, Nigeria, and Sierra Leone, in addition to a rifle company sent from The Gambia—and was accompanied by four Nigerian naval vessels and three Ghanaian vessels, as well as four jets, two helicopters, and nine Hercules C-130 from Nigeria and four jets from Ghana. ECOMOG's command structure reflected both its multinational composition as well as its predominance by Nigeria. The force commander was a Ghanaian officer, General Arnold Quainoo, a member of Ghana's ruling Provisional National Defense Council, who was seconded by Guinean deputy, Major General Lamine Magasoumba. The chief of operations was from Sierra Leone, while the chief of personnel and camp commander were from The Gambia. Nigerian officers occupied the key posts of chief of staff, chief logistics officer, chief intelligence officer, and chief communications officer. With the exception of the Gambian, all the officers on this mission to restore the constitutional government to Liberia came from countries ruled by military dictators whose democratic credentials and human rights records were little better than that of the embattled Samuel Doe—an irony that did not escape observers, including Charles Taylor whose radio station hailed ECOMOG contingent as the lackeys of a "club of dictators."

The split in the rebel movement had left Taylor and the NPFL controlling the eastern section of Monrovia as well as most of Liberia's interior, while Johnson and his INPFL held the northern part of the capital, including Bushrod Island and the market areas along the Mesurado River as well as the Caldwell neighborhood, where Johnson established his headquarters. President Doe held sway over very little aside from the Executive Mansion and the Barclay Training Center barracks, where the remaining units of the AFL were concentrated. By the time the ECOMOG contingent arrived, Johnson was hard pressed by Taylor's forces and, consequently, welcomed the intervention, which provided him with a much-needed respite. Taylor, on the other hand, harassed the landing of ECOMOG's units with artillery and small arms fire.

Despite splits—first between the francophone Guineans and the English-speaking units that made of the rest of the peacekeepers, then between the various English-speaking units along national lines—that quickly revealed themselves, ECOMOG secured a ceasefire between Johnson's INPFL and Doe's AFL and began the evacuation of ECOWAS nationals from Liberia. However, its long-term effectiveness was compromised by General Quainoo's decision to adopt an ill-conceived stratagem of convenience—he later explained it was based upon the notion that "the enemy of your enemy is your friend"[19]—and accept the collaboration of the INPFL fighters who controlled the Freeport that ECOMOG wanted for use as a base. In fact, the cooperation was so close that INPFL fighters and their leader were allowed free run of the ECOMOG base, access to which was secured by checkpoints under joint ECOMOG and INPFL control. Johnson soon became a familiar sight around ECOMOG headquarters, dropping by casually with his armed bodyguards and strumming a guitar while singly, absurdly enough, Christian Sunday school hymns. This unchecked access for Johnson was to have tragic results for the beleaguered President Doe.

Ever since the battle for Monrovia had begun, Doe had remained barricaded inside the Executive Mansion, abandoned by his ministers and even by his wife, who took the couple's four children abroad. Yet he resisted all entreaties to go into exile, despite his position becoming so weak that he was forced to sign, on September 5, a humiliating two-week ceasefire with Johnson in which the president promised not to enter areas under INPFL control without the rebel leader's permission. This accord notwithstanding, on Sunday, September 9, 1990, Doe inexplicably ventured out of the Executive Mansion and drove to ECOMOG headquarters in Johnson's zone of control. Although the evidence suggests that the subsequent events—events that became emblematic of the brutal violence of the Liberian civil war—were the tragic result of misunderstanding and unfortunate coincidence, the fact that rational calculation cannot explain the visit has left many Liberians with the conviction that he was lured away by Nigerian conspirators—with U.S. complicity according to some versions—eager to eliminate him and clear the way for a quick settlement of the civil war.

At 1:45 P.M. Doe's twenty-car motorcade, including the black presidential Mercedes-Benz stretch limousine flying the Liberian and presidential ensigns, left the Executive Mansion for the first time in months with sirens blaring. The seventy-five-member presidential party apparently caught the Nigerian guards on duty at ECOMOG headquarters off guard. After some discussions, the security guards prevailed upon the party to check their weapons at the entrance to the Freeport area, leaving only the president and a few others with side arms. The motorcade then pulled up to the main port building where Doe encountered the ECOMOG commander, Ghanaian General Quainoo, who was accompanied by his Guinean deputy, Major General Lamine Magasoumba, and his chief of staff, Nigerian Brigadier General Cyril Iweze. The president began to berate the generals, complaining:

> As Africans, you know our tradition; when you enter a village or town, the first thing you do is you go and call on the chief. Since you came here, you have not paid a courtesy call on me.[20]

The president was hectoring the ECOMOG officers ten minutes later when Prince Johnson drove up with an escort, all armed with AK-47s which, unlike the members of Doe's presidential entourage, they had not been required to surrender at the entrance to the port. A shooting spree broke out when one of Doe's bodyguards was overheard calling the INPFL fighters "rebels." Johnson shot Colonel Harrison

Pennue, a relative of Doe's and commander of the AFL's death squad, in the head. Doe took a bullet wound in the leg. Accounts vary about what happened next, but it seems that the ECOMOG officers fled the scene while Johnson's men mowed down Doe's all-but-unarmed entourage. With their commanding officers no where in sight, the ECOMOG peacekeepers stood aside and watched as Johnson bundled the injured president back into the presidential limousine and drove off with his victim.

Doe was brought back to INPFL headquarters, where he was stripped of his five-star general's uniform and exhibited by Johnson to a crowd of onlookers. The events that ensued were filmed by a Palestinian journalist who was covering the civil war for an Arab news service—the plummeting fortunes of Doe, who was friendly with Israel, at the hands of the Libyan-backed NPFL (and INPFL) had been popular fare on the Arab street in the months before the Iraqi invasion of Kuwait. Copies of the edited video chronicle, complete with scratchy martial music and production credits, was subsequently handed out to distinguished visitors not only by Johnson, but by the others foes of the Doe regime, including Taylor's NPFL. The copy in the possession of this author is labeled: "The Capture of Samuel K. Doe by Field Marshall [*sic*] Prince Yeduo Johnson and His Gallant Men and Women of the Independent National Patriotic Front of Liberia on Sunday, September 9th, 1990."

This ghastly home movie opens with Johnson seated behind a massive desk drinking an American beer—a Budweiser, to be precise—with a garland of hand grenades around his neck and a young woman fanning him. The woman occasionally wipes the perspiration from his brow with a cloth. On the wall behind Johnson is, ironically enough, a large devotional picture of Jesus Christ. Opposite the INPFL leader, Doe is shown kneeling on the floor, surrounded by armed fighters who appear to be drunk. The president is stripped down to his white briefs and has his hands cuffed behind his back. Blood is visible on Doe's face and legs. In his lap is a bundle consisting of the various protective *juju* amulets that had been found on his person.

An interrogation of sorts takes place until Johnson, apparently upset, pounds the table and shouts: "That man won't talk! Bring me his ear!" The video shows Doe being held down while one of Johnson's men cuts off his left ear. The ear is handed to Johnson who eats part of it before tossing the remaining part over his shoulder. The rebel leader then bangs the desk again, shouting: "Now the other ear! The right ear!" The video continues with further interrogation and torture with various persons coming and going to watch the spectacle. Doe was apparently half dead from blood loss by the time the *coup de grâce* was administered in the early hours of September 10. One ECOMOG officer described the end:

> [Doe] was crying and blood was running down his cheeks from his face and head. But you know how when sweat runs down your chest it sometimes collects in the center—well, the blood was collecting and he was trying to blow on it, to make it run down. Blowing, you know? He kept blowing. That's all he did. Then one of Johnson's men thought he was trying to do some kind of *juju*, blowing on himself to make himself disappear. So he shot him again. He was nearly dead by then, anyway, from loss of blood.[21]

Doe's body is then shown tossed into a wheelbarrow and paraded around by INPFL fighters before taking—still in the wheelbarrow to be certified dead by a Nigerian physician. The body was subsequently displayed at a medical clinic on Bushrod Island for several days, where throngs of Monrovians braved passage through the various checkpoints to view it. Prince Johnson then proclaimed himself "Brigadier General and Field Marshal"—obviously oblivious to the difference between the two titles—and "President of Liberia," parading around Monrovia in Doe's presidential Mercedes-Benz while flashing the late president's sunglasses and Rolex watch. Johnson's presidency did not last long: Nigerian soldiers commandeered the vehicles in the motorcade and, having embarrassed ECOMOG not so much by his brutality but by his lack of discretion in filming and distributing evidence of it, the rebel leader was bundled off to a comfortable exile in Nigeria where he "found Jesus" and is presently "the Evangelist Johnson" of the Christ Deliverance Ministry in Lagos.[22]

Doe's abduction right out of its headquarters destroyed the credibility of the ECOMOG peacekeepers. Quainoo quickly left Monrovia, citing the need for consultations with ECOWAS chairman Dawda Jawara of the Gambia, and never returned. He was replaced by a Nigerian officer, Major General Joshua Dogonywaro, a member of the Armed Forces Ruling Council, the ruling junta of Nigeria, who brought in two extra battalions, one each from Nigeria and Ghana, doubling the size of the

ECOMOG contingent. A sustained offensive led by the new commander, who shed all pretense of impartiality in the Liberian civil conflict, drove NPFL fighters from central Monrovia and forced Taylor to accede to a ceasefire during an extraordinary ECOWAS summit in Bamako, Mali, on November 27, 1990. The Bamako agreement permitted the resumption of the flow of humanitarian aid to Monrovia as well as the partial restoration of electrical and water utilities. An uneasy truce was in force by the time Dogonywaro was replaced in February 1991 by another Nigerian officer, Major General Rufus Kupolati (all eight ECOMOG commanders after the disastrous Quainoo came from Nigeria).

THE WIDENING CONFLICT

ECOMOG's partial success in securing the capital permitted Amos Sawyer to be sworn in as president of the Interim Government of National Unity (IGNU) on November 23, 1990. In February 1991, the three Liberian armed factions—the AFL, NPFL, and INPFL, signed an agreement in Lomé, Togo, agreeing to ECOWAS-supervised disarmament and the establishment of a new interim government. The subsequent All-Liberia Conference, meeting in Monrovia through March and April to establish the new government, fell apart when Taylor insisted on the presidency—he had been offered one of two vice presidencies—and twenty of the fifty-one seats in the provisional legislature. When NPFL delegates walked out of the meeting, Sawyer was reconfirmed as interim president by the rump of the Conference and new elections were scheduled for October 1991.

By this time, the situation was causing massive instability throughout the region as the number of Liberian refugees in neighboring countries had doubled over the course of the year. By July 1991, there were 342,000 refugees in Guinea, 227,000 in Côte d'Ivoire, 10,000 in Sierra Leone, 6,000 in Ghana, and 4,000 in Nigeria. Further complicating the situation was the civil conflict that broke out in Sierra Leone. On March 23, 1991, a group calling itself the Revolutionary United Front (RUF) and led by a former corporal in the Sierra Leonean army, Foday Sankoh, who had trained in Libya with Taylor, invaded Sierra Leone from Liberia. This new conflict caused 107,000 additional refugees to flee into Guinea from Sierra Leone by July.

Having avenged himself on the late Samuel Doe, Ivorian President Houphouët-Boigny was now ready resume his role as the region's elder statesman by brokering a peace agreement. Between June and October 1991, *le Vieux* hosted four peace conferences at his showpiece capital of Yamoussoukro. As a result of these talks, a complex and, ultimately overly ambitious, agreement was reached that called for the deployment of an expanded ECOMOG throughout Liberia, the encampment and disarmament of the Liberian factions under the aegis of ECOMOG and former U.S. President Jimmy Carter's International Negotiations Network, the creation of a buffer zone along the Liberian-Sierra Leonean border, the repatriation and resettlement of Liberian refugees, and the creation of yet another interim government.

Taylor, who was allowed by the Yamoussoukro agreement to continue to administer those areas of Liberia under NPFL control, had consented to the deal because he hoped that the buffer zone between Liberia and Sierra Leone would ease the armed pressure that he had recently come under from a new faction calling itself the United Liberian Movement for Democracy (ULIMO). Founded on May 29 with the stated goal of attacking Taylor, ULIMO military force consisted of a collection of former AFL officers leading an estimated three thousand fighters drawn mainly from Krahn and Mandingo refugees in Sierra Leone. ULIMO's leadership included the Mandingo leader Alhaji Kromah, who was based in Conakry, Guinea, and two Krahn leaders based in Freetown, Sierra Leone, George Boley, who had served in Doe's cabinet successively as minister for presidential affairs, minister of communications, and minister of education, and Albert Karpeh, Doe's onetime defense minister.

Increasingly marginalized during the process was Liberia's nominal head of state, Amos Sawyer. As the only party in the conflict without his own military force, Sawyer was entirely dependent upon ECOMOG for his security, allowing his Liberian opponents to portray him as little better than the puppet of foreign invaders. As one African commentator observed: "The cerebral professor was in a situation where madness and mayhem reigned over order and oratory; one sometimes had the impression that he was in over his head."[23]

By the time another ECOWAS peace conference was convened in the Geneva, Switzerland, winter home of the ailing Ivorian leader, Houphouët-Boigny, in April 1992, it was clear that the Yamoussoukro agreement of the previous year had been overly ambitious: virtually none of its terms had been implemented. Nonetheless, the meeting reconfirmed the agreement with modifications to its timetable. That same month, a group of Sierra Leonean soldiers on leave from the fighting in that country's civil war, led by a twenty-seven-year-old infantry captain named Valentine Strasser, overthrew the government of President Mo-moh, replacing its with a new military junta. By August, Sierra Leone's civil war had caused an estimated 425,000 people to be displaced inter-nally, while 170,000 were refugees in Guinea and 12,000 even fled to Liberia.

During 1992, ECOMOG came under increasing pressure despite the tenuous truce that was still holding. The peacekeepers were plagued from the beginning with logistical problems, lacking both the equip-ment necessary to fight what was effectively a counterinsurgency cam-paign and the maintenance for such equipment that they had. In fact, the only well-supplied ECOMOG personnel were the 1,200 Senegalese soldiers who arrived in late 1991 and early 1992 in accord with the Ya-moussoukro agreement. The Senegalese were beneficiaries of a $15 million contribution from the United States, which was appreciative for Senegal's participation in the international coalition that fought the Gulf War the previous year. With losses mounting, ECOMOG's com-manders desisted from their efforts to deploy across Liberia and, by Au-gust 1992, had withdrawn their forces back to Monrovia.

On October 15, the NPFL launched "Operation Octopus," a surprise attack on Monrovia that targeted ECOMOG headquarters, the Ducor Hotel seat of Sawyer's IGNU, the Freeport, and, tellingly enough, the Nigerian embassy compound. The command centers for the Nigerian and Sierra Leonean units, located in suburban Topoe Village, quickly fell to NPFL fighters. Among the civilian casualties during the fierce fighting were five American nuns from the Ruma, Illinois-based Pre-cious Blood Sisters—Barbara Ann Muttra, Mary Joel Kolmer, Shirley Kolmer, Kathleen McGuire, and Agnes Mueller—who were taken from their convent in NPFL-controlled territory at Gardnersville, near Monrovia. When there bodies were recovered several days later, NPFL and ECOMOG commanders accused each other of the crime.[24]

While ECOMOG ultimately managed to beat back the offensive by mid-December, "Operation Octopus" was, over the long term, a victory for Taylor. ECOMOG had been forced to rely on AFL and ULIMO units to defend Monrovia, destroying what was left of its impartiality in the eyes of many Liberians. Reports of ULIMO's Kromah trading in diamonds with the complicity of Guinean officials hardly reinforced the credibility of any ULIMO allies, especially ones such as ECOMOG

whose Nigerian soldiers were seen looting refrigerators, air condition-
ers, and other appliances from Monrovia homes as they retook the city.
And, during the fighting, ECOMOG had evacuated Prince Yormie
Johnson after his Caldwell headquarters fell to the NPFL. Johnson
went into a comfortable exile in Nigeria, leaving many of his INPFL
fighters to rejoin Taylor's NPFL. In the aftermath of "Operation Octopus," Senegal's President Abdou Diouf withdrew his country's contingent from ECOMOG, officially citing the need for the soldiers to guard
polling stations at home during the upcoming presidential elections.

In the midst of "Operation Octopus," on November 18, 1992, the
UN Security Council intervened in the Liberian civil war for the first
time with the full weight of that body, passing Resolution 788, which
imposed a complete arms embargo on all the Liberian factions. France,
however, prevented the adoption of economic sanctions out of consideration for the French firms that had commercial interests in Taylor's
"Greater Liberia."

The arms embargo, coupled with the loss of the Roberts International Airport and the port of Buchanan to the ECOMOG counterattack, temporarily placed Taylor on the defensive. ULIMO forays into
Lofa, Bomi, and Grand Cape Mount Counties, cut the NPFL off from
its RUF allies in Sierra Leone. These developments led Taylor to resort
to guerrilla tactics that relied on surprise attacks on isolated ECOMOG
units, rather than conventional assaults. The heavy-handed ECO-
MOG response, brought further disrepute on the peacekeepers, who
were criticized by human rights groups for inflicting civilian casualties
with incidents such as the April 18, 1993, bombing of a Médicins sans
Frontières aid convoy that was mistaken for an NPFL arms shipment.[25]
Nonetheless, by July, Taylor controlled only half of Liberia's national
territory, whereas he controlled some 95 percent of it barely three years
earlier.

Effectively bombed back to the negotiating table, the Liberian factions
signed a new peace agreement at Cotonou, Benin, on July 25, 1993. The
civil war, up to that moment, had exacted a toll of an estimated 150,000
lives and had turned 700,000 Liberians into refugees.[26] The Cotonou
agreement stipulated that a ceasefire would be in effect from August 1. A
Liberian National Transitional Government (LNTG) would be formed
consisting of a five-member Council of State and seventeen-member
cabinet made up of representatives of the three parties—IGNU, NPFL,
and ULIMO—and a thirty-five member national legislature created by

merging the IGNU legislature in Monrovia with the NPFL legislative assembly in Gbarnga. Presidential elections were to be scheduled within seven months. During the interim, ECOMOG—to be reinforced by OAU units as well as new United Nations Observer Mission in Liberia (UNOMIL), authorized by Security Council Resolution 856 on August 10, 1993[27]—would be deployed throughout Liberia and would establish buffer zones on Liberia's frontiers with Sierra Leone, Guinea, and Côte d'Ivoire. The accord also granted an amnesty to all parties for any crimes they may have committed during the conflict.[28]

After the signing of the Cotonou agreement, the 368-man UNOMIL contingent as well as a 1,500-man East African (Tanzanian and Ugandan) force joined the ECOMOG peacekeepers. Their hopes for peace buoyed, some 60,000 Liberian refugees returned to Monrovia and Bong County only to find that the fighting had resumed. Personal rivalries and ethnic tensions were too deep to be easily effaced by an agreement that was essentially forced upon the parties by outsiders.

George Boley, the American-trained educator who had headed ULIMO's political affairs committee, broke away from that movement and formed his own group, the rather ironically named Liberian Peace Council (LPC). Although the LPC was ostensibly a nonethnic, nonreligious, and nonpartisan group, in fact it was a Krahn movement, consisting mainly of ethnic Krahns who had taken refuge in Côte d'Ivoire and Krahn soldiers who had served in Doe's AFL. Supported by Nigeria, whose new military ruler, General Sani Abacha, was angered by Charles Taylor's repeated humiliations of the Nigerian military commanders of ECOMOG, LPC—its name notwithstanding—fought the NPFL in Sinoe and Rivercress Counties in October 1993 for control of the Liberian southeast.

Before it could take advantage of the new fight on the NPFL's hands, ULIMO faced a challenge in Lofa County from the Lofa Defense Force (LDF), a militia formed by François Massaquoi, an ethnic Loma who had studied economics at New York University, and consisting primarily of ethnic Loma from Lofa County in the Liberian northwest. The LDF's self-described mission was to protect Loma villagers from attacks by marauding bands of ULIMO's largely ethnic Mandingo fighters. With arms provided by the NPFL as well as from ethnic Loma soldiers in ECOMOG's Guinean contingent, the LDF drove ULIMO from several Lofa villages after fierce battles in November and December 1993.

In early 1994, ULIMO split into two factions, a predominantly Mandingo ULIMO-K headed by Alhaji Kromah and a predominantly Krahn ULIMO-J headed by Roosevelt Johnson.

Two aspects characterized the conflict during the year that followed the Cotonou agreement of July 1993. The first was the increasing ethnic character of the violence with even previously allied groups, like the Krahn and Mandingo, falling out with each other. The second was the importance that economic calculations entered into the military campaigns. Kromah fought to retake the trading route that his Mandingo kinsman had lost along the Liberian-Sierra Leonean border regions. Taylor wanted the same area because the ULIMO invasion had cut him off from his weapons and diamonds traffic with his RUF allies in Sierra Leone. The NPFL revenues from the sale of timber, iron ore, gold, diamonds, and rubber from the areas that it controlled during this period were estimated to have been up to $250 million per year.[29]

While the fighting went on, the establishment of the LNTG was held up as the competing Liberian parties quarreled over the nominations to what they viewed as the four most important cabinet portfolios: foreign affairs, justice, defense, and finance. It was not until March 7, 1994, that the five-member Council of State was installed that included law professor David Dual Kpomakpor and Philip Banks representing the IGNU, Mohammed Sherif and Dexter Tayhor representing ULIMO, and Isaac Musa representing the NPFL. Kpormakor was designated to be chairman of the Council and, consequently, interim head of state. Even after its own installation, however, the LNTG remained ineffectual as competing factions continued their squabbles over appointments to governmental ministries and other agencies. The NPFL forbade its representatives in the LNTG to take up their posts until the disputes over the four contested ministries was resolved, as it was on April 19, when the NPFL was given the foreign affairs and justice portfolios, while ULIMO received finance, and the IGNU—which had no military force to speak of—took defense.

The disarmament process was even more painfully slow, even though separate demobilization camps were established for the AFL, NPFL, and ULIMO fighters. By August 22, 1994, only 3,612 combatants (out of an estimated 60,000) had been disarmed.[30] Disagreements arose between the commanding officers of UNOMIL and ECOMOG over their respective responsibilities. The ECOMOG contingents resented the better status and support that their UNOMIL counterparts enjoyed. UNOMIL personnel complained about lack of professionalism on the part of the ECOMOG troops. Both sets of peacekeepers provided useful pretenses that the various factions employed to excuse their failure to live up to their commitment to disarm: the LPC accused the peacekeepers of aiding the NPFL by blocking its attack routes, while the NPFL accused them of having helped the LPC along alternative routes, and so forth. As a result, the military observers were harassed and often attacked. Rather than fighting off the attacks, UNOMIL responded by withdrawing its observers to Monrovia and reducing the number of UN military observers from 368 to ninety.

The founding father of ECOMOG, Gambian President Sir Dawda Jawara, was overthrown in a military coup on July 22, 1994, led by the twenty-nine-year-old Lieutenant Yahya A.J.J. Jammeh. The new Gambian leader had served with ECOMOG in Liberia and cited the neglect of the Gambian soldiers serving with the peacekeepers among his grievances against the deposed regime. When coupled with the overthrow of Sierra Leone's President Momoh by the twenty-seven-year-old Captain Strasser two years earlier, it was becoming apparent that rather than containing instability, ECOWAS's involvement in the Liberian conflict was possibly spreading it. With this in mind, the new ECOWAS chairman, Ghanaian President Jerry Rawlings, convened the leaders of the Liberian factions to the resort town of Akosombo, Ghana, in early September 1994. Although the accord hammered out during this summit quickly fell apart, it differed from the preceding agreements in that it recognized for the first time that any hope for a settlement depended upon the warlords who held actual power in the country rather than the squabbling civilian politicians in Monrovia. Although bitter protests from the LNTG eventually scuttled the deal, the inclusion of the AFL chief of staff, General Hezekiah Bowan, as Monrovia's representative at Akosombo rather than a civilian statesman was probably an acknowledgement of reality rather than an attempt by Rawlings at a coup.

Several dramatic incidents in the fall of 1994 underscored the unpredictable nature of Liberian power politics. On September 14, General Charles Julu, a former AFL commander, entered Monrovia. Returning in disguise from several years of exile in the United States, Julu, an ethnic Krahn, rallied about three hundred AFL soldiers, all fellow Krahns. Storming the Executive Mansion the following day, Julu installed himself in Samuel Doe's presidential office and proclaimed himself president of Liberia. Although the attempted coup collapsed the following day when ECOMOG besieged the would-be rebels, the attack—carried out by a delusional military commander in a capital city supposedly guarded by thousands of soldiers—exposed the weakness of the international peacekeepers.

Later that same month, a trio of NPFL cabinet members—Internal Affairs Minister Samuel Dokie, Justice Minister Laveli Supuwood, and Labor Minister Thomas Woewiyu—broke with Taylor and formed the Central Revolutionary Council of the National Patriotic Front of Liberia (CRC-NPFL). Allying themselves with the LPC and ULIMO-K, the three renegade ministers managed to temporarily drive Taylor and those NPFL units that remained loyal to him from their "provisional capital" of Gbarnga.

As a consequence of these events, by the end of 1994, over 80 percent of the Liberian population had been displaced by the fighting that had engulfed no less than 80 percent of national territory. Excluding foreign military units that had been sent to intervene in the civil war, no fewer than seven major groups were involved in the conflict: the NPFL and the splinter CRC-NPFL, the rival J and K branches ULIMO, the AFL, the LDF, and the LPC. The two NPFL factions controlled Nimba, Bong, and Margibi Counties as well as the northern half of Grand Gedeh County. ULIMO-J controlled Grand Cape Mount and Bomi Counties and the southern half of Lofa County; while ULIMO-K controlled the northern half of Lofa County. The LDF controlled a handful of strategically situated Loma villages in Lofa County. The LPC controlled various territories in southeastern Liberia. The AFL was generally confined to Monrovia. UN Secretary-General Boutros Boutros-Ghali summarized the situation in rather uncharacteristically candid terms:

> Overall, the military situation remains confused, with groups aligning and realigning themselves depending on their short-term interests and the breakdown of command and control within the factions. The situation in Liberia is reaching the point where warlords, without any particular political agenda but with the control of a certain number of soldiers, are seeking territory for the sake of adding to their own claim to power…The current fighting in Liberia is small-scale bush fighting. The results are not large military victories, but deaths mostly of civilians, the decimation of entire villages and the breakdown of any semblance of law and order.[31]

A BIZARRE AND BRUTAL CONFLICT

Were it not for the exceptionally bizarre and brutal nature of the fighting, the Liberian civil war might have been dismissed as just another of the regrettably all-too-common conflicts that have blighted contemporary African history and, consequently, of not particularly noteworthy to outsiders. While a number of academics, perhaps reacting viscerally to vivid images described and sensational tones taken in many of the reports filed by Western correspondents during the conflict, have downplayed the "primitive" aspects of the fighting in West Africa, arguing, as one scholar does, that "in any war opportunist individuals or groups muddy the waters with atrocities and looting,"[32] the journalistic accounts nonetheless captured the flavor, if not always substance, of the events. During the conflict, the various competing factions, including the ostensible peacekeepers, perpetrated atrocities that have been well publicized.

Shortly after Charles Taylor's NPFL invaded Nimba County in December 1989, Samuel Doe's AFL loyalists began a campaign of reprisals in areas they controlled, especially Monrovia, against alleged rebel sympathizers. On January 5, 1990, Robert Phillips, a member of leading family that was thought to have ties with the late General Thomas Quiwonkpa, was found dead outside his Monrovia home with his throat slashed. This was the start of campaign of terror aimed especially at members of the Gio and Mano ethnic groups, hundreds of whose headless corpses were found in the morning after they had been last seen with soldiers the night before. In retaliation, the Gio and Mano in Nimba County who flocked to support Taylor, began attacking Krahn, whom they held responsible for the actions of their fellow Krahn tribesman, Doe, as well as Mandingo, who had prospered under the dictator's protection.

As the war progressed, the NPFL began recruiting children, many of them orphans whose parents had been killed in attacks by Doe loyalists, into special "Small Boy Units," whose fighters proved to be known for their fanatical loyalty to their *"papay,"* Charles Taylor. When the NPFL invaded Lofa County in July 1990, several contingents of these child soldiers were deployed against the town of Bakedu, slaughtering over five hundred Mandingo residents. Reportedly the imam of the local mosque was beheaded and his severed head was displayed on the copy of the Koran.[33]

On the night of July 29–30, government soldiers massacred some six hundred people—mostly Gio and Mano, including many women with children—who had taken refuge at St. Peter's Lutheran Church in Monrovia.[34] One Krahn officer who tried to limit the abuses by AFL soldiers, Colonel Chris Doe (no relation to the president), was himself arrested and taken to the Executive Mansion where, on August 14, he was hacked to death with machetes.[35]

After Prince Johnson broke with Taylor and formed the INPFL, he committed a number of atrocities during the siege of Monrovia in addition to his infamous videotaped execution of President Doe. On August 3, for example, he executed a Liberian relief worker accused of profiteering, while the victim was handcuffed to a Frenchman employed by Catholic Relief Services. The entire incident happened in front of international journalists, and a photo of the Johnson pointing at the victim was published worldwide.[36]

As the conflict became protracted, the new factions that entered the fray—ULIMO, LPC, etc.—likewise committed atrocities.[37] Units of the LPC in particular were implicated in cannibalism. One survivor described the LPC assault on her village to journalists:

> "They broke his ankles, and then when he was on the ground, they cut his throat," says Lucy, who is in her 40s. As her husband, Solomon, bled into the dirt, he was approached by a "heartman," a witch doctor who steals hearts for ritual purposes. The other guerillas, called him Young Colonel Killer. "I'm taking your main machine," Lucy recalls Young Colonel Killer saying. Then he cut Solomon's heart out. Lucy says Young Colonel Killer told the village women to scare up some cooking wood and boil the heart. The guerillas ate it, beheaded two more men and ordered the villagers out. Lucy's account was confirmed by seven other people who fled her village, which is not far from Buchanan.[38]

Another LPC unit was perhaps the wackiest outfit in the entire conflict: the "Butt Naked Battalion," commanded by Joshua Milton Blahyi, better known as "General Butt Naked." The unit and its commander acquired their moniker from the fact that they went into battle naked in the belief that this would render them impervious to enemy fire. After the 1996 battle for the capital, in which he played a prominent role, Blahyi underwent a religious conversion experience and presently runs his own Christian church, the Soul-Winning Evangelical Ministry in Monrovia. Nowadays, the former guerilla leader attributes his atrocities to a telephone call he claims to have received, when he was eleven-years-old, from the Devil who demanded nudity on the battlefield, acts of indecency and regular human sacrifices to ensure his protection, explaining:

> So, before leading my troops into battle, we would get drunk and drugged up, sacrifice a local teenager, drink their blood, then strip down to our shoes and go into battle wearing colorful wigs and carrying dainty purses we'd looted from civilians. We'd slaughter anyone we saw, chop their heads off and use them as soccer balls. We were nude, fearless, drunk and homicidal. We killed hundreds of people—so many I lost count. But…God telephoned me and told me that I was not the hero I considered myself to be, so I stopped and became a preacher.[39]

Even the ECOMOG peacekeepers ran afoul of international standards, committing various abuses including indiscriminate bombing, violations of medical neutrality, and summary executions.[40]

Some scholars have tried to make sense—if such can be the term—of the violence and brutality by arguing that the actions of the rival warlords and their fighters were reflections of ideas, even, as Stephen Ellis has convincingly suggested, deeply rooted religious ideas. Ellis has asserted that: "There is no doubt that some of the acts of war in Liberia which have been considered particularly atrocious contain…references to known repertoires of spiritual symbols."[41] Others held that the horrifying acts of brutality could not "in any way be taken to prove a reversion to some kind of essential African savagery."[42] Rather, as Paul Richards has contended, the violence possessed a "logic" of its own, even if its significance was not adequate communicated. Still others take the view advocated by journalist Robert Kaplan in his influential essay that the nature of the conflict was the result of a social breakdown caused by population pressure, environmental collapse, and economic desperation.[43] In his expanded book-length treatment of his thesis, however, Kaplan gave a rather more global explanation:

> The forest was to blame for the iniquities of humankind here—for President Doe disemboweling the previous president, Tolbert, and for Prince Johnson, in turn, cutting off Doe's ears; for Charles Tay-

lor's teenage soldiers breaking into the bridal shops of Monrovia, dressing up in women-*cum-juju* spirits, and going on boozy rampages that ended in ritual killings...

A forest reflects no light. In the forest there are no horizons. You cannot see more than a few feet ahead, so you are in fear of surprise. You are more prone to excitable rumors. The slightest pinprick or jab may lead to panic. In other words, in the forest, where one's view is blotted out by every manner of tree and creeper (each containing its own "spirit"), men tend to depend less on reason and more on superstition...

Liberia, with the wettest, densest forest in tropical West Africa, was, as the quality and scope of its violence indicated, still a forest culture: a land of spirits. Sustained population growth rates of over 3 percent and the importation of large quantities of automatic weapons were dominant factors in the initial implosion. Nevertheless, much of the violence was ritualistic in nature, amplified by drugs and alcohol, and carried out with machetes and other sharp implements. It made for an awful revelation: of how unprecedented birthrates, alcohol, mass-produced weaponry, and other artifacts of modern times could, under circumstances that are increasingly common in the third world, make for a new-age primitivism, far more deadly than the benign warrior cultures of old, characterized by ritualized—rather than real—combat.[44]

Whatever the theoretical explanation, many Liberians as well as outside observers came to agree with the existential conclusion that the long conflict—fought as it was with its peculiar intensity, savagery, and depravity—was somehow set apart.

THE BUSINESS OF WAR

As the conflict dragged on with its seemingly endless cycle of brutal violence, it became evident that while the inhuman circle of hatred, violence, and vengeance had its own momentum, the continuation of the civil war was also due to causes more rational than human—or better, inhuman—emotion. William Reno has argued that:

The war's cause can be traced to cutoffs of aid after the cold war's end and the collapse of patron-client politics that had bound Liberia's politicians to one man. Liberia's seemingly anarchic violence conceals a reshaping of politics. Individuals may fight for the sake of fighting, but rational interests motivate the country's war leaders. They fight for power — to control resources and people. The war has been as much a battle over commerce inside and beyond Liberia's borders as it has been a war for territory or control of the government.[45]

The particular novelty of the Liberian conflict was the extent to which the rival leaders who emerged as warlords at the head of armed factions used their forces to seize territories not so much to govern as to secure external commercial alliances so as to, in turn, dominate social networks. As Stephen Ellis notes, "the resulting *logique de guerre* crippled the Liberian state as an organ of administration and created a new set of economic opportunities based on plunder."[46]

During the 1989–1997 conflict, ULIMO gained control of large segments of mineral-rich Bomi County in western Liberia in 1993. When the movement split into rival factions in early 1994, the faction led by Alhaji Kromah edged those of Roosevelt Johnson out and took control of the Bomi mining operations, with the help of several Nigerian ECOMOG commanders who received a cut of the trade in exchange for their military support. Likewise with the connivance of Nigerian "peacekeepers," George Boley's LPC took control of the timber trade in Maryland County on the eastern border with Côte d'Ivoire. Boley also ran several abandoned rubber plantations with forced labor, exporting through the ECOMOG-controlled port of Buchanan an estimated three thousand tons, worth about $1.5 million, in 1994 alone.[47] Not content with their "commissions," ECOMOG commanders went into business for themselves, concentrating—as will be discussed subsequently—on stripping Liberia of its fixed assets, which they sold abroad.

However, the undisputed master of the "business of war" among the competing warlords was Charles Taylor. Reno, perhaps the leading expert on the economics of civil conflict in the developing world, has noted that "the force of Taylor's political authority lay in his ability to manipulate foreign firms to secure foreign exchange, weapons and political support and to use them as tools to manage various internal conflicts in his favor."[48]

At the start of the civil war, the most valuable economic asset in the country was the high-grade iron ore project at Mount Nimba on the Liberian border with Guinea. The most active member of the consortium of investors was the *Bureau de recherches géologiques et minières* (BRGM), which was partly controlled by the French government. BRGM secured funding from Japan's Sumitomo Corporation as well as investment commitments from the London-based African Mining Consortium Limited, which brought together various American, British, and Japanese investors, including some Liberian exiles living in the United States.[49] As he besieged Monrovia in June 1990, Taylor contacted the African Mining Consortium—using his American lawyer, former U.S. attorney-general Ramsey Clark, according to Stephen Ellis—and proposed restarting the Nimba project as well as to ship the stockpiled ore down a railroad line controlled by the NPFL to the port of Buchanan, then controlled by the rebels. Soon, some seventy thousand tons of ore were being exported from Buchanan, earning Taylor a monthly royalty of $10 million.[50] Most of the ore was shipped to the French port of Dunkerque.

Through his ties with Côte d'Ivoire's Félix Houphouët-Boigny, Taylor forged close ties with influential French diplomatic and commercial circles, particularly Jean-Christophe Mitterand, son of French President François Mitterand, who ran the *Cellule Africaine*, the presidential office in the Elysée that managed French interests in Africa, and Michel Dupuch, the French ambassador in Abidjan who would later become the chief advisor of African affairs to Mitterand's successor, President Jacques Chirac.[51] Sollac, a French firm that supplied iron ore to the state-owned Usinor steel mills became one of Taylor's largest trading partners. When Taylor's scheme to develop more ore mining in Nimba County with the Nimba Mining Company (NIMCO) consortium ran into international opposition over concerns of its environmental impact the project was located in the midst of West Africa's largest remaining rainforest—French diplomats succeeded in blunting the criticism of the United Nations.[52] France also became the principal customer for timber products exported from Taylor's "Greater Liberia." Using Lebanese-owned firms based in Côte d'Ivoire as intermediaries, "Greater Liberia" became the third largest supplier of hardwood to the French market by 1991, shipping to the ports of Bordeaux and Nantes.[53] John Hirsch, who served as U.S. ambassador to Sierra Leone during the period has commented:

> In fact, France maintained an active but hidden involvement in the entire sub-region, primarily promoting its economic interests, which

included extensive timber operations in Liberia. In 1992, at the height of the Liberian civil war, France successfully blocked Security Council sanctions against Liberia's factions. Shortly after Taylor's election, President Jacques Chirac invited him to Paris on an official state visit. More recently, France has used its role as a permanent member of the Security Council to exclude timber exports from the United Nations sanctions on Liberia.[54]

After backing Foday Sankoh's Revolutionary United Front (RUF) rebellion in Sierra Leone, Taylor and the NPFL became heavily involved with the trade that the RUF conducted in diamonds to pay for arms through the unofficial diamond dealers who dominated smuggling of the precious minerals through "Greater Liberia."[55] Shortly after the RUF invasion, migrant Mandingo and Fula traders who were long involved in the cross-border diamond traffic, were tortured and summarily executed by the rebels.[56] In their stead, by 1995, Taylor as well as other Liberian warlords, especially Kromah of ULIMO, were estimated to have been involved in the transit of somewhere between $300 million and $500 million in diamonds and gold.[57] Taylor in particular used his international business connections to bring the so-called "blood diamonds"—relabeled as being from Liberian sources—to market and supplying arms to the RUF fighters.[58] It has also been suggested that among the purchasers of the diamonds in recent years was Osama bin Laden's al-Qaʻeda, which sought to convert its assets into a form that could be more easily transported across national borders. In late 1998, Abdullah Ahmed Abdullah, said to be a top al-Qaʻeda operative involved in the planning of the attacks on the U.S. embassies in East Africa earlier that year, is believed to have bought a large quantity of diamonds in exchange for weapons and cash.

Taylor's goal was always the Liberian presidency. Had he been successful in 1990, it was likely that he would have set up a patrimonial state with a centralized patronage network similar to that of other African heads of sovereign states. However, the ECOMOG intervention prevented him from seizing the capital and the installation of the ineffectual IGNU regime of Amos Sawyer denied him the international recognition of juridical sovereignty. This left Taylor in a difficult situation: "he could not sell diplomatic support in exchange for aid or politically motivated foreign investment as Doe had done" nor could he "convincingly attract aid in return for promised to hold elections until he captured Monrovia,"[59] and his NPFL did not receive much by way of international relief aid. Consequently, his only option was to acquire resources for his military operations by resorting to a "warlord political economy" of tapping the assets in areas under his control and exploiting the commercial opportunities afforded by increasingly flexible global economic conditions, characterized by decentralization and lack of territorially defined markets. Insofar as his NPRAG regime was not internationally recognized, Taylor was not constrained by the traditional requirements of a state actor and, consequently, enjoyed the advantages of a global market while the de jure governments in Monrovia were saddled with its disadvantages, including accountability for past sovereign debt. In this sense, the economics of Taylor and the other Liberian warlords represent a new and troubling reality in geopolitics.

THE TORTUOUS ROAD TO PEACE

Not to be discouraged by the failure of the September 1994 Akosombo agreement, the indefatigable Ghanaian President Rawlings convened the Liberian factions as well as representatives from both interested ECOWAS countries (Benin, Burkina Faso, Côte d'Ivoire, The Gambia, Ghana, Guinea, Nigeria, Senegal, and Togo) and the East African peacekeeping states (Tanzania and Uganda) in Accra in late November 1994. The accord negotiated provided for a ceasefire to be followed, within ten days, by the establishment of yet another five-member Council of State with seats divided among groupings of the leading warlords (the NPFL; the two ULIMO factions; the LPC, LDF, CRC-NPFL, and AFL; the Liberian National Conference; and the LNTG) and the creation of nine ECOMOG-protected safe havens (Monrovia, Gbarnga, Buchanan, Greenville, Harper, Totota, Tubmanburg, Voinjama, and Zwedru).

The agreement was signed on December 21, 1994, but quickly fell apart amid acrimony. The so-called Coalition (the LPC, LDF, and CRC-NPFL) and the AFL could not agree on their joint representative on the Council of State. Then Charles Taylor, the NPFL representative, at insisted on the chairmanship of the Council. When this demand was rejected, he insisted on being the sole vice chairman. When this was rejected, Taylor angrily accused Nigeria of manipulating the negotiations against him and threatened to renew the conflict. The two most prominent Krahn leaders, George Boley and General Hezekiah Bowen, both vied to assume the leadership mantle of their ethnic kin that had been left by the late President Doe. When most Krahn elements backed Boley, Bowen threw his support to Taylor out of spite.

Persistent negotiations led to the compromise nomination of a thoroughly nonpartisan figure for the chairmanship of the Council of State in the person of the ninety-year-old Chief Tamba Tailor,[60] who had been paramount chief of Lofa County since 1955. Tailor, a polygamist with twenty wives and an indeterminate number of offspring, was widely respected for his probity and longevity despite his lack of education—observers are divided as to whether he was totally illiterate or had simply become too senile to read documents put in front of him. Nonetheless, the Council was not established because deliberations dragged on over its composition, with Taylor and other insisting on revisions of the Accra accord, while the LNTG's lame-duck chairman, David Kpomakpor, calling unrealistically for a return to the terms of the Cotonou agreement of 1993, which had excluded the warlords from the Council of State.

As the leaders continued to argue, the fighting continued sporadically throughout the spring of 1995. Fighting between the NPFL and LPC spilled over into Côte d'Ivoire, where the LPC accused its rival of maintaining bases in several border towns. The hostilities cause an additional thirty-five thousand Liberians to flee the Liberian border regions for safety deep in Côte d'Ivoire.[61] The NPFL, meanwhile, pursued some of its own dissidents into Guinea.

The logjam was broken finally in June 1995 when Charles Taylor surprisingly arrived in Abuja, Nigeria, to meet with the Nigerian head of state, General Sani Abacha. In August 1993, having annulled the presidential elections of the preceding June and jailed its presumed winner, Nigeria's General Ibrahim Babangida, whose notions of grandeur and regional hegemony had led to the creation of ECOMOG in the first place, retired after setting up an unelected interim government under a businessman, Ernest Shonekan. In November of the same year, Shonekan was forced to resign and was replaced by his defense minister, Abacha, who had been Babangida's loyal military deputy. One of the reasons for the coup was that Shonekan was preparing to bring Nigeria's 12,000-man ECOMOG contingent, whose deployment costing the country $500,000 per day, home from Liberia. Having staked its prestige upon the success of the Liberian mission, a withdrawal was anathema to the high command of the Nigerian military. The direct encounter between Taylor, who despite defections still led Liberia's strongest faction, and Abacha, who commanded strongest contingent in ECOMOG, resulted in a mutual understanding: the Nigerian leader needed Taylor's cooperation if he was to bring his peacekeepers home with honor and the Liberian warlord needed the assent of Abacha if he was gain the presidency of his country.

This meeting of the minds between the Liberian warlord and the Nigerian military strongman led to the late August summit in Abuja of ECOWAS heads of state along with representatives of the leading Liberian factions. Nigeria, in a *volte-face* from its position at previous negotiations, backed Taylor's contention that the Liberian factions were not equal in military strength and that only the inclusion of warlords who held effective control of the country would guarantee that any interim regime might be able to exercise leadership. Consequently the Abuja agreement was an exercise in *Realpolitik* that stood in contrast to the previous policy of idealistically propping up civilian political leaders with little sway. Power in the new Council of State would be concentrated in the hands of the three most powerful warlords—Taylor, Kromah, and Boley—who were designated its vice chairmen. As titular chairman of the Council, the warlords decided that the senile Chief Tamba would be too absurd, even for Liberia. While the unlettered old man was allowed to keep his seat on the Council, the warlords picked an innocuous writer, Wilton Sankawulo, for the chairmanship instead. A Lutheran seminary dropout who later earned a master of fine arts degree from the University of Iowa Writers' Workshop, Sankawulo's chief claim to fame was having published several collections of folktales in the 1970s. The other council member was Oscar Quiah, a member of the Liberian National Conference who was close to Boley. With three relatively weak figures sitting with the three most powerful warlords, it was clear where the power in the new body resided, although the accord did stipulate that the Council chairman was ineligible to run for president when the elections were organized and that any member who chose to run would have to resign from the Council three months before the poll. The Abuja agreement also distributed posts in the cabinet to other factional leaders, including Hezekiah Bowen, Samuel Dokie, Roosevelt Johnson, Thomas Woewiyu, and François Massaquoi.

The Abuja agreement was signed on August 19, 1995. It provided for a ceasefire that would take effect one week later, on August 26; between October 2 and December 14, ECOMOG and UNOMIL peacekeepers would deploy throughout Liberia; combatants (a list of 59,370 was provided by the various factions) would move to assembly points between November 9 and December 31; and disarmament would take place between December 1 and January 30, 1996.

On August 31, 1995, Charles Taylor entered Monrovia in triumph, thousands of Liberians lining the nine miles from the buffer zone between the ECOMOG peacekeepers and the NPFL advance positions to see the warlord-turned-statesman. While no doubt some of those lining the streets came out of curiosity and others were just glad that Taylor's presence heralded the coming of peace and stability, it cannot be denied even by his harshest critics that Taylor represented — and continues to represent — a significant constituency within the Liberian body politic. The Methodist bishop of Liberia, Arthur Kulah, noted that the reception that Taylor received contrasted with the ignored homecomings of the other signatories of the Abuja agreement:

> None of the warring faction leaders received the euphoric and exhilarated reception that Charles Taylor did. When Taylor arrived, the normal life of the city came to a halt, and people lined with streets... Taylor's arrival roused jubilation among the residents of Monrovia... Taylor was seen as a charismatic leader whose command of words and smooth talking ability convinced even the most serious antagonist. To many, Taylor was the hero who aroused courage; to others, he was the villain who stirred fear and masterminded the destruction of Liberia. To yet others he was a liberator, a revolutionary ready to lead Liberia into the twenty-first century, while others vowed to make life unpleasant for the warlords and their cronies. Taylor was loved and hated, worshiped and detested, adored and abhorred.[62]

The following day, the six members of the Council of State of the second Liberian National Transition Government were sworn into office at a ceremony presided over by Ghana's Jerry Rawlings. Despite the failure of no less than nine previous peace agreements, the new scheme was greeted with hopeful enthusiasm because of several reasons. Unlike its predecessors, the Abuja agreement had finally brought the warlords into direct participation in government. Furthermore, many of those with personal stakes in the continuation of the conflict—Houphouët-Boigny's vendetta against Doe, Doe's close personal ties with Babangida—were no longer around: the Ivorian leader had died on December

7, 1993, and the Nigerian strongman had retired on August 26, 1993. Fatigue over the long conflict had come to affect not only the Liberians, but also the peacekeepers: Nigeria's Abacha, facing numerous domestic difficulties as well as international pressure because of his abysmal human rights record, could ill-afford the continuing military adventure in a country that did not even border his country. And, finally, ECOMOG, once hailed as the model of African solutions to African problems, was becoming a caricature of all that was wrong with the continent. Human rights groups were accusing Nigerian soldiers of drug trafficking, while their Ghanaian counterparts were implicated in child prostitution. Some ECOMOG units were seen looting commercial establishments of goods, machinery, and even scrap metal. Helpless Liberians even joked that ECOMOG stood for "Every Car Or Moveable Object Gone."

Despite the auspicious start, neither the Abuja agreement nor the LNTG that it established lived up to expectations. Possessing neither a popular following nor a military force, Sankawulo was reduced to an ineffectual figurehead. Taylor, meanwhile, tried to usurp the role of *de facto* chairman of the Council of State, antagonizing the other warlords in the process. Consequently, low intensity hostilities continued between the NPFL in the southeast, between the two branches of ULIMO in the west, and between the NPFL and ULIMO-K in the central regions.

The next major outbreak of violence occurred when Nigerian peacekeepers, in accord with the Abuja agreement, deployed to Tubmanburg, an ULIMO-J stronghold in Bomi County, about sixty miles (ninety-six kilometers) from Monrovia, in late November 1995. On November 28, ULIMO-J fighters attacked the ECOMOG contingent and killed sixteen soldiers and wounded seventy-eight others, seizing ECOMOG's heavy weapons and other supplies. Buoyed by his battlefield success, Roosevelt Johnson then attacked the NPFL at Kakata, forty-five miles from Monrovia, but was driven back. Nonetheless, after sustaining further losses, ECOMOG retreated from Tubmanburg in March 1996. Meanwhile the fighting between the NPFL and LPC continued to spill, on occasion, into Côte d'Ivoire, leading the new Ivorian President Henri Konan Bédié to place his western region under a regime of military rule that proved harsh to Liberian refugees present there.

On March 2, 1996, the executive council of ULIMO-J removed Roosevelt Johnson as its chairman, replacing him with William Karyee. However, many of Johnson's fanatical Krahn fighters—who were known to strip themselves naked before battle—issued a declaration refusing to acknowledge the new leader. On March 4, the LNTG Council of State passed a resolution condemning ULIMO-J's attack on Tubmanburg, ordering the movement to return the stolen weapons, and demanded that both Johnson and Karyee appear before it the following day. When Johnson failed to present himself as ordered, the Council recognized Karyee as the new leader of ULIMO-J and suspended Johnson from his cabinet post as minister for rural development. The Council asked ECOMOG to search the Johnson's house in the Sinkor neighborhood of Monrovia for "illegal weapons." When ECOMOG sent a unit to Johnson's house on March 7, his loyalists abducted an accompanying UN observer and two other foreigners, threatening to kill them if Johnson was harmed.

On March 22, fighting broke out in Monrovia between the now-divided ULIMO-J partisans, during which three Karyee supporters were killed near Johnson's home. The following day, the Council of State issued a warrant for Johnson's arrest on murder charges. Johnson responded by barricading himself inside his house and surrounding it with loyal fighters.[63] On April 6, Charles Taylor and Alhaji Kromah ordered their NPFL and ULIMO-K fighters to "assist" the national police in effectuating the arrest. This led to fierce gun battles between the NPFL and ULIMO-K forces opposed by the Johnson elements of ULIMO-J, supported by some AFL and LPC units.

The largely Krahn coalition of ULIMO-J, AFL, and LPC fighters was forced eventually to retreat to the AFL's Barclay Training Center barracks. En route, the Krahn fighters seized some two hundred foreign nationals—mostly aid workers—for use as human shields. As the fighting continued, U.S. Marines evacuated the diplomatic corps and other remaining foreign nationals. A brief ceasefire on April 18 saw the release of the foreign nationals being held at the Barclay Training Center, but fighting broke out again on April 29. During the renewed fighting, press reports, later confirmed by the United Nations Secretary-General,[64] of looting by ECOMOG soldiers and their shipping home the "spoils"—including equipment belonging to the UN—further damaged the peacekeeping force's reputation, which was already suffering from its failure to intervene to prevent the fighting. Many observers thought that ECOMOG's Nigerian commander, General John Mark Inienger, had permitted the NPFL and ULIMO-K fighters to go after Roosevelt Johnson to avenge the humiliation his soldiers had suffered at the hands of the ULIMO-J leader at Tubmanburg. By the time the fighting died down in late May 1996, some three thousand civilians had lost their lives.[65]

The new ECOWAS chairman, Nigeria's General Sani Abacha, convened the foreign ministers of the ECOWAS nations of Benin, Burkina Faso, Côte d'Ivoire, The Gambia, Ghana, Guinea, Nigeria, Senegal, and Togo, in Abuja in mid-August 1996. During meeting Nigerian Foreign Minister Tom Ikimi proposed a revision of the Abuja agreement, suggesting a new timetable backed by sanctions to ensure compliance. Under the plan, eventually known as Abuja II, elections in Liberia were postponed from the originally scheduled August 20, 1996, to May 30, 1997, with the new government to be installed no later than June 15, 1997. The Liberian factions were expected to disengage their forces by August 31, 1996. Fighters were to be disarmed and demobilized demobilized by January 31, 1997. Members of the Council of State and other government officials who wanted to participate in the UN-supervised elections had to resign their offices by February 28, 1997. The plan was to implemented in five stages with monitoring missions authorized to recommend sanctions—including restrictions on travel, seizure of assets, and exclusion from the elections—against any violators. Apparently the Abacha regime was not sufficiently embarrassed by its status as an object of international sanctions—imposed after the November 10, 1995, hangings of Ken Saro-Wiwa and eight other Ogoni environmental and human rights activists—to advocate sanctions against Liberia's warlords.

In support of the new peace plan—the eleventh of the Liberian civil war—four francophone nations—Benin, Burkina Faso, Côte d'Ivoire, and Togo—agreed to send small units to reinforce ECOMOG. Nonetheless, despite the August 31 deadline for a ceasefire, fighting continued in Liberia with the two branches of ULIMO battling in the west and the NPFL and LPC struggling in the southeast.

The Abuja II plan had empowered the ECOWAS heads of state to remove any recalcitrant Liberian Council of State members. The first victim of this provision was Wilton Sankawulo, who was deposed in favor of Ruth Perry, a former opposition senator who had defected to Samuel Doe's National Democratic Party of Liberia. She was inaugurated in Monrovia as Liberia's first woman head of state on September 3, 1996. Tellingly, Charles Taylor was absent from her inauguration, choosing instead to travel to Tripoli to attend celebrations of twenty-seventh anniversary of the *coup d'état* that brought his benefactor, Colonel Muammar Qaddafi, to power in Libya. While Perry proved to be more energetic than her lackluster predecessor, she was still obstructed by the three warlords who not only dominated the Council of State, but also controlled ministries and other government offices through their appointees. Clearly, no improvement would be expected before the installation of a permanent government.

Despite various technical glitches, the peace process proceeded as scheduled with disarmament beginning on November 22, 1996. Fighters were provided food and transportation home in exchange for the surrender of a serviceable weapon or one hundred rounds of ammunition. Revised lists showed that approximately thirty-three thousand fighters needed to be demobilized; by the time that UN Secretary-General Kofi A. Annan reported to the Security Council on March 19, 1997, some 21,315 of them had been disarmed,[66] surrendering more than 9,570 weapons and 1.2 million rounds of ammunition. In addition, search operations conducted by the freshly reinforced UNOMIL and ECOMOG contingents netted another 917 weapons and 122,162 rounds of ammunition.[67]

On February 18, 1997, Nigeria's Sani Abacha—himself no paragon of democratic legitimacy—communicated ECOWAS's acceptance of five UN recommendations regarding the Liberian elections: the date would be May 30, as planned; the voting would be organized by an Independent Elections Commission with ten members, seven Liberians chosen by various civic and political groups and one representative each from ECOWAS, the UN, and the OAU; eventual disputes would be resolved by the Liberian Supreme Court; there would be a bicameral Congress with a sixty-four-member House and a twenty-member Senate, both elected by proportional representation because of the displacement of Liberians; and those Liberians abroad, including refugees, who wished to vote had to return home. The requirement to come home to vote came at the insistence of the Guinean and Ivorian governments, citing national sovereignty issues, but whose real preoccupation was to get the refugees out of their countries. Ultimately, only an estimated seventy-thousand to eighty-thousand refugees returned to vote, leaving more than half a million Liberians effectively disenfranchised.

On February 28, Charles Taylor, Alhaji Kromah, and George Boley resigned from the Council of State to run for president as the candidates, respectively, of the National Patriotic Party (NPP), All Liberian Coalition Party (ALCOP), and the National Democratic Party of Liberia (NDPL). The three were replaced by successors they designated. Interestingly, with both Taylor and Boley choosing women, the Council of State became the first African ruling body where half the membership consisted of women.

Amos Sawyer tried to organize a "grand coalition" of seven parties the Liberian Action Party (LAP), the Liberian People's Party (LPP), the Liberia Unification Party (LUP), the National Democratic Party of Liberia (NDPL), the True Whig Party (TWP), the United People's Party (UPP), and the Unity Party (UP)—to defeat Taylor's NPP. However, the March 25–26 convention of the Alliance of Political Parties (APP), as the coalition came to be called, revealed the petty jealousies and narrow vision of most of Liberia's civilian politicians. When the convention nominated the honest, but unassuming, geologist and former chairman of the Liberian Petroleum Refining Company, Cletus Segbe Wortorson, an ethnic Kru, as its candidate, Gabriel Baccus Mathews (UPP) and Togba Nah Tipoteh (LPP) walked out, withdrawing their parties from the APP, as did George Boley (NDPL). When, after some hesitation, Ellen Johnson Sirleaf decided to return to Liberia and contest the election, the LUP and TWP likewise withdrew from the coalition to endorse her.

The elections, scheduled for May 30, were delayed by ECOWAS on May 21. The previously announced timetable had proved to be too ambitious with electoral legislation still to be adopted, voters registered, and the poorly-organized civilian politicians unable to compete with the well-organized Charles Taylor (Ellen Johnson Sirleaf did not decide to run until April 18). The politicians asked for a six-month extension to get their acts together, a request opposed by Taylor. UN Secretary-General Kofi Annan suggested a two-month postponement. Ultimately, the date of July 19 was chosen.

The official campaign opened on June 16, 1997, with thirteen registered parties participating. From the onset, it was clear that Taylor enjoyed the advantage both in terms of popular support and in organization. His campaign resembled that of the stereotypical African "Big Man," Chief Nanga, described by Nigerian writer Chinua Achebe:

> Chief Nanga was a born politician; he could get away with almost anything he said and did. And as long as men are swayed by their hearts and stomachs and not their heads the Chief Nangas of this world will continue to get away with anything...This is of course a formidable weapon which is always guaranteed to save its wielder from the normal consequences of misconduct as well as from the humiliation and embarrassment of ignorance.[68]

Taylor established a "Charles Ghankay Taylor Educational and Humanitarian Relief Foundation" to help those disabled by the war. He was seen donating ambulances to the John F. Kennedy Memorial Hospital in Monrovia. A previously nonexistent "Charles Taylor Relief Agency" cropped up distributing rice and dairy products to the needy residents of Monrovia. NPP rallies became giveaways with t-shirts and food distributed freely. Taylor became the sponsor the national soccer team. He even announced that he had "found Jesus" and was ordained a Baptist minister. In contrast, his opponents ran lackluster campaigns:

> Johnson-Sirleaf, [Taylor's] closest rival, drove around in a convoy of battered old vehicles, condemned the violence and greed of the warlords (especially Charles Taylor), and blamed them for destroying the control. She called for a government of national unity to rebuild Liberia and flaunted her international credentials for attracting economic assistance to the country. Baccus Mathews promised free and compulsory universal primary education. Cletus Wotorson [sic] touted his reliable judgment and character. Harry Moniba, Samuel Doe's former vice president, promised peace and stability.[69]

On July 19, 1997, some 85 percent of the more than 750,000 voters registered by the Independent Elections Commission cast their ballots at 1,864 polling stations. The voting was one of the most closely scrutinized electoral contests in history.[70] In addition the UNOMIL and ECOMOG military contingents that were deployed to provide security, the UN had 330 election observers in place, the European Union sent sixty-four, the OAU thirty-five, and the Carter Center forty (including the former U.S. president and his wife). Nongovernmental organizations deployed another five hundred international and 1,300 local observers. In effect, there was one observer watching every 280 voters. UN Secretary-General Annan pronounced himself satisfied that the entire process "impartial and transparent"[71] and that "the Liberian people were able to freely associate themselves with political parties of their choice...there was no evidence to suggest organized or widespread acts of violence or intimidation."[72]

The final results, announced on July 24, gave Charles Taylor a landslide victory with 75.3 percent of the vote. Ellen Johnson Sirleaf ran a distant second with 9.5 percent of the vote. Alhaji Kromah received 4 percent, while Cletus Wortorson and Gabriel Baccus Mathews received

2.5 percent each and Togba Nah Tipoteh received 1.6 percent. The remaining seven parties all received even fewer votes. Taylor's NPP carried twenty-one of the twenty-six seats in the Senate and forty-nine of the sixty-four seats in the House of Representatives. The UP led the opposition, winning three and seven seats in the two chambers, respectively. The rest of the congressional seats were apportioned to other parties. Regarding the results, Stephen Ellis observed:

> Liberia held the fairest elections in its history, in which some 80 percent of the eligible population voted. Three-quarters of those who went to the polls voted for Charles Taylor. In some cases people may have reasoned that a vote for Taylor was the best hope for peace, since they knew that of Taylor did not win the election, he was likely to restart the war. But many may have also voted for Taylor because his very determination made him appear strong; when he argued that he was destined by God to be president of Liberia, it carried the ring of conviction. Some older Monrovians were shocked by the song sung by young NPFL supporters:
>
> > *He killed my Pa*
> > *He killed my Ma*
> > *I'll vote for him.*
>
> After seven years of ECOMOG presence, the result was exactly the one which the ECOWAS countries had set out to prevent in August 1990: Charles Taylor was president of Liberia.[73]

At last, it was hoped, the more than seven years of civil war were over. UN Secretary-General Annan was generous in his congratulations, even as he sought to underline the role played by the international organization:

> With the establishment of the democratically elected Government in Liberia, the principal objective of UNOMIL has now been achieved. I congratulate ECOWAS and ECOMOG, which played a leading role in bringing peace to Liberia through a successful partnership with the United Nations. I also wish to express my appreciation to all Member States that have contributed to the process, whether bilaterally or through the Trust Fund. Above all, however, the credit goes to

the Liberian people, who, through the electoral process, demonstrated their commitment to peace and their desire for the establishment
of a democratically elected Government in their country.[74]

DEBATING ECOMOG

With the conclusion of the Liberian conflict in 1997, the ECOWAS intervention was almost universally applauded. ECOMOG—which went
on to intervene in Sierra Leone that same year and in Guinea-Bissau the
following year—was hailed as "a credible African initiative to maintain
regional peace and uphold various peace accords at a time when some
of the African countries engulfed in conflict no longer enjoy their 'Cold
War privileges.'"[75] On the other hand, the intervention force has been
accused—not only by Charles Taylor, but also by a number of more objective observers—of political bias, corruption, and brutality. There also
remained the question of whether or not the intervention needlessly
prolonged the civil war.

Prescinding from the question of the rather shaky juridical basis for
ECOWAS's establishment of ECOMOG in general and the force's intervention in the Liberian conflict in particular,[76] the formal rationale
given by the regional body included concern over the nationals of the
member states caught up in the Liberian conflict, worries about the humanitarian situation faced by the Liberian population; fears about the
flow of refugees; and a desire to prevent the spill-over of the conflict into
neighboring countries.[77] However, Charles Taylor, who at the time controlled nearly all of Liberia's national territory, rejected the intervention
as an ill-disguised move to deprive him of the fruits of a victory that was
nearly consummated. Consequently, the then-warlord could hardly be
expected to view ECOMOG as a neutral and benevolent peacekeeping
force operating under the classic conditions of consent of the belliger-
ents, use of force for self-defense only, and, most importantly, impartiality.[78] Rather, the NPFL saw the intervention, which was welcomed by
its AFL and INPFL rivals, as an inherently hostile action. Taylor's suspicions were reinforced when, shortly after its deployment, ECOMOG
moved again the NPFL, rather than other warring factions including
the INPFL of Prince Johnson that had been responsible for President
Doe's abduction from ECOMOG headquarters and his murder.

For similar concerns about bias, as noted previously, the decision to intervene was also rejected from the start by Côte d'Ivoire and Burkina Faso, who were eventually joined in their opposition by other francophone states, including Mali and Togo. In a regional context, these countries furthermore viewed ECOMOG as a tool of Nigeria for the advancement of its hegemonic ambitions. With South Africa still under an apartheid regime, Nigeria had long attempted to establish itself as the political, economic, and military arbiter of Africa, or at least of the West African region. Even an apologist for Nigeria's role in ECO-MOG, Adekeye Adebajo, admitted that "Nigeria's leaders almost gave the impression that all the country had to do was simply appear on the African state and all other states would bow in deference at the splendor of the new African colossus that the gods had sent to fulfill their messianic mission in Africa."[79] In fact, with their dim view of the creation of ECOMOG, some of the francophone statesmen of Africa no doubt saw in it the ominous fulfillment of the ambition of Shehu Shagari, Nigeria's president from 1979 to 1983, who declared that: "Just as [U.S. President James] Monroe proclaimed the American hemisphere free from the military incursions of European empire builders and adventurers, so also do we in Nigeria and in Africa insist that African affairs be left to Africa to settle."[80] The former Nigerian ambassador to the United States, E. Olu Sanu, was even more explicit: "We have to be recognized as a regional power in West Africa. This is our region and we have a right to go to war. It is a Monroe Doctrine of a sort."[81] Such rhetoric was hardly comforting to the states that opposed the intervention. In fact, until very late in the conflict, the only French-speaking country with a significant participation in ECOMOG was Guinea, which was flooded with Liberian refugees and whose president, General Lansana Conté, bore significant personal animus toward Charles Taylor.[82] The French foreign ministry interpreted the Nigerian intervention in the light of Nigeria's claims on the oil-rich Bakassi peninsula held by Cameroon, a French client state, and, consequently, kept the topic of Liberia — to say nothing of the ECOMOG intervention — off of the agenda of the UN Security Council through 1990.[83]

Suspicions about the rectitude of Nigeria's intentions increased over the course of the civil war. Although ECOMOG was theoretically under the control of the ECOWAS Authority—composed of the heads of state of the member nations presided over by a rotating chairman—acting through the regional body's executive secretary, in practice the Nigerian force commanders reported to their own defense ministry's

Committee on ECOMOG. By 1993, a number of international leaders, including former U.S. President Jimmy Carter, who was trying to mediate the deadlocked conflict, were complaining that ECOMOG had ceased to be an impartial peacekeeping force and had turned into just another combatant.[84]

Even as ECOMOG was drawn into the mire of the Liberian civil war, components of the force soon joined the contending warlords in exploiting the economic potential of the conflict, undermining their very mission to end the fighting. The poorly financed peacekeepers soon fell under suspicion of looting, profiteering, corruption, and other abuses:

Many individual Nigerians, possibly up to the level of ministers, tried to enrich themselves. Among the small movable goods that were stolen by Nigerian officers were videos, motorcycles, and air-conditioners. More serious incidents occurred as well. Expensive equipment was stolen from a hospital in Buchanan, while LIMINCO's iron ore refinery in the same city was stripped bare for an amount estimated at fifty million U.S. dollars. This happened in a restricted zone under the exclusive control of ECOMOG and must have required the logistical involvement of an entire military unit. Similarly, underground cables were dug up and exported as scrap metal. In Nigerian ports observers reported the importation of various goods from Liberia, such as cars, electrical equipment, refrigerators and other household items. Upon completing their ECOMOG duty, some Nigerians later returned to Liberia as civilian businessmen.[85]

It is no wonder that cynical Liberians began to pun that ECOMOG stood for "Every Car Or Movable Object Gone" and other even less flattering variants. In addition, ECOMOG commanders also took "commissions" from the commerce carried out by the various Liberian factions. Some even went into business for themselves. Guinean officers serving with ECOMOG, for example, routinely received diamonds from ULIMO militiamen in exchange for weapons that Guinea acquired from Eastern Europe. The Eastern Europeans, mostly Ukrainians, were paid, in turn, with shipments of Guinean bauxite.

All the ECOWAS-led efforts to resolve the Liberian conflict faltered until the Abuja accord of 1995 created the second Liberian National Transitional Government headed by a six-member Council of State that included the principal warlords. Before then, the mediation efforts had high-mindedly tried to form interim governments with the various groups—established political parties, civilian political leaders, religious figures, non-governmental organizations, and others—that constituted Liberia's "civil society," most of whom were based in the parts of Monrovia controlled by ECOMOG.[86] While the approach was defended as not rewarding those who had caused the conflict, it was also unrealistic to expect to achieve anything by favoring those who did *not* exercise effective authority to the detriment of the groups that *did*. Not only did many of these "civil society" groups have memberships that consisted of little more than the self-appointed "leaders" and their family and friends, but their dependence upon ECOMOG cost them what little credibility they had enjoyed with the Liberian populace. In fact, if not in dearly held theory, their contributions to bringing the conflict to a peaceful end were negligible.

In the end, because ECOMOG operated effectively as a party to the conflict—both for reasons of animus against Taylor and for Nigeria's regional interests—the ostensible peacekeepers were precluded from serving as mediators capable of impartially monitoring a cease-fire and overseeing a lasting peace process. While the landing of the force in August 1990 prevented Taylor's takeover of Monrovia—a result that certainly was a limited blessing for the inhabitants of the besieged capital—it also only delayed the result that came seven years later with Taylor's election as Liberia's president. During the interim, the casualties piled up as the peacekeepers adopted the strategy of multiplying factions to combat the NPFL, a means that only exacerbated Liberia's ethnic and political divisions and prolonged the conflict. And, while it would be an exaggeration to assert that ECOMOG was *only* an instrument for either the assertion of Nigerian regional hegemony or the advancement of private interests, it is true that both of these factors did influence the actions undertaken by the peacekeepers.

Furthermore, an important lesson is to be learned from the experience of the ECOWAS attempt at resolving the Liberian conflict with a military force. The intervention was doomed from the start because a self-described "monitoring group" was sent to oversee a ceasefire that did not, in fact, exist. At the point when ECOMOG entered the scene, Taylor was on the verge of victory and had no incentive to give any quarter. To impose a cessation in the hostilities, ECOMOG had to engage the NPFL by force, weakening not only its claims to neutrality, but also the legitimacy of Amos Sawyer's IGNU that it propped up as an alternative to Taylor's National Patriotic Reconstruction Assembly Government.

Perhaps the lesson to be learned from the early internationalization of the Liberian civil war is a hermeneutical one: that intervention, while it can be motivated by commendable concerns, is not *ipso facto* a neutral act. An intervention can just as easily worsen or even create a conflict as it can prevent one. In Liberia, the former proved, unfortunately, to have been the case.

ENDNOTES

1. See Matthew Brelis, "Rebel's Saga: Mass. Jail to Showdown for Power," *Boston Globe* (July 31, 1990).
2. See Asteris Huliaras, "Qadhafi's comeback: Libya and sub-Saharan Africa in the 1990s," *African Affairs* 100/1 (2001): 5–25.
3. Stephen Ellis, *The Mask of Anarchy: The Destruction of Liberia and the Religious Dimension of an African Civil War* (1999; New York: New York University Press, 2001), 70–71.
4. See Jon Lee Anderson, "The Devil They Know," *The New Yorker* (July 27, 1998). Lester Hyman has recently published a policy book that amounts to an apologia for the Taylor regime, *United States Policy Towards Liberia, 1822–2003: Unintended Consequences* (Cherry Hill, New Jersey: Africana Homestead Legacy Publishers, 2003).
5. See Douglas Farah, "The Tyrant We're Too Willing to Live With," *Washington Post* (August 3, 2003). Robertson has subsequently published a "clarification" of his relationship with Taylor and Liberia; see <www.patrobertson.com/PressReleases/taylor.asp>.
6. D. Elwood Dunn, Amos J. Beyan, and Carl Patrick Burrowes, *Historical Dictionary of Liberia*, 2nd ed. (Lanham, Maryland/London: Scarecrow Press, 2001), 366, define *zo* as "a term used in central and western Liberia to refer to an individual, male or female, who is a respected elder. Often these individuals are considered to have medicinal and spiritual powers."
7. The importance that Taylor attached to this title can be seen in his insistence that it be included alongside his name and political title of "President of the Republic of Liberia" in the text of the July 7, 1999, Lomé Agreement for peace in Sierra Leone.
8. See Nancy Kiakula, "When a Psychopath Rules a Nation," *The Perspective* (April 30, 2002). Kiakula, a Liberian journalist living in exile in the United States, asserts that: "Dahkpannah engages in voodoo and other witchcrafts to obtain and hold onto power. Once he gains power, Ghankay surfaces, breaks all rules, torture [sic] the people of Liberia and West Africa, and gets into trouble with the international community. When his back is pushed against the wall hard enough, Charlie will blame everybody but himself. He will say or do anything to get out of trouble. Once the crises are over…Dakhpannah emerges to give Charlie the power he needs, Ghankay surfaces, and the circle continue [sic]."
9. See Byron Tarr, "Extra-African Interests in the Liberian Conflict," in Karl Magyar and Earl Conteh-Morgan, *Peacekeeping in Africa: ECOMOG in Liberia* (New York: St. Martin's Press, 1998), 150–170.
10. See Pierre Englebert, *Burkina Faso: Unsteady Statehood in West Africa* (Boulder, Colorado/Oxford: Westview, 1996), 159.
11. Quoted in Neal Henry, "Doe to Bush 'Help Your Stepchildren': In Desperate Letter, Liberian Leader Likens Himself to Nixon," *Washington Post* (August 9, 1990).
12. Chayee Doe, "In Defense of Sam Doe," *Washington Post* (June 28, 1990).
13. Quoted in David Hoffman, "U.S. Explains Reluctance to Intervene," *The Washington Post* (July 31, 1990).

14. Denis Johnson, "The Civil War in Hell," *Esquire* (December 1990): 46.

15. The name "Prince" is a common one in West Africa and is not a title. The is some discrepancy as to the middle name of this figure some authors (e.g., Adebajo) citing it as "Yeduo," while others (e.g., Dunn *et al.*) give it as "Yormie."

16. Adekeye Adebajo, *Liberia's Civil War: Nigeria, ECOMOG and Regional Security in West Africa* (Boulder, Colorado/London: Lynne Rienner Publishers, 2002), 51.

17. Wole Soyinka, *Open Sore of a Continent: A Personal Narrative of the Nigerian Crisis* (Oxford/New York: Oxford University Press, 1996), 14.

18. Carl Patrick Burrowes, "Democracy or Disarmament: Some Second Thoughts on Amos Sawyer and Contemporary 'Politicians'," *Liberian Studies Journal* 20/1 (1995): 117.

19. Quoted in Adebajo, *Liberia's Civil War*, 78.

20. Quoted in "Last Moments of Doe," *West Africa* 3815 (October 15, 1990): 2650.

21. Nkem Agetua, *Operation Liberty: The Story of Major General Joshua Nimyel Dogonywaro* (Lagos: Hona Communications, 1992), 51–52.

22. Festus Eriye, "I'm sorry I murdered the president," *[South African] Sunday Times* (July 6, 2003).

23. Adebajo, *Liberia's Civil War*, 92.

24. See Mary Ellen McDonagh, "Nuns Gave Lives in Liberia's 'No-Name War'," *National Catholic Reporter* (November 13, 1992).

25. See the 1992 report of Human Rights Watch at <www.hrw.org/reports/1994/WR94/Africa-03.htm#P103_48247 >.

26. See United Nations Secretary-General, *Further Report on Liberia* (S/26200, August 2, 1993).

27. See United Nations Security Council, *Resolution* (S/Res/856, August 10, 1993).

28. For the texts of the Cotonou agreement as well as other accords during the Liberian civil war, see Jeremy Armon and Andy Carl (eds.), *Accord: The Liberian Peace Process, 1990–1996* (London: Conciliation Resources, 1996).

29. See William Reno, *Warlord Politics and African States* (Boulder, Colorado/London: Lynne Rienne Publishers, 1998), 99; also see idem., "The Business of War in Liberia," *Current History* 95/601 (1996): 211–215.

30. See United Nations Secretary-General, *Sixth Report on the United Nations Observer Mission in Liberia* (S/1994/1006, August 26, 1994).

31. See idem., *Seventh Report on the United Nations Observer Mission in Liberia* (S/1994/1167, October 14, 1994).

32. Paul Richards, *Fighting for the Rain Forest: War, Youth, and Resources in Sierra Leone* (Oxford/Portsmouth, New Hampshire: James Currey/Heinemann, 1996), xvii.

33. See Ellis, *The Mask of Anarchy*, 78–79.

34. See Human Rights Watch, *Human Rights Developments 1990: Liberia Country Report* at <www.hrw.org/reports/1990/WR90/AFRICA.BOU-04.htm#P209_44481>.

35. See Africa Watch, *Liberia: A Human Rights Disaster. Violations of the Laws of War by All Parties to the Conflict* (New York: Human Rights Watch, 1990), 14–15.

36. See "Marines Evacuate 21 More in Liberia," *The New York Times* (August 8, 1990).

37. See Janet Fleischman, *Human Rights Abuses by the Liberian Peace Council and the Need for International Oversight* (New York: Human Rights Watch, 1994); Ellis, *The Mask of Anarchy*, 94–104; and Africa Watch, *The Cycle of Abuse: Human Rights Violations Since the November Cease-fire* (New York: Human Rights Watch, 1991).

38. Jeffrey Goldberg, "A War Without Purpose in a Country Without Identity," *The New York Times Magazine* (January 22, 1995): 38.

39. See Paul Gains, "Where Angels Will Not Tread," *(South African) Sunday Herald* (August 17, 2003).

40. See Africa Watch, *Waging War to Keep the Peace: The ECOMOG Intervention and Human Rights* (New York: Human Rights Watch, 1993).

41. Ellis, *The Mask of Anarchy*, 22.

42. Richards, *Fighting for the Rain Forest*, xvi.

43. Robert D. Kaplan, "The Coming Anarchy: How Scarcity, Crime, Overpopulation and

Disease are Rapidly Destroying the Social Fabric of Our Planet," *The Atlantic Monthly* 273/2 (February 1994): 44–76.

44. Robert D. Kaplan, *The Ends of the Earth: From Togo to Turkmenistan, From Iran to Cambodia — A Journey to the Frontiers of Anarchy* (1996; New York: Vintage, 1997), 27–29

45. Reno, "The Business of War in Liberia," 211.

46. Stephen Ellis, "Liberia Warlord Insurgency," in Christopher Clapham (ed.), *African Guerillas* (Oxford/Bloomington, Indiana: James Currey/Indiana University Press, 1998), 162.

47. See Reno, "The Business of War in Liberia," 214.

48. William Reno, "Reinvention of an African patrimonial state: Charles Taylor's Liberia," *Third World Quarterly* 16/1 (1995): 113.

49. See Ellis, *The Mask of Anarchy*, 165–166.

50. Economist Intelligence Unit, *Ghana Country Report* (December 1992): 32.

51. See Patrick de Saint-Exupéry and Sophie Roquelle, "La 'montagne de fer' que convoite l'Elysée,» *Le Figaro* (January 8, 1992).

52. See Reno, "Reinvention of an African Patrimonial State," 115.

53. See Justice and Peace Commission, *Exploitation of Natural Resources by Liberia's Warring Factions* (Monrovia: National Catholic Secretariat, 1995).

54. John L. Hirsch, "War in Sierra Leone," *Survival: The International Institute for Strategic Studies Quarterly* 43/3 (Autumn 2001): 155.

55. See David Keen, "Greedy Elites, Dwindling Resources, Alienated Youths: The Anatomy of Protracted Violence in Sierra Leone," *Internationale Politik und Gesellschaft* 10/2 (2003): 67–94.

56. See Richards, *Fighting for the Rain Forest*, 8.

57. Philippa Atkinson, *The War Economy in Liberia: A Political Economy* (London: Overseas Development Institute, 1997), 9.

58. See William Reno, "Political Networks in a Failing State: The Roots and Future of Violent Conflict in Sierra Leone," *Internationale Politik und Gesellschaft* 10/2 (2003): 62.

59. Reno. *Warlord Politics and African States*, 93.

60. There is some confusion as to whether Tailor was the surname of the chief or a description of his occupation as a repairer of garments (i.e., "Tamba *the* Tailor") or both.

61. Amnesty International, *Annual Report on Liberia* (London: Amnesty International, 1996), 2.

62. Arthur F. Kulah, *Liberia Will Rise Again: Reflections on the Liberian Civil Crisis* (Nashville, Tennessee: Abingdon Press, 1999), 42.

63. One anecdote from this episode is illustrative of the complexities of the highly personalized and rather arbitrary nature of Liberian politics that escapes many outsiders. After the arrest warrant was issued but before the fighting broke out, Taylor, acting apparently in the name of the Council of State, asked the Inter-Faith Mediation Committee to intercede with Johnson and obtain his peaceful surrender. When the religious leaders met with Johnson, he refused to turn himself in, arguing that if leaders were to be tried for the crimes of their subordinates, then the leaders of all the factions ought to be tried. This response was erroneously leaked to the press as a "proposal" of the interfaith committee. This infuriated the Council of State, which then ordered the arrest, on April 3, of the committee's chairman, Lutheran Bishop Ronald Diggs, who was charged with obstruction of justice. The Lutheran prelate was released on one thousand dollars bail, but ordered to appear for an April 5 hearing notwithstanding that the date was that of Good Friday. It was later learned that the charges against Bishop Diggs were the result of a personal grudge against him on the part of the ineffectual Council of State chairman, Wilton Sankawulo. Sankawulo had attended Pacific School of Theology in Glendale, California, in the hope of pursuing a career as a Lutheran minister. However, his ordination was blocked by Bishop Diggs.

64. See United Nations Secretary-General, *Seventeenth Report on the United Nations Observer Mission in Liberia* (S/1996/362, May 21, 1996), 7.

65. See United Nations Secretary-General, *Eighteenth Report on the United Nations Observer Mission in Liberia* (S/1996/684, August 22, 1996), 7.

66. See United Nations Secretary-General, *Twenty-second Report on the United Nations Observer Mission in Liberia* (S/1997/237, March 19, 1997), 14.

67. *Ibid.*, 3–4.

68. Chinua Achebe, *A Man of the People* (1966; New York: Anchor Books, 1989), 66–67.

69. Adebajo, *Liberia's Civil War*, 222.

70. See United Nations Secretary-General, *Twenty-fourth Report on the United Nations Observer Mission in Liberia* (S/1997/643, August 13, 1997).

71. *Ibid.*, 1.

72. *Ibid.*, 2.

73. Ellis, *The Mask of Anarchy*, 109.

74. United Nations Secretary-General, *Twenty-fourth Report on the United Nations Observer Mission in Liberia*, 9.

75. Rasheed Draman and David Carment, *Managing Chaos in the West African Sub-Region: Assessing the Role of ECOMOG in Liberia* (Centre for Security and Defence Studies Occasional Paper 26; Ottawa: Norman Paterson School of International Affairs/Carleton University, 2001), 1.

76. See, *inter alia*, K. Otent Kufuor, "The Legality of the Intervention in the Liberian Civil War by the Economic Community of West African States," *African Journal of International and Comparative* Law 5 (1993): 523–560; Klaas van Walraven, *The Pretence of Peace-keeping: ECOMOG, West Africa and Liberia (1990–1998)* (The Hague: Netherlands Institute of International Relations *Clingendael*, 1999), 13–28; and Adebajo, *Liberia's Civil War*, 63–65.

77. See Economic Community of West African States Authority, *Decision* (A/DEC. 1/8/90).

78. See David Carment and Patrick James, *Peace in the Midst of Wars: Preventing and Managing International Ethnic Conflicts* (Columbia, South Carolina: University of South Carolina Press, 1998).

79. Adebajo, *Liberia's Civil War*, 44.

80. Shehu Shagari, *My Vision of Nigeria: Selected Speeches* (London: Frank Cass Publishers, 1981), 75–76.

81. Quoted in Terry Mays, "Nigeria's Foreign Policy and Its Participation in ECOMOG," in Karl Magyar and Earl Conteh-Morgan (eds.), *Peacekeeping in Africa: ECOMOG in Liberia* (Hampshire/New York: Macmillan/St. Martin's Press, 1998), 112.

82. Personal conversation with Guinean Prime Minister Lamine Sidimé (November 18, 2001).

83. See Reno, "Reinvention of an African Patrimonial State," 115; also see Soyinka, *The Open Sore of a Continent*, 22.

84. See Max Ahmadu Sesay, "Bringing Peace to Liberia," *Accord: An International Review of Peace Initiatives* 1 (1996): 9–26, 75–81.

85. Van Walraven, *The Pretence of Peace-keeping*, 67–68.

86. See Samuel Kofi Woods II, "Civic Initiatives in the Peace Process," *Accord: An International Journal of Peace Initiatives* 1 (1996): 27–32.

FIVE

THERE GOES THE
NEIGHBORHOOD

CHARLES TAYLOR AND THE MOTLEY BAND of disaffected Americo-Liberians, aggrieved tribesmen, and foreign mercenaries who marched with him into Nimba County on Christmas Eve 1989 fired the first salvos of the Liberian civil war that, despite no fewer than eleven separate "peace agreements," continued virtually unabated until his presidential inauguration more than seven years later on August 2, 1997. In the mean time, the conflagration not only consumed Liberia, both literally and figuratively, but also ignited already precarious situations in all three neighboring countries: Côte d'Ivoire, Guinea, and Sierra Leone. While it has become facile convention to place the onus for the social, economic, political, and military upheavals across the subregion on Liberia and its warlords—and the latter certainly deserve to bear their full share of moral and legal responsibility—it is also necessary to note, as has been shown in the preceding chapters, that these other countries and their leaders are not entirely blameless for either lighting or at least feeding the fire in Liberia that eventually flared back to consume them as well.

Some of the subregional instability was the almost inevitable consequence of the tremendous displacement and economic strain that the arrival of Liberians seeking refuge caused in their ill-equipped host countries. In the first year of the civil war alone, a full third of Liberia's estimated pre-war population of 2.64 million had fled the country. Of the estimated 889,500 refugees, Côte d'Ivoire received 235,000, Guinea 409,000, and Sierra Leone 235,000, while Ghana took in 8,000, Mali 1,500, and Nigeria 1,000.[1] As late as the end of 2002, despite the relative peace established in the immediate aftermath of the 1997 elections and extensive efforts at repatriation or third-country asylum, the United Nations High Commission for Refugees still counted 274,516 Liberian refugees, with Côte d'Ivoire hosting 43,000, Guinea 119,293, and Sierra Leone 63,491.[2]

However, the greater part of the instability is attributable to these countries being drawn into the Liberian conflict either directly, such as through their participation in ECOMOG, or indirectly, such as through proxy forces like ULIMO that operated in Liberia with assistance from the Sierra Leonean and Guinea governments or the Revolutionary United Front (RUF) that operated in Sierra Leone with the assistance of Charles Taylor and the NPFL.

The dictum that "nature abhors a vacuum" is as applicable to geopolitics as it is to geophysics. In the vacuum of a failed state, which was what Liberia had clearly become during if not before its civil war, it was almost inevitable that the neighboring states would be drawn in. And once they were involved, any discussion of restoring the peace to Liberia required taking into account the regional situation.

CÔTE D'IVOIRE

That Taylor and the NPFL were able to enter Liberia at all, much less sustain their fight for so long, was largely thanks to Ivorian President Félix Houphouët-Boigny, who led Côte d'Ivoire to independence from France on August 7, 1960, and ruled it until his death on December 7, 1993. While he was no liberal democrat, Houphouët-Boigny presided over three decades of stability, founded on both economic prosperity—funded by Côte d'Ivoire's cocoa industry and its commercial port of Abidjan, as well as French economic and technical assistance—and *le Vieux*'s astute balancing of ethnic diversity. During his rule, Houphouët-Boigny, scion of a royal lineage of the Baoulé tribe, carefully appointed officials from different ethnic, regional, and religious backgrounds and welcomed migrant workers from throughout West Africa, using them to build one of Africa's largest economies. He also maintained close ties with the former colonial power, France, and became the chief conduit for French interests in the subregion. The French, in turn, were more than generous with both technical and financial assistance.[3]

The origin this partnership between France and her former African colonies, particularly Côte d'Ivoire, was the choice of four alternatives that French President Charles de Gaulle offered the African territories in 1958: (1) incorporation into the French state as departments with representation in the National Assembly on an equal basis with the departments of mainland France; (2) retention of their status as overseas territories; (3) autonomy as self-governing nations within the newly created French Community of Nations with a view toward gradual complete independence; and (4) immediate independence and departure from the French Community. Of the fifteen territories that held referenda on the proposal, only one, Guinea, voted for a complete break with the colonial power—with consequences that will be seen shortly. As a scholar of African affairs, Thomas Melady, who was later to serve two tours as a U.S. ambassador in both formerly British and French Africa as well as U.S. ambassador to the Holy See, observed at the time:

> While this may be regarded as a slap at French rule or even at France herself, Guinea's action actually validated the whole election. It proved that there was no trick, that a country could, and indeed did, vote itself right out of any control and relationship with France and become an independent, separate nation.[4]

That, aside from the two small colonies that voted to become overseas territories of metropolitan France, twelve of the colonial territories—Chad, the Central African Republic, Congo, Dahomey (later Benin), Côte d'Ivoire, Gabon, Madagascar, Mali, Mauritania, Niger, Senegal, and Upper Volta (later Burkina Faso)—voted to become autonomous republics within the French Community that, by the end of

1960, had acquired full independence as sovereign states, was in large measure due to the influence of Côte d'Ivoire's Houphouët-Boigny who, as a member of the French cabinet that had drafted the scheme for gradual independence, was committed to continuing close ties between African states and their former colonial rulers. As the Ivorian leader explained it at the time:

> France has suppressed slavery wherever it existed and has put an end to the quarrels which set different ethnic groups against one another. It has given an education to the African masses and its culture to an elite. It has instituted sanitary and medical improvements without precedent. In French ranks, in turn, we have poured out our blood in the battlefields for the defense of liberty and we have won a place in the history of France and of the free world. We do not want to abandon this recent heritage…These arrangements which we have chosen, and which are going into effect now, offer assurances of stability and security – conditions that are indispensable to the creation of an economic and social environment in which the African people can attain a standard of living comparable to that of the peoples of the great modern nations. These institutional arrangements are such as to attract investments in all forms – imports of capital, technicians and methods—which are indispensable to our territories.[5]

France generously rewarded Houphouët-Boigny's loyalty. As a result of the Franco-Ivorian post-colonial alliance, the West African country prospered—at least apparently—while many of its neighbors languished. Such was the wealth that Côte d'Ivoire enjoyed during Houphouët-Boigny's heyday that the old president built a showcase political capital for the country in his home village of Yamoussoukro, complete with its own marble Roman Catholic basilica that was second in size only to St. Peter's Basilica in the Vatican. Yamoussoukro was a visible manifestation not only of Houphouët-Boigny's religious faith and political ambitions, but also of his sense of familial loyalty. The Ivorian leader used the Liberian civil war to settle a personal, family score with Liberia's Samuel Doe for the 1980 murders of his close friend, Liberian President William Tolbert, and Tolbert's son, Adolphus, who was married to Houphouët-Boigny's adopted daughter, Désirée "Daisy" Delafosse.

The Ivorian interest in bringing down the Doe regime was reinforced by ties of ethnic kinship between Houphouët-Boigny's military chief of staff, General Robert Gueï and the indigenous peoples of Liberia who supported Taylor during the Liberian civil war. Gueï hailed from the Gouéssesso district north of the Man, in the Ivorian west. Gouéssesso is inhabited by the Yacouba people, who are related to the Gio of Nimba County, who rallied to Taylor's NPFL when he launched his revolt against Doe. Throughout the Liberian conflict Gueï funneled arms to Taylor, while the Yacouba towns of western Côte d'Ivoire profited from the conflict by serving as markets and transit points for commerce with the NPFL-controlled areas of Liberia. Perversely, these western Ivorian areas even profited from the influx of Liberian refugees fleeing the war that Côte d'Ivoire helped launch:

> Before Gbarnga became the headquarters of the NPFL, Taylor and the top brass of the Front lived in Danané. In order to establish his presence in Danané, it is believed Taylor contributed immensely to the development of Danané. If this was to be his base, he had to spend money to give it a facelift and to ensure security for himself. The money Taylor used may have been taken from the resources of Liberia. Looting was a favorite method of operation of his men and the majority of the goods looted from Liberia ended up in the Ivory Coast…In addition to the role of Taylor in helping to develop parts of the Ivory Coast, the Liberian refugees themselves played significant roles in the socioeconomic development of many Ivorian towns. The Ivory Coast never declared Liberians as refugees and consequently never established refugee camps as was the case in several other West African nations. Refugees in the Ivory Coast were considered as tourists and guests and were treated as such. When they rented rooms or homes they were required to pay far beyond the worth of the house or room. They were also made to pay all kinds of fees; and whenever relatives of Liberia's refugees (particularly in the U.S.) sent them money, they were forced to spend all of it. This did not only take place in Danané, it was true also in Tabou, Man, San Pedro, and other towns in the Ivory Coast.[6]

This cozy relationship cooled with the ascent of Houphouët-Boigny's successor, Henri Konan Bédié, in 1993. Bédié was more concerned with establishing his authority at home than with entanglements abroad, implementing a policy of *"Ivoirité"* ("Ivorianness") that was aimed at excluding his political rival, Alassane Ouattara, a former prime minister under Houphouët-Boigny, from the presidential elections scheduled for 1995. Ouattara was a Muslim hailing from Côte d'Ivoire's north with family ties to Burkina Faso, in contrast to Houphouët-Boigny, Bédié, and most of the governing classes, who were Catholic southerners—Bédié himself was a member of Houphouët-Boigny's Baoulé tribe. The ideology of *Ivoirité* soon permeated the entire political structure of the country as northerners were eased out of positions of responsibility in the government and military. As the bottom fell out on the cocoa-driven economy, non-Ivorian migrants (and Ivorian northerners who were indiscriminately lumped with them) were increasingly blamed for the crisis.[7]

Under Bédié, Côte d'Ivoire became a friendlier place for Liberians not associated with the NPFL, including some of Taylor's ethnic Krahn opponents like George Boley's LPC. As a result, the western areas of the country became the scene of cross-border raids by the NPFL on LPC sanctuaries and vice versa.

In December 1999, General Gueï mounted a coup that overthrew the Bédié government, replacing it with a military junta that he headed. While international pressure forced Gueï to hold presidential elections in October 2000, the general first revised the Ivorian constitution to require presidential candidates to provide proof of the Ivorian origins of both their parents, a standard that Ouattara could not meet. When the vote count in the poll went against him, Gueï stopped the counting and proclaimed himself the victor. Laurent Gbagbo, the presumed winner, responded by organizing protests led by members of his *Front Populaire Ivorien* party. When gendarmes loyal to Gueï opened fire on the demonstrators, units of the military turned against the general. At this point, it seems that Charles Taylor tried to intervene in support of his ally, sending what is reported to have been one hundred crack NPFL fighters to reinforce the general in Abidjan. Eventually, Gueï flew into exile in Benin—although he returned home after two months—and Gbagbo was sworn in as president. As president, Gbagbo developed links with opponents of Liberian President Taylor to counter Taylor's continuing support of General Gueï, who was suspected of plotting another coup.

Although a National Forum for Reconciliation met in October 2001 and the country's four "big leaders"—President Gbagbo, former President Bédié, General Gueï, and former Prime Minister Ouattara—met in Yamoussoukro in January 2002, Gbagbo has maintained the policy of

Ivorité, finding it a useful in preserving his hold on the reins of power and promoting his own Bété ethnic group. As it was under Houphouët-Boigny and Bédié previously *"Ivorité"* is less a coherent ideology than a political order founded upon the pillars of the administrative control of the mechanisms of the Ivorian state, the political and economic support of France, and the cultural and religious preeminence of Catholic southerners. Nowhere is this vision more tangibly illustrated than in the posh promontory that overlooks the central plateau of the *de facto* capital of Abidjan. As Houphouët-Boigny's architects laid out the city, they created a triangular plaza bordered—one on each side of the triangle—by the official residences of three incarnations of the *"Ivorité"*: the Ivorian president, the French ambassador, and the papal nuncio.

On September 19, 2002, a group of soldiers calling itself the *Mouvement Patriotique du Côte d'Ivoire* (MPCI) attempted a coup. Failing to take the *de facto* capital of Abidjan, the rebels retreated to Bouaké in the north central part of the country, where they were joined by other insurgents, who were thought to be Ouattara supporters who had deserted the army and taken refuge in Burkina Faso during Gueï's rule. The rapid deployment of a unit of one thousand soldiers by his French patrons enabled Gbagbo, who was visiting the Vatican at the time of the coup, to keep the MPCI confined to the north and an uneasy ceasefire, mediated by France, was signed at the end of October. A complex power-sharing accord, the so-called Linas-Marcoussis agreement, was signed January 23, 2003.[8]

On the first day of the coup, soldiers loyal to the Ivorian government of Gbagbo killed Gueï, who they accused of having a hand in the coup. Subsequently, two new rebel groups emerged among Gueï's former supporters in the western part of the country, the *Mouvement pour la Justice et la Paix* (MJP) and the *Mouvement Patriotique du Grand Ouest* (MPIGO), both claiming to avenge the general's death by overthrowing President Gbagbo. Reports indicate that these two movements include not only Gueï loyalists, but also former RUF fighters from Sierra Leone and some Liberian elements. By the end of 2002, the MJP had surrounded the key city of Man, while the MPIGO had captured the towns of Blolékin and Touba, and the southern half of Toulépleu.

On May 13, 2003, the United Nations Security Council authorized the creation of a United Nations Mission in Côte d'Ivoire (MINUCI).[9] A resolution passed on August 4 reaffirmed legal authorization for an ECOWAS peacekeeping force to operate alongside the French unit deployed previously, as well as reaffirmed a commitment to the country's "sovereignty, independence, territorial integrity and unity."[10]

The involvement of the Sierra Leonean and Liberian components of the MJP and MPIGO would indicate that the rebellion enjoys at least the tacit, if not the explicit, support of Liberia's Taylor. In response, Gbagbo has strengthened his ties with the anti-Taylor Liberian exiles in Côte d'Ivoire. Once more, the overlay of personal considerations of African leaders on preexisting ethnic loyalties and tensions has proven to be a lethal combination, both for individuals and nations.

While France's military and diplomatic interventions—including the interposition of a four-thousand-strong peacekeeping force to establish a demilitarized "zone of confidence" between government and rebel forces and the bringing of pressure for the two sides to agree on power-sharing—have been hailed by some as an example for the sort of forceful effort that the United States ought to exert in Liberia, a closer examination reveals that it constitutes a more of warning about unintended consequences than a model to be imitated by other Western nations confronted with African civil wars. While the French army managed to stop the fighting, the truce came at the cost of a prolonged *de facto* partition of Côte d'Ivoire between two stalemated sides. Like Taylor's NPFL in the wake of the ECOMOG intervention in the Liberian civil war in 1990, the MPCI (and its two come-lately allies in the rebellion) has reason to believe that the French military intervention deprived its forces of a relatively quick and decisive victory against the relatively weak forces loyal to President Gbagbo. Consequently, peace may have been bought in the present at the cost of renewed turmoil and violence in the future. Meanwhile, given a reprieve by the presence of the peacekeepers, Gbagbo's regime has been slow to implement the power-sharing arrangement and other concessions agreed to in the Linas-Marcoussis accord, causing the rebels to disavow the peace plan and begin rearming in late 2003. In the long run, it is questionable how long the French commitment will last given its financial drain on the French treasury—an estimated 30 million euros a month—as well as its diplomatic costs as the traditionally Francophile southern Ivorians blame their erstwhile allies for having effectively prolonged the conflict situation.

GUINEA

The sending of seven hundred soldiers by Guinea's brutal dictator Ahmed Sékou Touré to help Liberian President William Tolbert put down the Rice Riots of April 1979 became one of the grievances that propelled the rank-and-file of the AFL to support Samuel Doe's overthrow of the Americo-Liberian oligarchy the following year. However, the price that Guinea has paid once it was caught up in the maelstrom unleashed by Doe's *putsch* has far exceeded any notion of poetic justice. The first year of the Liberian conflict spilled 409,000 refugees into Guinea. The following year, the outbreak of the civil war in Sierra Leone sent another 170,000 fleeing into Guinea. Consequently, it was almost a foregone conclusion that the competing factions in the conflicts engulfing its neighbors would use the porous border zones of the eastern Guinean forest regions for refuge and provision. And it was almost as inevitable that Guinea would be drawn into an attempt to manipulate the situation to its advantage by provoking tensions that, ultimately, may come back to haunt it in future years.

Guinea's modern history is almost a reverse mirror image of that of Côte d'Ivoire. Félix Houphouët-Boigny was born into a royal Baoulé lineage and educated as a physician. He practiced medicine for fifteen years and established a prosperous cocoa plantation before entering politics and was elected to the French National Assembly, where he served from 1945 to 1956. At the Bamako Conference of francophone African nationalists in 1946, he was elected president of the *Rassemblement démocratique africain* (RDA), subsequently a powerful force in African politics and the eventual ruling party in Côte d'Ivoire. From 1956 to 1959, he served as a minister in French President Charles de Gaulle's cabinet, helping to formulate colonial policy. In 1958, when Côte d'Ivoire was preparing to become a self-governing republic within the French Union, Houphouët-Boigny was president of the constituent assembly. He became prime minister in 1959 upon autonomy that year, and president of the independent republic in 1960, serving until his 1993 death. A fervent Catholic, he constructed a monumental virtual reproduction of St. Peter's Basilica on the plains next to his native village of Yamoussoukro. The seven-thousand-seat—each individually air-conditioned—edifice, christened "Notre-Dame de la Paix," is only slightly shorter than the Vatican basilica and has more stained glass than the cathedral of Chartres. Workers labored around the clock in near secrecy for four years to complete the structure in time for Pope John Paul II to dedicate it in September 1990. His political longevity and the long stability of his country were due to the relative economic prosperity induced by his policies of slow Africanization, encouragement of foreign investment, and French aid given in reward for his close ties.

In stark contrast, Ahmed Sékou Touré was the son of a poor Muslim farmer (although later he would claim putative descent from the nineteenth century warlord Samory Touré). His schooling consisted only of attendance at a Koranic school and one year of studies at a French technical school in the Guinean capital of Conakry before his expulsion. He subsequently became a labor activist and entered politics. In 1958, he led Guinea's rejection of autonomy within a French Community in the September 28 referendum and opted for immediate independence, declaring in response to Charles de Gaulle's threat that those who refused the French offer should be prepared to "assume the consequences" that he preferred "poverty in freedom than riches in slavery."[11] He soon got his wish as the angry General de Gaulle gave Guinea its independence on October 2, 1958—after removing the entire French colonial infrastructure, including all four thousand French administrators, physicians, and teachers. The recalled teachers constituted three-quarters of all educators in the newly independent country and their withdrawal precipitated an education setback from which Guinea has yet to recover. Some of the departing officials even took imported office equipment, including telephones and light fixtures. Not only did aid cease but all financial ties were cut by the government in Paris, including a planned $80 million investment program.

A Marxist in orientation, Sékou Touré turned to the Soviet bloc for assistance. Two days after the Guinean National Assembly declared independence on October 2, 1958, the new country was recognized by the Soviet Union. By December 1958, the new regime had been offered an arms deal by Czechoslovakia. By February 1959, the Kremlin concluded a trade agreement with the government in Conakry. In August 1959, the Communist Party of the Soviet Union sent delegates to attend the fifth Congress of the *Parti Démocratique de Guinée* (PDG). Sékou Touré paid an official visit to Moscow in November 1959, a call reciprocated by Soviet Premier Nikita Khrushchev the following January.[12]

Abetted by his new Communist bloc patrons, Sékou Touré led his country into a period of totalitarian rule that saw the persecution of political opponents, religious leaders, and intellectuals as well as the social and economic ruination of what is potentially one of West Africa's richest countries. In 1961, the Guinean government announced that it had discovered a "conspiracy of teachers." A large number of teachers and their students—some as young as the elementary grades—were arrested together with trade unionists and PDG cadres. Governments of Soviet bloc countries where Guinean students were pursuing their studies, including those of the U.S.S.R., Czechoslovakia, and the German Democratic Republic, were asked to arrest the students and summarily repatriate them, so that they might be interrogated. In 1967, Sékou Touré announced a "cultural revolution" along the Chinese model—he had visited Mao Zedong in Beijing in September 1960 and pronounced his "high regard" for the political and economic system installed by the "Great Helmsman." A little volume modeled on the Chinese leader's *Little Red Book* and entitled *Thoughts of Sékou Touré* was published, with the Guinean people being commanded to purchase and "meditate" on its contents. Another aspect of this "cultural revolution" was a hasty decision to abolish the French language and give equal status as official languages to no less than eight local dialects (as a result of this last measure, today fewer than forty percent of the Guinean popular has a rudimentary knowledge of the official language, once again French).

Present-day Guinea continues, by inertia if not commitment, to bear the marks of its independence leader's ideologically motivated foreign policy. The country does not diplomatically recognize the State of Israel, but maintains diplomatic relations with the "state" of Palestine whose "ambassador" in Guinea, Jamal Ghoniem, also known as Abu Mohammed, has been the long-time *doyen* of the diplomatic corps in Conakry. Guinea also has no relations with the Republic of Korea and has rebuffed lucrative deals with South Korean firms over fishery rights, but maintains diplomatic relations with Kim Jong-Il's Democratic Republic of Korea, which maintains an experimental rice project in the hills of Coyah, near the Guinean capital—the irony of turning to starving North Koreans for agricultural assistance apparently escaping the senior bureaucrats in the Conakry government who were weaned on Sékou Touré's ideas of revolutionary solidarity.

Under Sékou Touré's rule, Guinea suffered a repressive, personal rule that arrested the development of any autonomous political or social institutions. The ruling party and the state became one, and all organs of the state were subordinated to the executive, in the person of the president. Corruption became the norm as the Sékou Touré's favored his own ethnic group, the Malinké. The regime purged or forced into exile members of other ethnic groups, while others were imprisoned, tortured, killed, or otherwise "disappeared" into the Guinean gulag. Among the "guests" detained at the notorious Camp Boiro in Conakry was the country's outspoken Roman Catholic archbishop, Raymond-Marie Tchidimbo, who spent nine years there.[13] This period also saw the economic decay of the country: by the time Sékou Touré died in 1984 as he was preparing another purge, Guinea was worse off than it was at the time of independence by every socioeconomic measure, including life-expectancy.

Sékou Touré was succeeded by his former hangman, Colonel (subsequently self-promoted to General) Lansana Conté, who literally made his career carrying out executions ordered by the late dictator by hanging victims from the Fidel Castro Bridge in central Conakry. Although Conté gradually liberalized both the economy and political life partially, he retained a tight grip on the reins of power, even as he has aged. Elected president at the end of 1993 on the basis of a constitution he promulgated, Conté survived a February 2, 1996, coup attempt led by junior officers, including Major Gbago Zoumanigui, scion of a prominent Guinean clan.

Conté was reelected for a second five-year term in 1998. Barred from seeking a third presidential mandate by his own constitution (the charter specifies a two-term limit) as well as his age (the constitution restricts candidacy to individuals between the ages of 40 and 65, the president was then sixty-six) Conté engineered a farcical referendum in 2001 to amend the law to permit another presidential term as well as to extend the term of office from five to seven years. The official results had the amendments passing with 98.36 percent of the votes in favor to 1.64 percent against, with 87.2 percent of the electorate participating—despite diplomatic and other international observers reporting a turnout of less than twenty percent. In long-delayed parliamentary elections, held in June 2002, the governing *Parti de l'unité et du progrès* (PUP) swept all thirty-eight constituencies. With the addition of the seats allocated by proportional representation, the PUP and its allies finished with ninety seats in the National Assembly, while the various opposition parties that participated in the poll settled for twenty-four seats.

A presidential election is scheduled for December 21, 2003, although the results are hardly in doubt. The Guinean supreme court—all of whose judges are appointees of the incumbent President Conté—has disqualified six of the seven opposition candidates on a variety of pretenses ranging from failure to document payment of the fees for candidacy to failure to present proof of one candidate's date of birth. The ruling leaves a virtual nonentity as the sole symbolic challenger to the country's ruler in the poll. Subsequently, the opposition has announced a boycott of the election, a move that should assure that Conté will win a seven-year mandate, however dubious its legitimacy.

Conté's favoritism of his own Sousou ethnic group, who comprise approximately twenty percent of the Guinean population, has roused deep resentment among the Fula (or Peul), who account for an estimated forty percent, and Malinké, Sékou Touré's ethnic kin, who make up thirty percent. These ethnic tensions threaten to tear the country apart in should the aging autocrat pass away without arranging an acceptable succession. Observers report that the Guinean leader, who is a diabetic, suffers from a renal disorder and regularly makes trips to a clinic in Morocco for dialysis. Despite his deteriorating health, General Conté has done little to groom a successor, perhaps out of fear that any successor would be a potential rival. While the constitution designates the president of the National Assembly as the successor to the head of state, the present incumbent of that position, Aboubacar Sompaoré, secretary-general of the ruling PUP, is a presidential lackey who enjoys widespread support in neither the government nor the military.

There is also concern over the presence of nascent Islamist tendencies among certain opposition quarters. Although some 85 percent of Guineans are at least nominally Muslim, Guinean Muslims—who traditionally have followed the gentle Mālikī school of Sunni Islam—have peacefully co-existed with the eight percent of their fellow countrymen who are Christian (primarily Roman Catholic) and have mixed their Islam with indigenous beliefs. However, in recent years an increase in Islamist activities has been observed, driven in large part by foreign elements whose entry into the country has been facilitated by certain— mainly Shī'a—members of the resident Lebanese community that plays a prominent role in the country's commercial sector as well as Arab missionaries of the Wāhhabī school, financed by Gulf benefactors. The proliferation in the poorer neighborhoods of Conakry as well as in the political opposition stronghold of the interior highlands of mosques not associated with the official National Islamic League—often accompanied by the erection of Koranic schools—threatens to inject a religious element into future conflicts.

During the Liberian civil war, it was no secret that the Malinké tribesmen of the Guinean eastern provinces lent aid to their Mandingo kin in ULIMO-K in their fight against Charles Taylor's NPFL. Alhaji Kromah and other Liberian figures maintained residences in Conakry as well as bases in the forest region of the Guinea's east. Once in power, Taylor responded by aiding Guinean dissidents and Sierra Leonean RUF fighters in their campaign against the government in Conakry, culminating in a September 2000 invasion that was driven back. More recently, it is an open secret that the battlefield successes of the anti-Taylor Liberians United for Reconciliation and Democracy (LURD) are directly attributable to the support they receive from the Conté regime. Like many other political bonds, there are personal as well as ethnic bonds at play: LURD's military commander, Sekou Conneh is married to General Conté's natural daughter and court seer, Aïsha. The couple has a large residence in Conakry that is guarded by the red-bereted units of the Presidential Guard.

Conté, it should be recalled, was the only francophone leader who did not criticize the establishment of ECOMOG and, in fact, contributed a battalion to the original contingent. Although the influx of Liberian refugees into Guinea as well as Taylor's ties to anti-French Guinea's traditional nemesis, the pro-French Houphouët-Boigny's Côte d'Ivoire, certainly concerned the Guinean leader, he was also motivated by his concern that Taylor's militias of disaffected youth presented a threat to all incumbent elites.

In 2002, a Special Forces unit of the United States Army trained an eight-hundred-man rapid reaction force for the Conté regime that is now deployed on the Guinean border with Liberia and is said to protect the rear of the LURD forces fighting the Liberian government. This blatant intervention in Liberian affairs could rebound on Guinea in the future when the Liberia-based Guinean dissidents no doubt exploit the power vacuum that will development in their homeland when the increasingly weak Conté finally passes away.

SIERRA LEONE

From the beginning, the histories of Sierra Leone and Liberia have unfolded along parallel lines. The Freetown colony was founded in 1792 by a private group of British philanthropists, the Sierra Leone Company, as a haven for freed black slaves, including some 1,200 who had supported the British during the American War of Independence—as well as deported British criminals. The company managed the Freetown settlement until the corporation was dissolved in 1808, and Sierra Leone became a crown colony, the first modern political state in sub-Saharan Africa. The founders of Liberia even took refuge there when the first expedition on the *Elizabeth* was decimated by disease.

The principal ethnic groups in the territory of the colony were the Christianized Creole (or "Krio," as they call themselves in Sierra Leone) who descended of the freed black slaves and paroled British convicts and who today make up approximately 10 percent of the population; the mainly Muslim Temne tribes that migrated out of the north and today comprise approximately 25 percent of the country's estimated five million population; and the heavily animist (albeit with a significant Christian segment) Mende tribes that have spread from the interior toward the southern coastal regions and likewise make up approximately twenty-five percent of the population. While Sierra Leone's civil war was not a war between ethnic groups, ethnic tensions nonetheless contributed to shaping the violence.[14]

British colonial officials, while active along the coast—the first sub-Saharan African university, Fourah Bay College (now University), was founded in 1827—were slow to extend their political rule into the interior. It was not until 1896 that a protectorate was declared over the interior territories that are part of present-day Sierra Leone. Even then, the colonial rule in the interior was indirect, being through tribal chieftains, whereas the coastal regions were directly administered. A legacy of this history continues to this day as twelve paramount chiefs still enjoy *ex ufficio* seats in Sierra Leone's 124-seat parliament. During the colonial period, the education system was largely in the hands of Christian missionaries, thus benefiting the Creole and Christian Mende populations most of all. The political and educational disparities proved to be the source of many later difficulties.

When Sierra Leone was given its independence within the British Commonwealth on April 27, 1961, Sir Milton Margai, a Mende physician who had been chief minister in the last years of British rule, became prime minister in a government led by the Sierra Leone People's Party (SLPP). When Sir Milton died in 1964, his half-brother, Sir Albert M. Margai, succeeded him at the head of another SLPP ministry. Sir Albert was a less capable politician than his older sibling and his government was beset by charges of mismanagement and corruption.

In the general elections in 1967, the Temne-based All Peoples' Congress (APC) won 32 seats compared to the 28 seats won by the incumbent SLPP. Four of the six independents elected declared their support for the APC's leader, Siaka Probyn Stevens, an ethnic Limba although he hailed from the Temne north. Stevens, who had been an associate of the elder Margai until he broke with him, was asked by the Governor General, Sir Josiah Lightfoot Boston, to form a new government. Minutes after Stevens was sworn in as prime minister on March 21, 1967, however, he was overthrown in a military coup led by Brigadier David Lansana, a Mende like the Margai brothers, who intended to restore Sir Albert. Lansana was himself overthrown three days later by another military group, led by Colonel Andrew Juxom-Smith, who established a regime that styled itself the National Reformation Council (NRC). The NRC government was overthrown in April 1968 by yet another army revolt, this one restoring Stevens and the APC to power.

This regime change was followed by several years of considerable unrest caused in part by the purge of Mende officers and officials by the restored Stevens—and marked by heightened ethnic tension as well as labor and student unrest. In 1971, supported by military forces he had borrowed from the brutal dictator of neighboring Guinea, Ahmed Sékou Touré, to put down yet another coup attempt, Stevens proclaimed Sierra Leone a republic with himself as president. His APC swept the farcical elections of 1973, and set about creating a *de facto* one-party state and nationalizing the diamond and mineral trade that were the principal sources of the country's export revenue (the monopoly on diamond exploitation had been held previously by Sierra Leone Selection Trust, a De Beers subsidiary, that shared revenues with the government). In 1978, Stevens staged a referendum that declared the APC to be Sierra Leone's only legal party.

In 1985, Stevens, then 80-years-old, retired after designating the army chief, Major General Joseph Saidu Momoh, as his successor as head of state (Stevens retained for himself the chairmanship of the APC). (Unlike many African strongmen, Stevens managed to retire peacefully and died in 1988.) His chosen heir, Momoh was duly "elected" president with 99 percent of the vote in a 1986 plebiscite. Under the APC's increasingly more corrupt stewardship, despite the country's rich natural resources and relatively small population, by the end of the decade, Sierra Leone was rated the fourth worst country in the world to live in by the UN Human Development Index (neighboring Guinea, which during the same period made a transition from the totalitarian terror of Sékou Touré to the relatively-benign kleptocracy of General Lansana Conté, enjoyed the dubious distinction of being the worst place in the world to live). Eighty percent of the population of Sierra Leone was illiterate and only twenty percent participated in the wage economy. Sierra Leone's official diamond exports fell from two million carats in 1970 to barely 48,000 in 1988—more an indicator of corruption than of declining natural resources.[15]

As previously seen, Momoh betrayed Charles Taylor when the latter came to him asking for the use of Sierra Leonean territory for his invasion of Liberia. Instead he sold his support to his fellow dictator Samuel Doe. To make matters worse so far as the NPFL forces were concerned, Momoh not only permitted ECOMOG to use the Lungi International Airport, near Freetown, to bomb areas controlled by the Liberian rebel movement, but sent Sierra Leonean units to join the intervention force. Taylor never forgave the Sierra Leonean ruler. On March 23, 1991, Foday Saybana Sankoh, a charismatic former army corporal who had been jailed for several years in the 1970s for his alleged role in the failed 1971 revolt against the Stevens regime and who subsequently underwent military training with a small group of Sierra Leonean dissidents in Muammar Qaddafi's Libya on the "art of revolution" alongside Charles Taylor and his companions, invaded eastern Sierra Leone from Liberia. Ironically, during his military service Sankoh had been posted to Congo (Zaire) as part of a failed UN peacekeeping operation. Sankoh, supported by the NPFL forces of Taylor, issued a call for antigovernment uprising in the name of the previously unknown "Revolutionary United Front" (RUF). The RUF, originally a diminutive force consisting only of several dozen disaffected rural youth to whom Sankoh had promised free education and medical care and who hailed him as "Papa," ostensibly fought for a redress of the iniquities of Sierra Leonean society whereby the APC regime exploited the rich diamond resources for the benefit of its elite even as the living standards in the country sunk to the very bottom of international scales. As former U.S. Ambassador to Sierra Leone John Hirsch has observed:

> Contrary to conventional wisdom, control of Sierra Leone's alluvial diamond fields was not the motivating factor for the RUF invasion of 1991. Sankoh had been imprisoned in the 1970s for a foiled coup attempt against Siaka Stevens, and was thirsting for revenge against

Momoh, his chosen successor, and his ministers. Sankoh's followers were unemployed, ill-educated young men with a mixed bag
of grievances. Exploitation of the alluvial diamond fields has been a
major factor, however, in the war's continuation.[16]

William Reno commented: "To the economist, this is war motivated
by greed. For the young fighter, it is injustice."[17]

Whatever its motivations, the RUF quickly earned a savage reputation, as the rebels amputated limbs of civilians as a terror tactic, routinely raped women and girls, and abducted young boys to join their
army. Young recruits were often forced to rape or kill a family member or neighbor, thus preventing a return to their previous lives, either
because of trauma or out of fear of retribution. Human rights groups
reported that the RUF's child soldiers were often forcibly injected with
drugs before being sent into battle in order to heighten their frenzy.[18] In
any event, the RUF rebellion caught the government forces unprepared
and, within a few months, Sankoh held sway over the southeastern fifth
of the country, including the diamond fields that financed his ongoing
military struggle over the next decade. Only the timely intervention of
military forces from Nigeria and Guinea prevented a total collapse of
the Freetown government.

Meanwhile the RUF quickly transformed itself from a ragtag collection of disaffected youth to a much larger, highly mobile and destructive guerilla force. At its height, the rebellion boasted as many as twenty
thousand members, including an estimated five thousand child soldiers,
although many of these served in non-combatant support roles. While
many members of RUF units were coerced into joining, others, drawn
from the marginalized segments of society, volunteered willingly in
exchange for the perceived "opportunities"— through looting, control,
and the impression of power — to be had through violence. It was not
by coincidence that Sankoh first raised the standard of the rebellion in
the southern Pujehun area, as the APC government had used the army
there to crush supporters of the rival SLPP during a campaign in the
early 1980s that was known locally as the *ndogboyosoi* ("bush devil")
war. The still-extent anti-government resentment provided the RUF
with ready recruits when it swept through in early 1991.

Throughout the conflict, in addition to the military and financial assistance provided by Libya, the RUF was kept supplied by elements of
the same elaborate network of international arms deals and diamond

buyers that assisted Taylor's NPFL, with the Liberians acting in many cases as the trans shipper. Later, after 1997, when the NPFL became the governing party in Liberia, Sierra Leonean diamonds were exported to Europe with Liberian labels to finance weapons shipments, primarily from Eastern Europe.[19] As previously mentioned, there is also evidence that similar arrangements existed with groups in the Middle East.

In April 1992, a group of soldiers on leave from the fighting on the front, led by a 27-year-old infantry captain named Valentine Strasser, overthrew the President Momoh. The coup was actually popular at the time as most Sierra Leoneans had grown disgruntled with the APC's corrupt rule against the backdrop of deteriorating social conditions. The present president of Sierra Leone, Ahmed Tejan Kabbah, then a United Nations official, even offered himself as an advisor to the APC. Even the RUF initially welcomed the regime change and declared a cease-fire, perhaps expecting to be invited to share power. Strasser, however, formed a National Provisional Ruling Council (NPRC) that grew increasingly despotic in its turn. According the Amnesty International, within months of taking power, the NPRC had executed twenty-six (or twenty-nine, reports differ) prominent political opponents. The human rights organization also reported that "Strasser's men attacked several villages, and, in the guise of rebel forces, lopped off the hands and feet of civilians while using others for bayonet practice." Eventually the NPRC also adopted another tactic out of the RUF's play book: by 1993, one well-placed Canadian diplomat estimated by that it had more than a thousand child soldiers under arms. Despite his increasing more abusive rule, the swashbuckling Strasser was courted by a succession of prominent African-Americans, who lent him an aura of respectability.[20]

The repressive measures by the Strasser regime, a government in which many Sierra Leoneans had placed their hopes led to disillusionment and had the effect of shifting popular momentum to the RUF, which not only seized control of the diamond fields, but subsequently also took the iron mines, the other major source of state revenue for the Freetown government. Strasser then turned to mercenaries, bringing in the Jersey-based Gurkha Security Group, a firm with close ties to the British government. The fifty-man outfit sent by Gurkha quickly lost its Canadian commander in a minor skirmish and its unsuccessful attempt to recover his body turned into a frenzy of indiscriminate killing. Strasser then spent $35 million to hire the South Africa-based firm Executive Outcomes, which had been assisting the government of Angola against Jonas Savimbi's UNITA guerillas, to assist in pushing back the RUF offensive. The mercenaries' military operations were financed by the sale of diamonds from the fields they drove the RUF from. In January 1996, Strasser was overthrown by his deputy, Brigadier Julius Maada Bio. (Strasser has met a kinder fate than many deposed African rulers. The British government procured for him a scholarship—funded by the United Nations—to study at Warwick University. His academic career proved, however, to be short-lived: the military ruler-turned-scholar was recognized by a fellow student from Sierra Leone and ensuing campus protests led to his removal.)

Under increasing foreign and domestic pressure, the new Sierra Leonean leader, Julius Bio, was forced to hold elections which were boycotted and sporadically disrupted by the RUF—to discourage people from voting, Foday Sankoh ordered his guerillas to cut off the hands of people who had cast a ballot (those who voted received an indelible ink mark on their hands to prevent them from voting more than once). In the rural areas where these amputations took place, they were especially cruel since they destroyed the livelihoods of the subsistence farmers who were thus rendered incapable of working if they survived their injuries. The elections took place nonetheless and were won, after two rounds, by the newly revived Sierra Leone People's Party, led by Ahmed Tejan Kabbah, a Mende who had survived the conflicts of the previous decades by living abroad as a career functionary with the United Nations Development Program.

On November 30, 1996, a peace agreement was signed in Abidjan, Côte d'Ivoire, between the new SLPP government of President Kabbah and the RUF.[21] The agreement granted an amnesty for all acts committed prior to its signing and called for the transformation of the RUF into a political party. The agreement quickly unraveled, however, as violence continued after a brief lull. When Sankoh was arrested, allegedly for arms trafficking, while visiting Nigeria in March 1997, the complicity of the Kabbah government in the arrest was widely believed and led to the final collapse of the peace accord. The rich irony of Sankoh being arrested on arms charges by the brutal military dictator of Nigeria, General Sani Abacha, himself the object of well-deserved international opprobrium for his own less-than-unblemished human rights record, was not lost on observers.

On May 25, 1997, yet another group of disgruntled Sierra Leonean soldiers, this time led by Major Johnny Paul Koroma, overthrew President Kabbah, replacing his government with an Armed Forces Revolutionary Council (AFRC) that invited the RUF to join it. The country fell into complete chaos as most of the judiciary system—judges, attorneys, police officers, and other law enforcement professionals who had previously been targeted by RUF rebels—fled the country before what it imagined to be the imminent entrance of the RUF into government. Consequently, as Amnesty International described it in one report: "The rule of law completely collapsed and violence engulfed the country." The angry populace, fearful not only of the RUF but also of the continuing decline of the country as schools, banks, and commercial services ceased to function, launched a series of civil disobedience campaigns. When, on October 8, the UN Security Council unanimously adopted Resolution 1132, imposing economic sanctions against the AFRC, it was scrupulously enforced by another ECOMOG contingent. Koroma quickly capitulated and promised to allow Kabbah to return to power by April 1998.

However, when Koroma appeared to renege on the deal, ECOMOG forces, under the command of a Nigerian general, and supported by the British mercenary company Sandline International, which had been hired by the exiled President Kabbah, launched an offensive against the now-combined AFRC/RUF forces in February 1998. The up to $10 million with which the exiled President Kabbah used to hire Sandline is believed to have come from a businessman, Rakesh Saxena, who arranged the initial meeting between Kabbah and Sandline executive Tim Spicer. In exchange for financing Kabbah's restoration, interests controlled by Saxena are reported by diplomats in Freetown to have received lucrative diamond concessions. Sandline's involvement proved to be a minor embarrassment to the government of British Prime Minister Tony Blair as it was in breach of the UN Security Council's arms embargo. Eventually, aided by irregular units of Mende tribesmen known as the *kamajors*, Kabbah was returned to power in March. The newly restored Kabbah took steps to begin demobilizing the army. Courts martial were held and twenty-four officers convicted of major responsibility in the AFRC regime were executed. Several civilian trials were also held, with some forty-seven individuals being convicted of treason and other charges associated with the AFRC regime and sentenced to death, including Foday Sankoh, who had been returned from Nigeria.

The restoration, however, quickly ran into difficulties as the intervention forces were routed outside Freetown and United States Marines had to enter Freetown in June to evacuate some 1,200 foreign citizens trapped by the fighting. During this period, the AFRC/RUF forces carried out a violent rampage throughout the country, despite being chased unsuccessfully by the Nigerian-led ECOMOG forces. As an Amnesty International Report noted at the time: "Human rights abuses have reached unprecedented levels. Several thousand civilians have been brutally killed or mutilated." The RUF itself referred to its campaign by the rather ominously descriptive designation "Operation No Living Thing."

Increasing numbers of Nigerian soldiers were required—by the end of the year nearly a quarter of the Nigerian army, some twenty thousand men, were in Sierra Leone—to prop up the Kabbah government. The RUF military commander, Sam "Mosquito" Bockarie, backed by Major Koroma, now designated deputy commander of the RUF, threatened to make the country ungovernable if Sankoh, who was appealing his conviction and death sentence, was not freed and included in the government. With RUF forces threatening to take the capital again, the Nigerians released Sankoh to participate in peace negotiations. The talks failing, UN Observer Mission in Sierra Leone (UNOMSIL) evacuated its foreign personnel in January 1999 as rebel forces threatened to storm Freetown. During this phase, apocalyptic scenes—at one point, for example, 40,000 people sought refuge in Freetown's National Stadium—were commonplace at every rumor. Using women and children as human shields, some RUF units managed to bypass ECOMOG forces and join comrades who had already infiltrated the city.

Eventually the ECOMOG forces managed to reestablish the Kabbah government's control over the capital and its environs in ferocious fighting, but at the cost of some 7,000 dead civilians and two-thirds of the city leveled. As the RUF units retreated, they abducted some three thousand. As a consequence of the mayhem, an about 600,000 of Sierra Leone's estimated four million inhabitants sought refuge in neighboring countries while two-thirds of those who remained were internally displaced.[22]

As in Liberia, the record of the ECOMOG contingent in Sierra Leone was a mixed one. One report by Human Rights Watch, recorded that the advocacy group "taken the testimonies of witnesses to over one hundred eighty summary executions of rebel prisoners and their suspected collaborators, mostly by ECOMOG forces."[23] Among the abuses detailed were:

Prisoners, some of whom had surrendered and many of whom were wounded, were frequently executed on the spot. Suspected rebel collaborators or sympathizers were often killed with little or no effort to establish their guilt or innocence. Some of the victims were rounded up during small mopping up operations, and many were executed at ECOMOG checkpoints after being found with weapons, determined to have improper identification, or denounced by the local population ... Several witnesses described the ECOMOG execution of over fifty rebels in and around Connaught Hospital on January 11, in violation of the laws of war protecting those no longer capable of fighting. Wounded rebels were dragged from their beds and executed within the hospital grounds, or shot directly in their beds or as they tried to flee on crutches and in wheelchairs. Others were executed in the morgue where they were caught trying to hide among the corpses.[24]

In addition to human rights abuses, the ECOMOG contingent, especially its Nigerian component, was implicated in illegal diamond mining and trading schemes with the very RUF forces it was supposed to be fighting. According to Indian Major General Vijay Kumar Jetley, who commanded the UN forces in Sierra Leone, Nigerian Brigadier General Maxwell Khobe, allegedly received ten million dollars to permit RUF activities, earning him the nickname "Ten Million Dollar Man." Jetley detailed his accusations in an acrimonious open letter to the United Nations, that also implicated UN Secretary-General Kofi Annan's special representative, reporting that ECOMOG and RUF enjoyed a relationship:

> ...of non interference in each other's activities, the total absence of ECOMOG deployment in RUF held areas is indicative of this. Keeping the Nigerian interest was paramount even if it meant scuttling the Peace Process and this also implied that UNAMSIL was expendable. To this end the Representative to the Secretary General (SPSG) and Deputy Force Commander (DFC) cultivated the RUF leadership—especially Foday Sankoh—behind my back.[25]

Eventually, the Nigerians, worn out by the fighting which claimed an estimated eight hundred of their peacekeepers and was costing them about $1 million daily, announced their intention to withdraw, forcing the two Sierra Leonean parties to enter into negotiations which resulted in the July 7, 1999, Lomé Peace Agreement,[26] signed in the Togolese capital. The deal made Sankoh the "Chairman of the Board of the Commission for the Management of Strategic Resources, National Reconstruction and Development" and accorded him "the status of Vice-President answerable only to the President of Sierra Leone." The accord also promised the rebel leader and his followers a "complete amnesty for any crimes committed...from March 1991 up to the date of the agreement." The Lomé Agreement was initialed by the two parties as well as by a special representative of the UN secretary-general, although the latter signed with the reservation that the amnesty provisions did not apply to "international crimes of genocide, crimes against humanity, war crimes, and other serious violations of international humanitarian law."[27]

The Lomé Agreement was ratified by the Sierra Leonean National Assembly on July 15, and endorsed by the UN Security Council in Resolution 1260 on August 20. The UN resolution authorized the expansion of UNOMSIL to 210 military observers. This group was renamed the United Nations Mission in Sierra Leone (UNAMSIL) by Resolution 1270 of October 22, which authorized six thousand military personnel, who were charged with assisting in the implementation of the peace agreement and facilitating humanitarian assistance.

The Lomé accord, like its predecessors, quickly fell apart. In several incidents in late 1999 and early 2000, UN peacekeepers were themselves disarmed by RUF forces. In response, the Security Council, in Resolution 1289 of February 7, 2000, increased UNAMSIL's personnel to 11,100. This resolution also revised UNAMSIL's mission to include protecting the government of President Kabbah. The situation only worsened, however. In early May, the RUF killed seven UN peacekeepers and captured fifty others. The number of peacekeepers taken prisoner soon increased to over five hundred as the UN forces under General Jetley, who was experiencing difficulties with the Nigerian component of his command, apparently surrendered to the rebels without firing a shot. British forces, operating independently of the UN command structures, then landed in Freetown, ostensibly to help evacuate foreign nationals, but in fact to shore up the Kabbah regime.

The capture of Sankoh while he led an incursion on Freetown, however, saved the situation as the UN prisoners were released as the leaderless RUF forces began to disintegrate after their leader's arrest.

Meanwhile the Security Council, through Resolution 1299 on May 19, authorized UNAMSIL to increase its strength to 13,000 military personnel. This limit was raised to 17,500 with Resolution 1346 on March 30, 2001. Resolution 1346 also stretched UNAMSIL's brief, already expanded from mere peacekeeping to protection of the government, even further, declaring that: "The main objectives of UNAMSIL in Sierra Leone remain to assist the efforts of the government of Sierra Leone to extend its authority, restore law and order and stabilize the situation progressively throughout the entire country, and to assist in the promotion of a political process which should lead to a renewed disarmament, demobilization and reintegration program and the holding, in due course, of free and fair elections."

As the country was gradually pacified during 2001, UNAMSIL celebrated the success of its disarmament program with an arms destruction ceremony on January 17, 2002, although informed observers have noted that the not all the elements of the RUF have been disarmed. Rather, estimates are that up to five thousand have simply moved to a different conflict, taking service with the RUF's longtime ally, Liberian President Charles Taylor, in his own ongoing civil conflict. In any event, the war was officially declared ended the following day. Estimates are that there were up to seventy-five thousand war-related deaths during the decade-long conflict, although the figure is difficult to verify. The social and psychological toll of the conflict is even more difficult to assess, although one preliminary study by Médicins sans Frontières indicated that almost all of those surveyed suffered from starvation or had witnessed someone being killed or wounded, and about half had lost a family member. A year later, the first reliable economic forecasts are hardly encouraging: with a population presently estimated at approximately five million and a gross domestic product of less than $1 billion, Sierra Leone will require at least a real GDP growth rate of at least 8 percent sustained over at least a decade to even begin to turn around.

President Kabbah, who was triumphantly reelected in May 2002 elections, had, in a letter addressed to the UN Security Council, dated June 12, 2000, requested the Council's assistance "in establishing a strong and credible court" that would meet the twin objectives of bringing those guilty of atrocities to justice and ensuring the future peace of the country by thus establishing the rule of law. The Sierra Leonean head of state admitted that not only did his country lack the resources and expertise to carry out the judicial proceedings, but that there were "gaps in Sierra Leonean criminal law as it [did] not encompass such heinous crimes as those against humanity and some of the gross human rights abuses committed."[28] Tellingly, President Kabbah's letter mentioned only offenses committed by the RUF—an annex to the communication suggested that "the mandate of the court could be designed to be narrow in order to prosecute the most responsible violators and the leadership of the Revolutionary United Front"—and ignored any abuses carried out by other forces in the decade-long conflict, including those perpetrated by forces that back his government.

Consequently, on August 14, 2000, the Security Council adopted Resolution 1315, which requested the "the Secretary-General to negotiate an agreement with the Government of Sierra Leone to create an independent special court" whose jurisdiction would include "crimes against humanity, war crimes and other serious violations of international humanitarian law, as well as crimes under relevant Sierra Leonean law committed within the territory of Sierra Leone." The resolution also entrusted the UN secretary-general with the responsibility for producing a detailed plan for the proposed tribunal.

Following negotiations with Sierra Leonean government, Secretary-General Annan issued his report to the Security Council on October 4, 2000.[29] The report contained a draft agreement between the UN and the Sierra Leonean government establishing the Special Court and a draft Statute for the tribunal. Although some of those slated for trial by the court were already in custody, various events diverted the world's attention and prevented any action on the proposals until the end of 2001 when, in a letter dated December 26, Annan informed the Security Council that he was authorizing the commencement of operations for the Special Court for Sierra Leone (SCSL), beginning with the dispatch of a planning mission to the West African country. During the a whirlwind twelve-day tour of the war-torn country in January 2002 the mission was joined by UN Under-Secretary-General for Legal Affairs, Hans Corell, who, on January 16, signed the agreement formally establishing the SCSL with Sierra Leone's Attorney General and Minister of Justice, Solomon E. Berewa. The agreement signed by the two was essentially the one contained in Annan's October 2000 report, albeit with several notable amendments, including the abandonment of two trial chambers in favor of a one. Annan communicated the accord, along with the statute that formed an integral part of it, to the Security Council on March 6.[30] Meanwhile, the implementing legislation for the tribunal was passed by the parliament of Sierra Leone on March 19, and signed by President Ahmed Tejan Kabbah on March 29.

On April 17, 2002, the UN secretary-general appointed David M. Crane, a veteran attorney with the U.S. Department of Defense who had most recently served as the Pentagon's senior Inspector General, to a three-year term as the chief prosecutor for the Court. The appointment of judges for the three-member trial chamber and the five-member appeal chamber—the SCSL statute called for the Sierra Leonean government to appoint one trial judge and two appeals judges and the UN secretary-general to appoint two trial judges and three appeals judges and the two parties to agree on two alternate judges—was delayed until July 29, 2002, as the UN Secretariat's bureaucracy struggled to create a slate that reconciled the competing interests that it juggled just as the choice of an American for the role of chief prosecutor had been carefully crafted to allay to the doubts of the American administration regarding international criminal assizes, especially as the U.S. was expected the bear the major burden for paying the tribunal's bills.

The court has thus far indicted twelve of "who bear the greatest responsibility for serious violations of international humanitarian law"[31] committed during the continuing Sierra Leonean civil war after the Abidjan Peace Accord of November 30, 1996. Of the twelve men indicted, one—RUF leader Foday Sankoh—died in custody on July 29, 2003, while awaiting trial, and two—RUF military chief Sam "Mosquito" Bockarie and former APRC junta leader Johnny Paul Koroma—died in Liberia. Eight are in custody awaiting trial. One remains at large: Charles Ghankay Taylor who, according the indictment

> To obtain access to the mineral wealth of the Republic of Sierra Leone, in particular the diamond wealth of Sierra Leone, and to destabilized the State...provided financial support, military training, personnel, arms, ammunition and other support and encouragement to the RUF, led by Foday Saybana Sankoh, in preparation for RUF armed action in the Republic of Sierra Leone, and during the subsequent armed conflict in Sierra Leone.[32]

ENDNOTES

1. See Human Rights Watch, *Human Rights Developments 1990: Liberia Country Report.*
2. See United Nations High Commission for Refugees, *2002 Annual Statistical Report: Liberia* (July 23, 2003).
3. For a good discussion of the background context on French postcolonial policy in Africa, see James O. Goldsborough, "Dateline Paris: Africa's Policeman," *Foreign Affairs* 33 (Winter 1978–1979): 174–190.
4. Thomas Patrick Melady, *Profiles of African Leaders* (New York: Macmillan, 1961), 8.
5. Quoted in *ibid.*, 122.
6. Arthur F. Kulah, *Liberia Will Rise Again: Reflections on the Liberian Civil Crisis* (Nashville, Tennessee: Abingdon Press, 1999), 61–62.
7. See Corinne Dufka *et al.*, *The New Racism: The Political Manipulation of Ethnicity in Côte d'Ivoire*, edited by Peter Takirambudde (New York: Human Rights Watch, 2001).
8. For the full text of the Linas-Marcoussis agreement, see the website of the French Ministry of Foreign Affairs at < www.usip.org/library/pa/cote_divoire/cote_divoire_ 01242003.html >.
9. See United Nations Security Council, *Resolution* (S/Res/1479, May 13, 2003).
10. See United Nations Security Council, *Resolution* (S/Res/1498, August 4, 2003).
11. Ahmed Sékou Touré, *Expérience guinéenne et unité africaine* (Paris: Éditions «Présence africaine», 1961), 88.
12. See Robert Levgold, *Soviet Policy in West Africa* (Cambridge: Harvard University Press, 1970), 63.
13. Like the Hungarian Cardinal Joszef Mindszenty of Esterzgom and the Czech Cardinal Joseph Beran of Prague, Archbishop Tchidimbo was a victim of the post-Vatican II papal diplomacy's compromises with Communist regimes. The prelate was released from his imprisonment in August 1979 to learn that the pope had accepted his "resignation" from his office. Archbishop Tchidimbo has since lived in exile in France. See his memoirs, *Noviciat d'un évêque. Huit ans et huit mois de captivité sous Sékou Touré* (Paris: Éditions Fayard, 1987).
14. See David Keen, "Greedy Elites, Dwindling Resources, Alienated Youth: The Anatomy of Protracted Violence in Sierra Leone," *Internationale Politik und Gesellschaft* 10/2 (2003): 67–94.
15. See Robert D. Kaplan, *The Ends of the Earth: From Togo to Turkmenistan, From Iran to Cambodia — A Journey to the Frontiers of Anarchy* (1996; New York: Vintage, 1997), 50–51.
16. John L. Hirsch, "War in Sierra Leone," *Survival: The International Institute for Strategic Studies Quarterly* 43/3 (Autumn 2001): 150; also see idem., *Sierra Leone: Diamonds and the Struggle for Democracy* (Boulder, Colorado/London: Lynne Rienner Publishers, 2001).
17. William Reno, "Political Networks in a Failing State: The Roots and Future of Violent Conflict in Sierra Leone," *Internationale Politik und Gesellschaft* 10/2 (2003): 66.
18. In fairness, it should be noted that while the reputation that the RUF earned for brutalities was especially heinous and its use of child soldiers particularly notorious, atrocities were committed on both sides during the conflict. The post-war report by the United Nations High Commissioner for Human Rights, released in February 2003, admitted that a number of the atrocities blamed at the time of the conflict on the rebels were, in fact, perpetrated by the peacekeepers from the monitoring group sent by the Economic Community of West African States (ECOMOG). During the conflict in fact, UN forces arrested over one hundred of their own military personnel, principally West Africans, on charges of summary executions (including the infamous massacre of twenty patients at Connaught Hospital on January 20, 1999) and mistreatment of relief workers from the Red Cross and other agencies. The contrast, however, remains both in the relative scale of the abuses committed and in that the peacekeepers attempted to rein in their own for excesses while the rebels seemed to encourage systematic rights violations on their side.

19. See Dena Montague, "The Business of War and the Prospects for Peace in Sierra Leone," *The Brown Journal of World Affairs* 9/1 (2002): 229–237.

20. See Keith B. Richburg, *Out of America: A Black Man Confronts Africa*, rev. ed. (San Diego/ New York/London: Harcourt, 1998), 137–142.

21. For the complete text of the Abidjan agreement see <www.usip.org/library/pa/sl/sierra_ leone_10301996.html>.

22. International Crisis Group, *Sierra Leone: Time for a New Military and Political Strategy* (April 11, 2001), 2.

23. Human Rights Watch, *Getting Away with Murder, Rape, Mutilation: New Testimony from Sierra Leone* (July 1999), at <www.hrw.org/reports/1999/sierra/>.

24. *Ibid.*

25. Vijay Kumar Jetley, *Report on the Crisis in Sierra Leone* (May 2000).

26. For the complete text of the Lomé agreement see <www.usip.org/library/pa/sl/sierra_le- one_07071999_toc.html>.

27. See United Nations Secretary-General, *Seventh Report of the Secretary General on the United Nations Mission in Sierra Leone* (S/1999/836, July 30, 1999).

28. The correspondence is published in United Nations Security Council, *Letter dated 9 August 2000 from the Permanent Representative of Sierra Leone to the United Nations addressed to the President of the Security Council* (S/2000/786, August 10, 2000).

29. See United Nations Secretary General, *Report of the Secretary-General on the establishment of a Special Court for Sierra Leone* (S/2000/915, October 4, 2000).

30. See idem., *Report of the Planning Mission on the Establishment of the Special Court for Sierra Leone* (S/2002/246, March 8, 2002).

31. *Statute of the Special Court for Sierra Leone*, art. 1.

32. Quoted in Lester S. Hyman, *United States Policy Towards Liberia, 1822–2003: Unintended Consequences* (Cherry Hill, New Jersey: Africana Homestead Legacy Publishers, 2003), 88. Hyman, the legal counsel for Liberia in the United States, defends his former client from the charges in the book, especially at *ibid.*, 88–116.

SIX

A SLOW FAREWEEL
TO ARMS

With the Nigerian strongman Sani Abacha, incumbent chairman of ECOWAS, the presidents of Burkina Faso, Chad, Côte d'Ivoire, Guinea, Guinea-Bissau, Mali, and Niger, and the prime ministers of Benin and Togo, the vice president of The Gambia, the chairman of the Council of State of Ghana, the special envoys of the United States, Libya, South Africa, and Zimbabwe, delegations from the EU and the OAU, and the special representatives of the UN Secretary-General in attendance, Charles Ghankay Taylor was inaugurated as twenty-second president of the Republic of Liberia on August 2, 1997. Most Liberians hoped that the ceremony was not only the birth of a presidency, but the requiem for more than seven years of fratricidal conflict.

The question that arises, however, is why so many Liberians, after what they had been put through, turned around and gave their votes to one of the principal architects of their misery. Although no one mentioned it at the time, the explanation that has acquired currency is that Liberians "did not do so out of love for the man but from a desire for peace and stability."[1] Former U.S. President Jimmy Carter, who monitored the election, later attributed Taylor's victory to the fear of Monrovians who "felt that he might resort to violence if he lost."[2] One of Carter's senior aides explained that:

> The issue of peace dominated the July 1997 election and most voters seemed determined to use their franchise to maximize the chances of stability. Many Liberians believed that if Taylor lost the election, the country would return to war.[3]

This, of course, does not detract from the fact that those same Liberians also arrived at that conclusion in polls that, despite some technical difficulties, were judged by observers to have been "impartial and transparent."[4] However, it does render the objection specious on juridical grounds: constitutional arrangements in democratic polities exist to guarantee procedural justice, not moral.

While legitimate to a certain extent, the question of the motivations of some of the voters does not do justice to the fact that Taylor did represent a significant constituency within Liberia. Even Carter, who later became a critic of the new Liberian president, has reluctantly conceded that Taylor had the "strong support of people whom he had dominated in the rural areas."[5] The fact was that, as previously noted, Taylor started the civil war with the popular support of the Gio and Mano communities of Nimba County as well as that of his maternal Gola kinsfolk, all of whom felt themselves to be persecuted by the Doe regime. And, from his paternal Americo-Liberian roots, he also had a following among the descendants of settlers who were likewise alienated by Doe. Even in Montserrado County around Monrovia, Taylor won 55 percent of the vote.

Another factor in Taylor's success was his access to an estimated $250 million in annual revenues from the territories controlled by the NPFL during the civil war. He consequently could outspend all of his rivals combined in the distribution of pre-election largesse. He also had the benefit of a private radio station while his opponents vied for attention on public service broadcasters.

Perhaps, however, the most significant factor contributing to Taylor's electoral sweep was his opponents. Augustine Toure, cofounder of the nongovernmental human rights group Liberia Democracy Watch, has subsequently pointed out that:

> In explaining Charles Taylor's spectacular electoral victory in 1997, many analysts have pointed to the fears of many Liberian voters that, had Charles Taylor lost the July 1997 elections, he would have returned to the bush and resumed the war to he started. However, an equally important but often overlooked explanation, is the breakup of the alliance of political parties comprising seven civilian-based political parties which had been formed on the eve of the elections in a bid to deny Taylor an electoral victory. The breakup of the Alliance—as the coalition of parties was known in March 1997—virtually guaranteed Taylor's victory. The disintegration of the Alliance confirmed the worst fears of Liberians: that the civilian politicians were egoistic, power-hungry, disorganized, and disunited, and could not subsume their personal ambitions to the common good. The disintegration of the Alliance thus dissuaded a significant portion of the Liberian population who had held deep-seated suspicions of civilian populations from casting their votes for members of the Alliance.[6]

Despite Amos Sawyer's heroic efforts to put together a united opposition, the various civilian politicians vied with each other for spoils. Some of them—like Gabriel Baccus Mathews and Togba Nah Tipoteh—were fighting old battles from the pre-Doe era that were of little interest to most voters, as their poor showings revealed. Furthermore, the disastrous Alliance of Political Parties convention did little to reassure voters that these parties were capable of ensuring stability, the most important issue to the majority of Liberians. Baccus Mathews and Tipoteh had pulled their parties, the United People's Party (UPP) and the Liberian People's Party (LPP) respectively, from the Alliance when they each failed to win its presidential nomination. In the end, out of the seven parties in the Alliance, only two—the Liberian Action Party (LAP) and the Liberian Unification Party (LUP)—kept faith with their preconvention pledge to abide by the decision of the convention. Toure concluded that:

> A united front of civilian politicians could have presented the Liberian population with an alternative to the much discussed security

threat posed by Taylor in the event that he had lost the election. The fact that Taylor won the majority of votes cast in Monrovia—generally regarded as the stronghold of the civilian politicians and as an anti-warring factions—is reflective of the extent of the disillusionment felt by the population.[7]

Even Taylor's principal rival, Ellen Johnson Sirleaf, had problems of credibility. Voters with long memories recalled her backing of the brutal Doe when it suited her interests and even her endorsement of Taylor early in the civil war. Also, having lived abroad for more than a decade and only returning to Liberia to contest the election, she appeared detached from the sufferings of ordinary Liberians, who could only dream of the salary and standard of living she enjoyed as a senior international civil servant and successful private consultant.

In fact, the late Clarence Zamba Liberty, a professor at the University of Liberia who represented his country at the United Nations Educational, Scientific, and Cultural Organization (UNESCO), pointed out that many reports misunderstood the slogan that many Liberians chanted at the time of the election to the horror of many observers, including former President Carter: "He killed my Ma / He killed my Pa / I'll vote for him." Zamba Liberty attributes to the refrain not only a pro-Taylor, but also an antiestablishment meaning. In his version, the chant was: "*They say*, 'You killed my Ma' / *They say*, 'You killed my Pa' / *But* I will still vote for you!"[8]

In short, despite Taylor's reputation as a brutal warlord whose aim had always been the capture of power in Monrovia, the across-the-board victory for him personally and for the NPP that had formed out of his rebel movement in an election that, despite its difficulties, was judged free and fair by the international community could perhaps be best explained by the fact that the electorate faced an uncertain security situation and made a reasoned choice for the candidate who was most likely maximize the possibility for stability and, eventually, improved conditions.[9]

Some international observers, especially members of the press, evidently did not share the Liberian populace's preference for Taylor. After having depicted him—albeit not without reason—as villain, many foreign journalists were embarrassed to discover that their analyses were incorrect regarding popular sentiment. It was, of course, neither the first nor the last time that such an occurrence was verified in the history of war coverage in West Africa. As late as four years later, one of the veteran correspondents in Monrovia was still complaining about how inexplicable it was that the electorate had preferred Taylor to Ellen Sirleaf Johnson who had international experience and support – entirely missing the point that her long sojourns abroad were precisely what discredited her in the eyes of many voters. The author of a *New York Times* editorial commenting on the election clearly suffered from the same sense of disbelief, declaring that: "Mr. Taylor's landslide victory requires explaining, since tens of thousands of Liberian families lost relatives to his undisciplined rebel troops during an eight-year civil war that took 150,000 lives. Further, despite a professed conversion to peace and democracy, Mr. Taylor has a well-deserved reputation for violence and indifference to human rights."[10] The *Washington Post* was less circumspect:

> Liberians have chosen a strange way to end—if it is ended—the seven-year civil war that has shredded their 150-year-old West African country. They have overwhelmingly elected president the single person most responsible for Liberia's tragedy. Charles Taylor, a warlord, broke out of a Massachusetts jail where he was being held on embezzlement charges, invaded his country on Christmas Eve 1989 and soon toppled the government of Samuel Doe. Immense ethnic horrors followed.[11]

The *Post* made no secret of its preference in the poll:

> Respectful as Americans customarily are to the verdict of democratic opinion, they will not come easily to the notion of President Charles Taylor. Ms. Johnson-Sirleaf, a former World Bank economist and United Nations administrator, seemed a natural fit for a country desperately in need of massive rebuilding and integration into the regional and world economies.[12]

In this context of support at home and continuing hostility abroad, Taylor took office, assuring Liberians in his inaugural address that he would promote unity and national reconciliation, respect human rights, and reestablish peace and stability both at home and abroad. The events of the following years, unfortunately, would show that the goals eluded the Liberian president, if indeed he had pursued them at all.

WARLORD TURNED STATESMAN?

After more than seven years of fratricidal civil war, preceded by nearly a decade of the increasingly despotic misrule by the semiliterate Sergeant Doe, Liberia was in a precarious situation. The institutions of government had completely collapsed while the structures of vibrant civil society were nonexistent. The task of rebuilding Liberia would have required Herculean efforts, even for a statesman of the first caliber. Instead, the task fell to a former warlord. Taylor had promised in his inaugural address to build a government that respected human rights, stating that he was committed to an independent judiciary, human rights, the rule of law, and equal protection of the law. At first he seemed to honor the pledge, inviting members of the opposition to participate in rebuilding the country. However, Taylor soon turned to consolidate his power and institutionalize his control over Liberian society.

Shortly after his inauguration, Taylor fell out with ECOMOG's Nigerian commander, General Victor Malu, over the latter's insistence on a role for the regional contingent in restructuring the Liberian armed forces. By the end of the year, the Liberian president succeeded first in having Malu replaced with a more pliant officer and, by the end of 1998, in getting the peacekeepers withdrawn altogether. Shortly after Malu's withdrawal, Taylor forced 2,500 AFL soldiers, including most of the remaining Krahn officers, into retirement, replacing them with veterans of his NPFL. Taylor also established Anti-Terrorist Units (ATUs), not to be confused with the crack contingent of the same name trained for Samuel Doe by the Israeli military. The ATUs constituted essentially a private army—albeit one that received state largesse that eventually exceeded that given to the regular army—on whose loyalty Taylor could count. Most of the members of the ATUs were recruited from abroad to ensure their loyalty to the president above any domestic Liberian considerations. The ranks of this private army swelled after the demobilization of the RUF in neighboring Sierra Leone.

With the Taylor administration diverting funding to the ATUs, the regular Armed Forces of Liberia units resorted to looting to "pay" themselves, using as a pretense the continuing civil conflict between the government and the rebels of the Liberians United for Reconciliation and Democracy (LURD) and other dissident groups. In early March 2002, for example, two Catholic mission stations in the western part of the country near the Sierra Leone border, one in Bomi and one in

Mount Hope, were completely sacked. The attacks were almost fore-seeable: the two missions were among the only yet-unscathed institutions in there respective areas.

Less than four months after Taylor's inauguration, a former political ally who later defected from the NPFL during the course of the civil war to form the CRC-NPFL, former Interior Minister Samuel Saye Dokie,[13] was stopped at a police check point near Gbarnga on November 28, 1997. Dokie and three family members were taken to a Liberian National Police (LNP) station. The following day, five members of the Special Security Service (SSS) removed the Dokies from LNP custody. Their mutilated, burned bodies were discovered three days later. The head of the SSS later admitted that he had ordered the arrest, but disavowed participation in or knowledge of the family's murder. Five suspects, including three of the SSS officers involved in the Dokie abduction, were subsequently arrested, tried, and acquitted.[14]

The following year, it became the turn of Roosevelt Johnson, the only one of the warlords who had fought against Taylor during the civil war and still remained in the country. Since Taylor took office, Johnson had seen numerous followers killed in clashes with government forces. On September 18, 1998, security forces in the capital conducted a military assault, codenamed "Operation Camp Johnson Road," against Johnson himself. Hundreds of SSS officers and members of the police Special Task Force, joined by scores of fighters from Taylor's former NPFL faction, opened fire on Johnson's Monrovia compound with automatic weapons, rocket-propelled grenades, and mortars. Although Johnson managed to escape from Liberia, U.S. diplomats reported that as many as three hundred civilians, most of them Krahns, many of them women and children, were killed in the seventeen-hour gun battle, and in subsequent house-to-house searches and summary executions by government forces.[15]

Freedom of the press remained alive insofar as journalists were allowed to write or broadcast what they wanted—if they were willing to suffer the consequences. In 1999, the government pulled the short-wave frequency allocation from independent Star Radio. Although the station was allowed to broadcast via FM, the broadcast area was limited. In 2001, the government likewise refused to renew the short-wave license to Radio Veritas, a station owned by the Catholic Church. This left the only state-owned Liberian Broadcasting System and the Liberia Communications Network, which is owned by Charles Taylor personally, as the country's only two national broadcasters.

Critics of the Taylor government were increasingly subjected to routine harassment, with the more articulate among them being arrested, tortured, and imprisoned—as was the case with human rights prominent lawyer Tiawan Gangloe and Hassan Bility, editor of the independent *Analyst* newspaper, both of whom disappeared into custody in early 2002, the latter allegedly for communicating via e-mail with the LURD rebels. At the same time, Frances Johnson Morris, director of the Catholic Justice and Peace Commission and former Chief Justice of Liberia, was arrested after she presented a paper at a public forum questioning the validity of the "state of emergency" declared by President Taylor. She was detained at the central police prison among male inmates until international protests brought about her release. The official excuse that LNP Director Paul Mulbah gave to diplomats was that it was a case of "mistaken identity." In any event, Morris fared better than Henry Cooper, a ranking official of the opposition Unity Party. He was taken into custody at the same time she was. His body was found riddled with bullet holes fifty miles north of Monrovia. Meanwhile, five members of the National Human Rights Center of Liberia, an umbrella organization of nine non-governmental human rights organizations, were arrested on Good Friday 2002. When they managed to get a court to rule several weeks later that their arrest without charges went against the Liberian constitution and to order their release, they were immediately arrested again on charges of "criminal malevolence" and "resisting arrest." The basis of the latter charge was that they contested the previous arrest!

Even as the Taylor government cracked down on political dissent, it was unable to improve the general situation in the country. The Liberian dollar went from a 41.5-to-1 exchange rate with the U.S. dollar when Taylor became president to a 70-to-1 rate at the end of 2002. Despite the nadir that the country's economy had fallen to during the civil war, its economy continued to shrink, in real terms, during the peace.[16]

With the economy in shambles, crime and insecurity have plagued the lives of Liberian civilians throughout Taylor's presidency, even before the renewal of civil conflict in late 2001 and early 2002. Armed robbery and the looting of humanitarian supplies occurred in urban centers, while banditry thrived in the Liberian interior. The U.S. State Department even reported ritual murders:

Ritualistic killings, in which human body parts used in traditional rituals are removed from the victim, continued to occur. The number of such killings is difficult to ascertain, since police often described deaths as accidents even when body parts have been removed. Deaths that appear to be natural or accidental sometimes are rumored to have been the work of ritualistic killers. Most reported ritual killings were from the southeastern counties.[17]

In fact, by 2003, the average Liberian was, by most socioeconomic indices, worse off than he had been at the start of the civil war. Life expectancy in July 1990 had been 54 years for men and 58 for women. By August 2003, those same values for the 3.3 million Liberians were estimated to be 47.03 and 49.3, respectively. In its annual survey of the world, *The Economist* magazine awarded Taylor's Liberia the dubious distinction of being "the worse place to live in 2003."

ADVENTURES ABROAD AND TROUBLES FROM ABROAD

One of the first foreign policy concerns facing the newly installed Taylor administration was Sierra Leone where, in May 1997, a group of disgruntled Sierra Leonean soldiers, led by Major Johnny Paul Koroma, overthrew that country's newly elected president, former UN bureaucrat Ahmed Tejan Kabbah, and installed an Armed Forces Revolutionary Council (AFRC) that soon entered into an alliance with Taylor's allies from Foday Sankoh's Revolutionary United Front (RUF). As a result of the fears that the entrance of the RUF into government caused as well as the fighting that broke out when a new ECOMOG force was sent to restore President Kabbah, some 25,000 additional Sierra Leonean refugees fled into Liberia.[18] Sensitive about the control of the border areas not only because of the ULIMO attacks on his NPFL from across the frontier with Guinea during the Liberian civil war, but also recalling his own cross-border invasion of Nimba County, Taylor sent troops to the border and redoubled his support of the RUF.

In early 1999, Liberian dissidents based in Guinea launched attacks on the towns of Voinjama and Kolahun in the northwestern county of Lofa. In reprisal, Taylor's allies in the RUF attacked several villages in Guinea in May 1999. In September 1999, two Guinean villages close to the Liberian frontier were attacked Guinean dissidents backed by the Liberian government.

As this tit-for-tat game continued, Laveli Supuwood, the former NPFL-appointed minister of justice in the Liberian National Transition Government who broke with Taylor, called a meeting of anti-Taylor exiles in Freetown in February 2000. The groups represented at the meeting included an assortment of former members of the AFL as well as of the ULIMO-K, ULIMO-J, and LPC factions—all predominantly Mandingo and Krahn. The meeting resolved to establish a new anti-Taylor umbrella group, Liberian United for Reconciliation and Democracy (LURD). Finding a wider latitude allowed by the Guinean president, General Lansana Conté, who already hosted Alhaji Kromah and whose spiritual advisor and acknowledged natural daughter Aïsha was married to the group's military leader Sekou Damante Conneh, LURD transferred its activities to that country.

In July 2000, LURD fighters invaded Lofa County from Guinea. Two months later, after the LURD guerrillas had been driven back across its frontier, Guinea was invaded by a force composed of RUF fighters, Liberian irregular units, and Guinean dissidents led by Major Gbago Zoumanigui, who had led the failed 1996 coup attempt against the government of General Conté. While no regular units of the Liberian military were involved in the invasion, it was clearly carried out with Taylor's blessing. The invasion was a well-coordinated two-pronged maneuver, the invader entering Guinea both in the eastern forest region bordering Liberia's Lofa County and in the western coastal area across from Kambia in northwestern Sierra Leone. The invaders took the towns of Guéckédou and Macenta and reached the outskirts of Kissidougou in the east and penetrated a third of the way to the capital of Conakry in the west, before retreating in January 2001. In order to beat back the invasion, Conté—who worried about the loyalty of his own army, fearing that some elements might defect to Zoumagui—was forced to rely on LURD fighters as well as Sierra Leonean militiamen recruited from refugee camps. Subsequently, overtures to the United States, which wanted military pressure applied to the Taylor government, brought a special military mission in 2002 that trained an eight-hundred-man rapid deployment force for the Guinean president.

These adventures abroad, especially the continuing involvement with the RUF, soon brought Taylor into conflict with the United Nations. On December 20, 2000, a panel of experts commissioned by the UN Security Council to study the civil conflict in Sierra reported its findings, which were damning to the Liberian president.[19] The report concluded that the

RUF was heavily reliant upon the general, as well as training and safe haven, assistance given to it by Liberia. It also documented the financing of the RUF's war effort through Liberian-assisted participation in commerce in illicit diamonds. The panel recommended a stiff set of measures geared both to defeating the RUF and containing Taylor.

On March 7, 2001, the UN Security Council passed Resolution 1343 which placed an arms embargo on Liberia, prohibited the sale of Liberian diamonds, and banned international travel by "senior members of the Government of Liberia and its armed forces and their spouses and any other individuals providing financial and military support to armed rebel groups in countries neighboring Liberia, in particular the RUF in Sierra Leone." The resolution also called for the Secretary-General to monitor the situation and established a committee to enforce the sanctions.[20]

The arms embargo, however, did little to halt the fighting that shifted, once more, to Liberia. By late April 2001, heavy fighting between LURD forces and the Liberian army was taking place near Foya and Kolahun in Lofa County. Violence was also reported in Nimba County. Only the onset of the summer season brought a stop to the conflict.

Meanwhile, the relatively successful progress of the peace process in Sierra Leone, however, had the unintended consequence of fueling the renewed conflict in Liberia. The now unemployed Sierra Leonean combatants found employment as mercenaries fighting for the parties in what was to become the second Liberian civil war. By late 2001, an estimated two thousand former RUF fighters had been recruited into Taylor's ATUs, while around five hundred former *kamajor* fighters had joined LURD in the Guinea. Observers estimated that Liberian government were paying approximately bounties of $500 to each recruit, while LURD has openly admitted to employing the *kamajors* "on a contract basis" between $200 and $300 each.[21]

LURD began what it announced as a new offensive against the Liberian government of Charles Taylor in November 2001. Part of the fighting was "hit-and-run": one side would seize a town while the other side fled, leaving the invader to loot for several days. Then the invader would withdraw, while the party that retreated would return to loot what was left. This "tactic" was especially true in those areas where the AFL was deployed—trusting the official army less and less, Taylor diverted resources towards his ATUs, leaving regular military units unpaid for months at a time. Nonetheless the LURD offensive did lead to real combat as the towns of Voinjama, near the border with Guinea in

Lofa County, and Vahun, near the border with Sierra Leone in the same county, fell to rebel forces in December 2001. LURD forces penetrated as far as Bopolu before withdrawing to concentrate systematically on the campaign in Lofa County.

In February 2002, RUF military commander Sam "Mosquito" Bockarie, whom Taylor had assured the UN Secretary-General Annan had left Liberia a year earlier,[22] was rallying just-disarmed RUF along the Lofa County border. That same month, LURD vice chairman, Laveli Supuwood, an ethnic Loma, managed to convince remnants of the former Lofa Defense Force (LDF) to ally themselves with LURD, opening the way for the rebel force to advance on Gbarnga by way of Zorzor, which was captured on February 28. Meanwhile, another prong of the rebel invasion advanced into Bomi County and occupied Klay Junction, twenty-eight miles (forty-five kilometers) west of Monrovia.

Increasingly desperate, Taylor hastily complied with the demands of the 2001 UN resolution, except for the arms embargo,[23] which measure he protested constituted an unfair penalization of his government as it fought a rebel invasion. He attended a February 27 summit with Guinean President Conté and Sierra Leonean President Kabbah, hosted by King Mohammed VI of Morocco at Rabat, and agreed to further dialogue. Nonetheless, the UN Security Council adopted Resolution 1408 on May 6, 2002, that reaffirmed for the sanctions previously imposed on Liberia, extending for twelve months the arms embargo, the travel ban against Liberian officials and their families, and the prohibition on the import of diamonds from Liberia.[24]

On May 14, 2002, the main LURD force took the town of Gbarnga. The town, in addition to the strategic importance of its control of roads linking Monrovia with the Liberian interior as well as Monrovia and the southeastern part of the country, had symbolic significance as the capital of Taylor's NPFL-controlled "Greater Liberia" during the first civil war. Massive looting occurred upon the fall of the city. Some of the LURD fighters even smashed open the tomb of the Gbarnga's recently deceased Roman Catholic bishop, Benedict Dotu Sekey, in an apparent effort to steal his episcopal ring and pectoral cross. Other rebel units penetrated as far as Taylor's hometown of Arthington, twenty miles (thirty-two kilometers) from Monrovia on the St. Paul River, and shelled the capital from there. Meanwhile, the other prong of the LURD attack penetrated as far as Tubmanburg, to the west of Monrovia. However, the poorly disciplined LURD force soon became disintegrated as individual units peeled off to loot and pursue other personal agendas before the onset of the rainy season in June. As a result, the government managed to retake Gbarnga by the end of May and several months later drove back the other prong of the LURD offensive, retaking Tubmanburg, before heavy rains ended the campaigning season.

THE ENDGAME

By the middle of 2002, it was clear to many observers that the success Taylor had enjoyed in beating back the LURD offensive had little to do with the strength of either the government's military position or its popular support. Both were, in fact, rather weak, as one report of by the International Crisis Group, the high-level independent analysis and conflict resolution organization, noted:

> During his time in power, President Taylor has increasingly practiced a strategy of "balkanising" his security forces to ensure that no single military, police, intelligence or militia faction will be strong enough to challenge him. Individual security elements remain loyal to their immediate commander and to the President, but little exists in a normal operational chain of command. For example, many militia and security elements feel no compulsion to take orders from the relatively marginalized Minister of Defense in conducting field operations. Indeed, more often than not militias appear to have been given the lead in coordinating counterattacks on LURD positions, such as at Gbarnga and recently Tubmanburg.
>
> The end result of President Taylor's strategy to develop multiple redundancies within his security services has been a confusing proliferation of military groups: the elite Anti-Terrorist Unit (ATU) that serves as a palace guard; the Special Operations Division (SOD); the Special Security Services (SSS); the police; a very weak Armed Forces of Liberia (AFL) that serves as the traditional military; and a hodge-podge of militia groups including the Marines, the recently remobilized "Wild Geese" and a host of others...
>
> Competition, suspicion and rivalries between the many security organs, including fights over resources, appear to be on the rise. Military discipline has never been a particular strength in Liberia, and such a personality-dominated security structure would seem to be a recipe for trouble if fighting intensifies.[25]

Rather LURD's failure to take Monrovia was the direct result of its own internal difficulties, as Human Rights Watch reported at the time:

> The LURD does not appear to have a defined political program, other than to remove Charles Taylor from power. The organization has been plagued with internal power struggles, political rivalries and corruption, and there also appears to be some division between the Guinea-based political side of the movement, and it's field based military commanders. There seems to be little clarity or consensus on key political issues, such as whether or not to seek a negotiated settlement with the Taylor government, or what kind of government should replace Taylor in the event of a LURD military victory. In March 2002, at peace talks brokered by the Economic Community of West African States (ECOWAS) in Abuja, Nigeria, LURD did not send official representation that could speak on behalf of the group.[26]

The rebel movement was divided along political and ethnic lines. The first fissure was that between the movement's battlefield commanders, such as LURD Chairman Sekou Conneh, and its politicians, such as Vice Chairman Chayee Doe, brother of the late president, who enjoy diplomatic and other international contacts but who have little support among the rank-and-file fighters. The second fissure was between the members of the Mandingo and Krahn ethnic groups, who did not trust each other. In fact, these fissures led the emergence, in early 2003, of yet another group, the Movement for Democracy in Liberia (MODEL), among Krahn émigrés in Côte d'Ivoire. This breakaway, but still allied, group subsequently concentrated its attacks in the southeastern counties of Grand Gedeh, Sinoe, and Grand Kru.

As a result of these internal divisions, the government was able to retake several towns in Lofa County, including Kolahun and Foya, during September and October 2002. Despite the UN arms embargo, the government's forces received over two hundred tons of armaments from old Yugoslav stockpiles sold by a Belgrade dealer.[27] However, when these supplies were depleted, LURD began to regain ground, launching another major offensive from Lofa County in January 2003.

While the government beat off five different attempts to storm Foya in the first two months of 2003, it nonetheless lost Kolahun once more. On February 4, Tubmanburg fell to LURD forces again, cutting off the supply line to Foya from the capital. Taylor redeployed his forces to defend Monrovia, halting LURD's advance, but sacrificing the central government's ability to defend Grand Cape County in the process.

Under the sponsorship of the ECOWAS parliamentary assembly and the Inter-Religious Council of Liberia, ceasefire talks were held in early February in Freetown. However, follow-up discussions, scheduled for March 2003 in Bamako, Mali, were cancelled as fierce fighting continued. One explanation advanced for the breakdown in the talks was the deteriorating condition of Guinea's president, General Lansana Conté, LURD's principal patron. His worsening condition created an uncertainty over the future of his country and a sense of urgency on the part of the LURD leadership to take advantage of Guinean military assistance while it was still forthcoming.[28]

A government counterattack, with air support, to retake Grand Cape Mount County, failed and, by the beginning of April, LURD forces controlled all three major road axes leading to and from Monrovia: Tubmanburg and Klay Junction (Bomi County) to the west, Bopolu (Lofa County) to the northwest, and Gbarnga (Bong County) to the northeast. Meanwhile MODEL forces were besieging Buchanan, Liberia's second largest city and the principal port for lumber exports. In response, the Taylor government began to move several of the camps for internally displaced persons to new locations in order to ring the capital with a kind of human shield—a tactic that the regime had employed the previous year.[29]

On May 6, the UN Security Council decided that the Taylor regime had not yet complied with the demands of Resolution 1343 passed two years earlier and, consequently, voted once more to extend for another year the regime of sanctions against Liberia banning the sale of arms, international travel by senior officials and members of their families, and the importation of diamonds originating from the country. The Council also added a ten-month ban on the importation of logs and other timber products from Liberia.[30] The resolution also "reminded" states to cease arms shipments to "non-state actors," specifically mentioning the LURD, but without attaching sanctions.

By the end of May, with over 60 percent of Liberia's national territory loosely under the control of either LURD or MODEL forces, but with neither force sufficiently prepared to take the capital by storm, the parties agreed to meet in Accra for peace talks to be mediated by a former Nigerian head of state, General Abdulsalami Abubakar, under the auspices of ECOWAS. President Taylor's attendance at the parley, however, was cut short by the June 4 announcement by the prosecutor of the Special Court for Sierra Leone (SCSL), David Crane, of his indictment and the warrant for his arrest. Both documents had been signed by the presiding judge of the Trial Chamber of the SCSL on March 3 and 7, respectively, but had been sealed. Taylor hastily left the peace talks and returned to Monrovia, while African diplomats who had worked to set up the mediation sharply criticized the prosecutor's insensitive timing as well as his failure to notify Ghanaian President John Kufuor, who had personally guaranteed the immunity of all participants.

In Taylor's absence, Liberian Defense Minister Daniel L. Chea, LURD representative Kabineh Janneh, and MODEL representative Tiah J.D. Slanger, signed a ceasefire on June 17. The ceasefire also committed the parties to work towards the formation of a transition government within thirty days that did not include Taylor.[31] By the time the ceasefire was signed, however, the main LURD force, perhaps inspired by the indictment, had taken the offensive once more and was within a few miles of Monrovia, causing widespread pandemonium as rocket and grenade fire hit the capital.

Meanwhile international pressure began to mount on the Liberian president to step aside. On June 26, on the eve of his first trip to Africa, U.S. President George W. Bush declared in a speech to the Corporate Council on Africa: "President Taylor needs to step down so that his country can be spared further bloodshed."[32] The American president also affirmed that the United States was "determined to help the people of Liberia find the path to peace," although he left the specifics of how that was to be done out, sparking to a month of debate among policy makers over whether or not the U.S. would or should participate in an international military intervention. After a thirty-two-person military assessment team visited the besieged Liberian capital, the U.S. dispatched three warships—the amphibious assault ship U.S.S. *Iwo Jima*, the amphibious landing dock U.S.S. *Carter Hall*, and the transport dock U.S.S. *Nashville*—with a 2,300-strong task force of marines. Ultimately, fewer than ten marines landed on August 6, to coordinate American assistance to international peacekeepers, joining the eighty military personnel at the U.S. embassy (some two hundred marines were dispatched ashore at a later moment after Taylor's resignation, but the bulk of them—some 150 marines—were withdrawn to the warships after just eleven days, leaving only one hundred American military personnel in Liberia: seventy guarding the embassy, and thirty acting as liaisons with the West African contingent).

The fighting resumed in early July after Taylor appeared to have backed away from earlier promises to step down, with LURD forces virtually dividing the capital. Nearly six weeks of fighting, amid a population that had swelled to over 1.3 million people because of refugees from the fighting elsewhere, left over one thousand civilians dead, thousands more wounded, and hundreds of thousands starving as humanitarian organizations were unable to carry out their work.

After protracted negotiations, the first units of a new Nigerian-led West African peacekeeping force landed in Monrovia on August 4, just two days shy of the thirteenth anniversary of ECOWAS's decision to dispatch ECOMOG while Taylor and Prince Johnson besieged then Liberian President Doe inside the Executive Mansion. Unlike its predecessor, the new force, dubbed ECOWAS Mission in Liberia (ECOMIL), enjoyed the sanction of a United Nations Security Council Resolution authorizing "Member States to establish a Multinational Force in Liberia to support the implementation of the June 17, 2003, ceasefire agreement, including establishing conditions for initial stages of disarmament, demobilization and reintegration activities."[33] Things had come full circle, although Taylor did manage to escape Doe's fate. Finally accepting the offer of political asylum and residence in a villa in the southeastern Nigerian resort city of Calabar, Taylor resigned the presidency on August 11, 2003, handing power over to Vice President Moses Blah at a ceremony attended by South African President Thabo Mbeki, Ghanaian President John Kufuor, and other African and international dignitaries. In a rambling farewell address, the departing president alternately accused the U.S. of having "refused to acknowledge the existence of the war" and of being the "architect of the anti-Taylor policy." He concluding by promising—ominously to some, hopefully to others—"God willing, I will be back."

ENDNOTES

1. Arthur F. Kulah, *Liberia Will Rise Again: Reflections on the Liberian Civil Crisis* (Nashville, Tennessee: Abingdon Press, 1999), 42.
2. Jimmy Carter, "There's Hope in Liberia's History," *New York Times* (July 13, 2003). Amos Sawyer's caution concerning what he perceives to be the former American president's *naïveté* should be noted: "Jimmy Carter [is] a very naïve man. He brought elements of simplistic notions of redemption to a problem steeped in a culture he did not understand." Quoted in Adekeye Adebajo, *Liberia's Civil War: Nigeria, ECOMOG*

and Regional Security in West Africa (Boulder, Colorado/London: Lynne Rienner Publishers, 2002), 92.

3. Terrence Lyons, *Voting for Peace: Post-conflict Elections in Liberia* (Washington, D.C.: Brookings Institution, 1999), 59.

4. United Nations Secretary-General, *Twenty-fourth Report on the United Nations Observer Mission in Liberia* (S/1997/643, August 13, 1997), 1.

5. Carter, "There's Hope in Liberia's History."

6. Augustine Toure, *The Role of Civil Society in National Reconciliation and Peacebuilding in Liberia* (New York: International Peace Academy, 2002), 12.

7. *Ibid.*

8. See Clarence E. Zamba Liberty, "Butuo: A Lilliputian Testament to a Struggle — The NPFL Journey to State Power: How Charles Taylor Upset the Bowl of Rice and Took Home the Whole Hog," *Liberian Studies Journal* 23/1 (1998): 175–176.

9. See David Harris, "From 'warlord' to 'democratic' president: how Charles Taylor won the 1997 Liberian elections," *Journal of Modern African Studies* 37 (1999): 431–455.

10. Editorial "Liberia's Ambiguous Election," *New York Times* (July 24, 1997).

11. Editorial "Look Who's President of Liberia," *Washington Post* (July 23, 1997).

12. *Ibid.* The press was not the only part of the American establishment to be miffed by Taylor's victory. Although the source has its limitations, Liberia's former legal counsel in Washington has documented a long catalogue of fairly petty slights suffered by former client Taylor at the hands of officials or former officials of the U.S. government. See Lester S. Hyman, *United States Policy Towards Liberia, 1822–2003: Unintended Consequences* (Cherry Hill, New Jersey: Africana Homestead Legacy Publishers, 2003), 51–80.

13. For a personal profile of Samuel Saye Dokie, based on a number of interviews, see Bill Berkeley, *The Graves Are Not Yet Full: Race, Tribe and Power in the Heart of Africa* (New York: Basic Books, 2001), 21–61.

14. United States Department of State, *Liberia Country Report on Human Rights Practices for 1997* (January 30, 1998); see <http://www.state.gov/www/global/human_rights/1997_hrp_report/liberia.html>.

15. Idem., *Liberia Country Report on Human Rights Practices for 1998* (February 26, 1999); see <www.state.gov/www/global/human_rights/1998_hrp_report/liberia.html>.

16. Economist Intelligence Unit, *Country Report: Guinea, Sierra Leone, Liberia* (December 2002), 44.

17. United States Department of State, *Liberia Country Report on Human Rights Practices for 1999* (February 25, 2000); see <www.state.gov/www/global/human_rights/1999_hrp_report/liberia.html>.

18. Idem., *Sierra Leone Country Report on Human Rights Practices for 1997* (January 30, 1998); see <www.state.gov/www/global/human_rights/1997_hrp_report/sierrale.html>.

19. See United Nations Security Council, *Report of the Panel of Experts appointed pursuant to Security Council resolution 1306 (2000), paragraph 19, in relation to Sierra Leone* (S/2000/1195, December 20, 2000).

20. See idem., *Resolution* (S/Res/1343, March 7, 2001).

21. See the undated statement, posted to LURD's website, at <http://liberian.tripod.com/Post26.html>.

22. See United Nations Secretary-General, *First Report pursuant to Security Council resolution 1343 (2001) regarding Liberia* (S/2001/424, April 30, 2001), 1.

23. See idem., *Third Report pursuant to resolution 1343 (2001) regarding Liberia* (S/2002/494, May 1, 2002).

24. See United Nations Security Council, *Resolution* (S/Res/1408, May 6, 2002).

25. International Crisis Group, *Liberia: Unravelling* (August 19, 2002), 4–5.

26. Binaifer Nowrojee and Corinne Dufka, *Back to the Brink: War Crimes by the Liberian Government and Rebels. A Call for Greater International Attention to Liberia and the Sub-region*, edited by Bronwen Manby and Janet Fleischman (New York: Human Rights Watch, 2002), 7.

27. See United Nations Security Council, *Report of the Panel of Experts appointed pursuant to Security Council resolution 1408 (2002), paragraph 16, concerning Liberia* (S/2002/1183, October 7, 2002), 18–20.

28. See International Crisis Group, *Tackling Liberia: The Eye of the Regional Storm* (April 30, 2003), 6.

29. See United Nations Secretary-General, *Second Report of the Secretary-General Pursuant to Security Council resolution 1408 (2002) regarding Liberia* (S/2003/466, April 22, 2003), 6.

30. See United Nations Security Council, *Resolution* (S/Res/1478, May 6, 2003).

31. For the text of the "Agreement on Ceasefire and Cessation of Hostilities between the Government of the Republic of Liberia, Liberians United for Reconciliation and Democracy, and the Movement for Democracy in Liberia," see <www.usip.org/library/pa/liberia/liberia_ceasefire_06172003.html >.

32. For the text of the speech, see <www.whitehouse.gov/news/releases/2003/06/20030626-2.html >.

33. United Nations Security Council, *Resolution* (S/Res/1497, August 1, 2003).

SEVEN

LIBERIA AND
THE LESSONS OF A
FAILED STATE

TRAGICALLY, THE RECENT HISTORY of Liberia has been a case study *par excellence* of a failed state. As its formal structures of government collapsed in 1989-1990, Liberia showed signs of all the characteristics noted by Andrew Natsios in his definition of a complex humanitarian emergency.[1] First, the conflict was rooted in ethnic animosities of long standing: between Americo-Liberians and those assimilated to them on one side and the majority of Liberians who belonged to indigenous cultures on the other. These animosities were superimposed on already-existent tensions—some dating back to the slave trade—between the members of the various indigenous ethnic groups, splits that were exacerbated by Doe's bias in favor of his fellow Krahns as well as members of the Mandingo people whom he cultivated. Even if, against this evidence, one rejects the "tribalist" dimension of the civil war, a case can be made that once the conflict broke out, ethnic identity became a very useful tool for the mobilization of the populace, a phenomenon that, in the Balkan context, Steven Majstorovic called "primordialization" whereby historically rooted identities are recalled and enhanced.[2] Second, the authority of the national government quickly disintegrated once the conflict broke out into the open. Throughout most of the 1989-1997 civil war, the writ of the recognized national authority of the moment extended little beyond Monrovia—and then only on the sufferance of the ECOMOG peacekeepers. Third, the conflict caused the displacement of nearly half of the population, not only in Liberia, but also in neighboring Sierra Leone, in addition to disruptions in Guinea and Côte d'Ivoire. Finally, Liberia's prewar economic system collapsed completely, being replaced by an economy dominated by the warlords and characterized by the illicit traffic in diamonds, timber, and other natural resources.

Furthermore, in addition to exhibiting the traits characteristic of a complex emergency, in many respects, as seen from the history chronicled in the preceding chapters, both the causes and symptoms of state collapse manifested in Liberia are archetypical for a failed state one, in fact, that was in long-term decline. Consequently, it is worth reviewing these factors and characteristics before drawing conclusions as to some of the lessons that might be learned from the tragedy.

HISTORICAL ROOTS OF STATE FAILURE

While the Liberian civil war had a definite terminus *a quo* in the Christmas Eve 1989 invasion of Nimba County by the NPFL under the leadership of Charles Taylor, it would be inaccurate to employ the same date for the failure of the Liberian state. Rather, history shows that the collapse began much earlier and, in fact, the very foundation of the Liberian state contained within it the seeds of its own self-destruction.

While it is the place of neither the historian nor the political scientist to cast aspersions on the personal sincerity of the architects of the endeavor to resettle freed black slaves on the West African coast, one cannot but marvel at the almost willful blindness of leading members of the American Colonization Society to the difficulties that plagued their undertaking, including the alarming mortality figures among the early settlers as well as the hostility of the indigenous peoples that should have counseled for a serious reconsideration of the practicality of the enterprise. However, having persevered in establishing a foothold on the African mainland, the settlers themselves confounded the situation by seeking to distinguish themselves from the societies in which they were located and, for the most part, segregating themselves from the native inhabitants except for such minimal contact as necessary for trade. In fact, it was not until the twentieth century when, under pressure from imperialist European powers, did the most of the area of the country come under the authority of the government in Monrovia. The idea of a nation-state with a national identity was itself a foreign import to a territory whose peoples saw themselves in terms of ethnic and sub-ethnic identifications. Until very recent times, the national myth was such that people whose ancestors had lived in parts of what would become the territory of the Liberian state for centuries were not considered—legally or otherwise—Liberians by the Americo-Liberian descendants of the settlers. The official motto of the Republic of Liberia, "The Love of Liberty Brought Us Here," is hardly an inclusive statement of national unity: it presented the vision of the small settler minority against the indigenous majority who were *already* present—a point recognized, but never acted upon, by the Commission on National Unity (also known as the Deshfield Commission, after its chairman, TWP secretary-general McKinley Alfred Deshfield Sr.) appointed by President Tolbert in 1974.[3] At the time of the actual outbreak of the civil war in 1989, this meant that the official ideal of a Liberian nation and a Liberian state excluded all but a few thousand people out of a total population of nearly three million.

Nigerian Nobel Laureate for Literature Wole Soyinka once wrote: "Nation making from the top (what I earlier referred to as the objective manifestation of the will of one individual or a handful of individuals) never does, however, appear to have much staying power."[4] In fact, he warned that:

> Neither the tenacity of state repression nor the longevity of an illusion is adequate to guarantee an eternity to nationhood whose foundations are unsound and whose superstructures, however seductive, are constantly stressed as much by the incubus of collective memory as by the dynamics of human development, both the quantifiable aspects and the intangible.[5]

Such was clearly the case with the Liberian state right up to the 1979 murder of President William Tolbert and the overthrow of the True Whig oligarchy. The national vision of Liberia served to legitimize the America-Liberian settler class—as well as such Congo and native elements that were assimilated into the ruling oligarchy—in its self-identification as bearers of a unique mission, but it did little to bring the overwhelming majority of the population into the *polis* constituted by what was essentially a colonial frontier society. The patronizing sentiments of the ruling class were neatly summarized by President Arthur Barclay in his 1904 inaugural address:

> When we came here in 1822, the country was indeed divided among a large number of tribes, but there were signs, not only in this territory but along the whole West Coast, of a desire to merge tribal governments into wider political organizations which would secure the peace of the country, put a stop to incessant raids, devastations, and consequent loss of life and property...The more sagacious chiefs saw in our settlement the necessary center.[6]

Consequently, the demise of the settler autocracy at the hands of elements coming from the excluded majority was almost preordained: the historical record does not lend support to the view that a stable political culture accepted as legitimate and transcending ethnic ties can be imposed by political and cultural domination. As one observer sadly concluded:

> Liberia [was] the voluntary continuation of a slave society by slaves who did not wish to abolish an unjust order, but wanted to preserve it, develop it, and exploit it for their own benefit. Clearly, an enslaved mind, tainted by the experience of slavery, a mind born into slavery, fettered in infancy, cannot conceive or conjure a world in which all would be free.[7]

Unfortunately, under Samuel Doe, Liberia did not embark on a national reconciliation so much as the transfer of power to another minority, in this case to Doe's Krahn kinsmen and their Mandingo allies (as well as some co-opted America-Liberian technocrats). The ruling class of any nation-state with such shallow domestic legitimacy is condemned to almost certain collapse from its own weight once it had lost its foreign support. The mistake of Liberian leaders was that they never contemplated the possibility that they might find themselves abandoned by their presumed patrons in the United States. So long had the delusional myth of the country's "special relationship" with the U.S. been cultivated and perpetuated by many Liberian scholars, particularly those of Americo-Liberian descent, that many recent observers failed to note that, historically, the American government had repeatedly disavowed any particular claims on its attention that its Liberian counterpart advanced. For example, in the recently published memoirs of former U.S. Secretary of State Madeleine Albright, Liberia was mentioned only three times—none of which was in any detail—in almost six hundred pages.[8] The "love affair," it seems, was entirely one-sided.

At the end of the Cold War, when the increasingly despotic Doe became more of a liability than anything else, the United States cut off the flow of aid and his regime quickly crumbled. Hence, while it could be said that the end came quickly, the failure of the state in Liberia was a gradual, but no less terminal, process. However, a distinction needs to be made between the withdrawal of aid *occasioning* the collapse of a regime like that presided over by Doe (and the True Whig oligarchs before him), and that same withdrawal *causing* that failure. The roots of Liberia's national failure were already well entrenched long before there was even a Cold War. At most, America's Cold War policies, artificially prolonged the existence of a state whose myopic and improvident rulers has set it well along on the route to failure.

Another weakness of the Liberian state was its historical configuration as a highly centralized government centered in Monrovia. In this constitutional arrangement, there were no provisions for autonomous institutions of local government at the county or local levels that, in most liberal democracies, normally facilitate broad-based participation in the body politic. As a consequence of this institutional structure, aspiring politicians paid closer heed to the center than to any nominal constituents and Monrovia became a magnet in a way that goes beyond any "inside the beltway" Washingtonian could imagine. Graham Greene made a discrete observation of this phenomenon in his famed travelogue: "It is easy to make fun of this black capital city...of a town where almost every other man is a lawyer and every man a politician."[9]

Historically, most of the power of the centralized Liberian government was concentrated in the hands of the president. Unfortunately, from J.J. Roberts through William Tolbert, Liberia's leaders have shown more interest in vindicating their status on the international stage than establishing a solid foundation for the state at home, where their efforts were concentrated on building patronage networks personally dependent upon them than on capacity-building infrastructure, much less encouraging any national sense of common community. In this sense, the nineteenth century Liberian experiment in self-rule evolved into a form that was to presage the *de facto*—if not necessarily the *de iure*—arrangements typical of postcolonial regimes of twentieth-century Africa. The late Israeli diplomat and statesman Abba Eban has presciently noted of these regimes and their heads that:

> Africa and Asia have had brilliant leaders who carried them from colonial subjection to independence with all its external glories, such as embassies and seats in international agencies. But these leaders were much more brilliant in achieving independence than in knowing what to do with it. The flags are not enough. Men and women awaken on the morrow of independence celebrations to find that they may be free in every constitutional sense and yet lose the essence of their freedom in the throes of illiteracy, starvation, rampant disease, and want. Sometimes these legacies of colonialism are even aggravated by the transition from tutelage to freedom. Many such leaders have attracted world attention by the pathos of their struggle for freedom...few of [them] have shown the same consuming interest in the dull prose of economic planning as the in the more facile satisfactions of international diplomacy.[10]

Absent both the necessary constitutional framework and the experience of a continuous political tradition, the presidential rulers of Liberia—and the African states that would follow along the same path after their independence—saw the various tensions within their respective polities as "disloyalty," a threat the all-important "unity" of the state that must be protected by the imposition of uniformity. Amos Sawyer has observed that "the need to maintain this national unity becomes a justification for deeper state penetration, dominance, and repression"[11]—contributing to a vicious cycle that leads to only more tension and increased state intervention.

In countries where political authority is highly centralized in a national government—if not monopolized by a single individual—without autonomous structures for sharing power and responsibility on regional and local bases, the existence of alternative mediating institutions between the individual and the state takes on a capital importance. These institutions of "civil society"—including voluntary associations organized on the basis of ethnic, cultural, religious, professional/academic, and gender bases—serve a crucial role in not only as outlets for the expression of individual and communal sentiments, but also as means for the development and consolidation of democratic politics. These associations

> promote the stability and effectiveness of the democratic polity through both the effects of association on citizens' "habits of the heart" and the ability of associations to mobilize citizens on behalf of public causes. Emergent civil societies in Latin America and Eastern Europe are credited with effective resistance to authoritarian regimes, democratizing society from below while pressuring authoritarians for change. Thus civil society, understood as the realm of private voluntary association, from neighborhood committees to interest groups to philanthropic enterprises of all sorts, has come to be seen as an essential ingredient in both democratization and the health of established democracies.[12]

During most of the Liberia's history, many of the institutions that would normally have constituted the core of civil society were, in fact, co-opted by the ruling Americo-Liberian oligarchy. The Christian churches stood hand-in-hand with the settler aristocracy: President William Tolbert was also president of the World Baptist Alliance, while his vice president, Bennie Dee Warner, was also Liberia's United Methodist bishop. The Masonic craft was also transformed into yet another organ of the state: the roster of the grand masters of the Ancient Free and Accepted Masons of the Republic of Liberia include no fewer than four of the country's heads of state. It was not until the presidency of Tolbert that true civil society institutions developed in reformist movements opposed to the administration, especially the Movement for Justice in Africa and the Progressive Alliance of Liberia.[13] Unfortunately, the decade of repression under Doe and the ensuing civil war stunted the growth of many of these institutions, with a few exceptions such as the Catholic-sponsored Peace and Justice Commission.[14] While the conflict and the resulting flow of well-intentioned aid from abroad created a veritable cottage industry in local non-governmental organizations. One sympathetic observer noted: "Despite the havoc wreaked by war, Monrovia is filled with hundreds of non-governmental organizations (NGOs), churches, societies, trade unions, businesses, and political groups."[15] While Dave Peterson interpreted the phenomenon positively, it could also be seen as part of same selfish multiplication and fragmentation of society that has characterized Liberia's opposition political parties. In any event, there remains a substantial gap between the creation of structures and any substantive positive effect they may have on society.

In summary, lacking a unified and inclusive national vision, intermediate participatory structures of governmental authority, and a tradition of civil society institutions, and cursed with a highly centralized government that concentrated power in the hands of a single oligarchic class, it was virtually inevitable that Liberia should have stumbled into its civil war, given the significant amount of historical baggage and tension that it bore.

A COMPLEX EMERGENCY

The *coup de grâce* administered to the tortured Doe also unleashed a series of ethnic tensions that had long simmered below the surface. While it is true that many of the faction leaders in the ensuing civil war exploited ethnic ties to enrich themselves and their closest collaborators through a ruthless division of the natural resources of the country, it remains that they could not have done so had the strong sense of tribal identification not preexisted. Attempts to rationalize the conflict are precisely that: "politically correct" rationalizations.

And although there is some justification to complaints that members of the international media sensationalized the conflict the present study, in fact, sought to minimize the amount of attention devoted to recounting gory incidents that have been recorded elsewhere it is also true that the violence that followed the collapse of the Liberian state was indeed accompanied by a pattern of brutal violence that do not necessarily have to follow the breakdown of a previous order. State failure can cause disruptions of whole societies and, should this prove to be the case, the violence must be understood as part of an entire complex of social and cultural phenomena.

Even the nature of the failed state can evolve over the course of time. Throughout most of its history, Liberia was a failing state of the "abort-

ed" variety—following the scheme outlined Jean-Germain Gros—
where the government had not entirely consolidated its authority over
the territory it claimed. By the mid-1900s, Liberia had all the markings
of the failed state of the "captured" variety, with power monopolized
in a small minority, the Americo-Liberian ruling class. One of Liberia's
most eminent intellectuals, writer Edward Wilmot Blyden, an immigrant from the Virgin Islands who served as secretary of state, envoy to
Great Britain, president of Liberia College, and secretary of the interior
at various times in the late nineteenth century, admitted regarding the
Liberian state's expansion into the interior:

> The new government of Liberia was not the result of popular feel-
> ing. It was not the growth of the soil. It was forced upon the people
> as a protective measure in consequence of the impositions practiced
> upon their revenue by foreign adventurers.[16]

Finally, under Doe, the Liberia of the 1980s was "anemic," with the
authority of the central government slowly being eroded. During the
1990s, the state had become fully anarchic, with the complete collapse
of state power and its replacement by rival warlords who were often
allied with criminal elements. In each of these phases, the resolution of
the crisis would have required different approaches.

THE PERILS OF INTERVENTION

When a state fails, it has become fashionable to demand "action," usually understood to be some sort of international military intervention to
impose a ceasefire on the warring factions and push them to some sort
of new constitutional settlement. The case of Liberia was no exception.
However, the Nigerian-led decision of ECOWAS in August 1990 to
intervene in the then eight-month-old Liberian civil war demonstrates
some of the perils and unintended consequences of military intervention in a failed state situation. At the time of the intervention, Taylor's
NPFL controlled almost all of Liberian national territory and, in con-
junction with Prince Johnson's INPFL faction, was besieging President
Samuel Doe in his last stronghold in Monrovia.

The decision to establish ECOMOG was based on rather shaky legal
foundations within the framework of ECOWAS—a fact that alluded
to by the francophone members of the group who, with the exception

of Guinea which for historical reasons generally set itself against the other former French colonies, saw the peacekeeping force as little more than an ill-disguised instrument for furthering ambitions of Nigeria's military rulers to establish a regional hegemony.[17] A close reading of the texts cited at the time as the juridical justification for the intervention—the 1978 ECOWAS Protocol on Non-Aggression and the 1981 ECOWAS Protocol Relating to Mutual Assistance on Defense reveals that they do not say what ECOWAS officials claimed they said. The non-aggression pact obliges members with regard to their relations with each other and does not deal with internal matters like civil wars. And where there is an allegation of interference—as Côte d'Ivoire and Burkina Faso were clearly engaged in by supporting Taylor's anti-Doe rebellion—the protocol obliges the contesting parties to submit to a mediating committee of the regional body. The mutual defense agreement contemplated intervention only in the case of an extra-ECOWAS threat to an ECOWAS member. Even apologists for the Nigerian-led intervention, such as Adekeye Adebajo, have admitted that "the arguments used in establishing ECOMOG, in fact, had a more solid basis in politics than law, and ECOMOG was largely justified on humanitarian grounds."[18]

In point of fact, however, even if the good intentions are accepted *prima facie*, the political case for the ECOMOG intervention remains faulty.[19] One purported reason for intervening was that the Liberian civil war threatened the entire community. Although the fighting had forced Liberian refugees to flee into neighboring countries, the conflict only spilled over into other states when the intervention itself pushed Taylor to strike back by instigating Foday Sankoh's rebellion in Sierra Leone. The other justification advanced for the intervention was that the situation was militarily stalemated and could go on indefinitely, allowing anarchy to continue in Liberia that would destabilize the region. Consequently, ECOMOG was to mediate a ceasefire. In reality, there was no stalemate: the Doe regime was tottering on the brink of collapse and controlled little more than the Executive Mansion, while Johnson's INPFL faction was little more than annoyance to Taylor, who viewed the intervention as outside interference in his almost certain triumph. Rather, the evidence is convincing that the motivations for the intervention were more complex, including the attempt by Nigeria's military leaders to assert their status as a regional hegemon.

The ECOWAS intervention, as one analyst has observed, "demonstrates that well-intentioned military intervention to stop a war can have devastating unintended consequences."[20] As the NPFL attacked ECOMOG—which the former correctly perceived as being a last ditch effort to block its all-but-certain victory—the states in the would-be peacekeeping force abandoned their pretense of impartiality and began arming Taylor's rivals. This led to a downward spiral of new armed forces being created, violence proliferated, and even more armed forces created, thus complicating the challenge of forging a peaceful settlement. In this context, it is no wonder that more than twelve peace agreements and twenty ceasefires fell apart during the seven-and-a-half years between Taylor's Christmas Eve 1989 invasion of Nimba County and his July 19, 1997, landslide victory in the Liberian presidential elections.

The intervention turned what would have been a quick victory for the NPFL into a prolong conflict that ended with the same result: Taylor's installation in Monrovia's Executive Mansion. Although widely divergent figures—some of which were clearly over-inflated—have been circulated concerning casualties in the Liberian civil war, it would be reasonably accurate to conclude that between 20,000 and 25,000 people were killed during the first year of fighting.[21] Over the seven years of the conflict, it is commonly estimated that a total of 150,000 individuals lost their lives. In August 1990, there were a little less than 350,000 refugees in the region, almost all of them Liberians. As the conflict dragged on, it is generally thought that more several million people had been displaced at one point or another—including most of the populations of Liberia and Sierra Leone as well as significant numbers of Guineans and Ivorians. William Reno has made a convincing case that Taylor's adventurism in Sierra Leone can be attributed to the warlord's need for resources to fight to regain the military position he occupied when ECOMOG intervened, rather than any imperial ambitions.[22]

As Michael Barnett succinctly observed in his analysis of the moral responsibility for the Rwandan genocide, "peacekeeping was not a value-neutral activity."[23] Rather, peacekeeping interventions, by their very nature, imply political and ethical judgments that the existing institutions within the nation that is the object of the intervention are not only incapable of maintaining domestic security and the rule of law, but that their failure to maintain domestic order undermines the international order. However, with judgment comes the responsibility to not undertake a course of action that itself feeds the domestic conflict, increases

the security threat, and causes the regional insecurity—all of which intervention was meant to remedy. During the Liberian civil war of 1989-
1997, by being—or allowing itself to be transformed into, depending on
what motivations one attributes to ECOMOG's creators—a party to the
conflict rather than a neutral enforcer of law and order, the West African peacekeepers, regardless of any good intentions, ended up guilty of
all three offenses: intensifying the level of the conflict, thus exacerbating
the security threat, and leading directly into the spillover of the fighting
into neighboring countries.

Hence the political and ethical burdens rest with those who intervened in Liberia as well as with those who will advocate humanitarian
interventions there and elsewhere in the future to ensure that the military intervention does not itself create a set of circumstances where the
result that was supposed to be prevented becomes instead the inevitable,
even if unintended, consequence. Reflecting on the lessons of the Bal-
kans conflicts of the 1990s during his 2000 Tanner Lecture at Princeton
University, journalist and historian Michael Ignatieff, who heads the
Carr Center for Human Rights Policy at Harvard University's Kennedy School of Government, commented *à propos*:

> Intervention is also problematic because we are not necessarily com-
> ing to the rescue of pure innocence. Intervention frequently requires
> us to side with one party in a civil war, and the choice frequently
> requires us to support parties who are themselves guilty of human
> rights abuses…We are intervening in the name of human rights as
> never before, but our interventions are sometimes making matters
> worse.[24]

ENGAGEMENT FATIGUE AND CALCULATIONS
OF U.S. NATIONAL INTERESTS

Despite the perils of intervention, that course of action remains popular,
especially when the international media broadcasts gruesome images of
pitiful civilians suffering the consequences of state failure.[25] However,
Henry Kissinger has cautioned:

> In the end, civil wars are about who dominates. As political legiti-
> macy erodes, a vacuum develops which must be filled by some new

authority. As the United States engages in a humanitarian military intervention, media and other observers descend on the scene, certain to find conditions deeply offensive to Western sensibility. They will urge a whole variety of initiatives, from ending corruption to the administration of justice, that make sense in the Western context. None, however, can be accomplished without greater intervention, drawing the United States ever deeper into the political process. And, sooner or later, no matter how well intentioned, such conduct will begin to grate on African sentiments, and that, in turn, will tend to undermine domestic American and indigenous African support for the operation. Nothing is more likely to end a permanent American contribution to Africa than a military role in its civil wars.[26]

As the mixed record of the eight-year ECOWAS engagement in Liberia's internal conflict reveals, intervention has little potential for success without a clear understanding of the limited scope of what can be realistically accomplished and even less potential for long-term support without an unambiguous demonstration of national interest. Without those two factors—limited and clearly defined scope of mission and then only in the cases of national interest—the intervention is more likely to complicate the situation over the long run than to alleviate overall human suffering. While in certain circumstances the strife caused by state failure will necessitate international intervention to contain it (as in the former Yugoslav Republic of Macedonia where a multinational force has generally succeeded in interdicting the spillover of Albanian nationalism from Kosovo) or even to prevent outside forces from exploiting the localized political vacuum (as in Afghanistan under the Taliban), the capacity for these missions is limited. Throughout the history of Liberia's existence, in fact, the foreign policy of the United States has been one of benign neglect. While the American government certainly bore the West African state no ill will, it also saw little utility in immersing the full weight of the United States in a private initiative that, by its very nature, was precarious.

For the United States, with its military and political forces already stretched to new limits by the post-September 11 realities of the world, the decision whether or not to invest scarce resources has to be made on the basis of *Realpolitik*, weighing such factors as the dangers of weapons of mass destruction, the threat that the failed or failing state poses to neighbors as well as its potential threat to America, the risk of possible terrorist buildup, and the failed or failing state's inherent importance to U.S. political and economic interests. In a complex world where no capability is limitless, responsible national authorities in states removed from the immediate conflict zone can only take the potential humanitarian situation into account at a second moment and then in only relation to the primary interests encapsulated in the earlier questions. While such a stance courts criticism for being "coldhearted," it is, as Kissinger observed, ultimately the only one sustainable over the long term, once the moral satisfaction of having "taken action" wears thin and old patterns reemerge anew. While conflict resolutions imposed from without by an intervention may mitigate some of the worse consequences of state failure in the short-term, over the long run such measures weaken the capacity of the affected society to manage future difficulties.

Then President Bill Clinton put it succinctly in his first address to the UN General Assembly when, on September 27, 1993, he told the international body that: "The United Nations simply cannot become engaged in every one of the world's conflicts. If the American people are to say yes to UN peacekeeping, the United Nations must know when to say no."[27] The president proceeded to suggest that several questions should be answered before any intervention is contemplated in "failed state" situations: Is there a real threat to international peace? Does the proposed mission have clear objectives? Can an end point be identified for those who will be asked to participate? How much will the mission cost? As was previously seen, none of these queries was adequately confronted in the lead-up to the ECOMOG and UNOMIL deployments into Liberia.

During the escalating international campaign that ultimately led to the resignation and exile of President Charles Taylor during the summer of 2003, much was made of the supposed "national interests" of the United States that were at stake in the outcome of the crisis. After reciting well-documented human rights abuses committed in Liberia during Taylor's presidency as well as some anecdotal evidence that an al-Qaʿeda operative may have purchased illicitly mined Sierra Leonean diamonds from the RUF with Liberian connivance, Ryan Lizza, associate editor of *The New Republic*, perhaps won the prize for conditional hyperbolic argument when he hypothesized that:

> Since 1989, when Taylor started Liberia's civil war, conflict spread to neighboring Sierra Leone, Guinea, and Côte d'Ivoire. While all these

states are west if of the big oil-producing countries along the Gulf of Guinea – from which the United States projects it will receive some 20 percent of its oil imports in a few years – there are plausible scenarios under which the chaos could spread further. Nobody would have predicted that Taylor's original 1989 Christmas Eve invasion would one day engulf Côte d'Ivoire, long a rock of stability in West Africa, but now it has. And, as *The Economist* pointed out this week, "if Côte d'Ivoire were to go the way of Liberia, it would cripple" Burkina Faso, Mali, and Niger, bringing the conflict to the doorstep of Nigeria, the already precarious oil-rich hegemon of the region.[28]

Even aside from the fact that, as the proverbial crow flies, no fewer than 920 miles (1,481 kilometers) as well as four countries separate Monrovia from Lagos, Nigeria, Lizza's scenario is farfetched at best. It was, however, typical of many editorials published during the period, all of which raised ambiguous "national interest" as a fig leaf for want of concrete strategic concerns that would justify long-term entanglement. The truth is while there may be, according to one's beliefs, compelling moral reasons for America to engage in "nation building" in Liberia, there are no real national interests—geopolitical, economic, or military—that would require such a long-term commitment as a matter of national security. Any concerns of this sort could—and was—dealt with in short order with brief pressure that achieved the objective of Taylor's resignation. About the only area where contemporary Liberia might possibly impinge upon the security interests of the United States is potential for mischief that its "flag of convenience" presents, but that is an issue that must be addressed more globally with a regime involving other countries engaged in the practice.[29] However, viewing the question of America's relationship with Liberia objectively will require the realistic vision that Hans Morgenthau admitted would be difficult to sell when he observed that "it is inevitable that a theory which tries to understand international politics as it actually is and as it ought to be in view of its intrinsic nature, rather than as people would like to see it, must overcome a psychological resistance that most other branches of learning need not face."[30] It will also require a national discourse within the United States that has yet to commence, as Michael Ignatieff recently observed:

But what has been the national interest once the cold war ended and
the threat of a growing Communist empire evaporated? No clear national interest has emerged. No clear *conversation* about the national
interest has emerged. Policy – if one can speak of policy – has seemed
to be mostly the prisoner of interventionist lobbies with access to the
indignation machine of the modern media.[31]

A TASK FOR THE NATION

Ultimately, while international intervention—whether American or
otherwise—may provide some measure of relief in the short term, outsiders will never be able to address the root structural causes—cultural,
social, economic and political—for state failure. The usual *écoutre-
ments* in the diplomatic toolkit—sanctions, peacekeeping contingents,
power-sharing arrangements, etc.—can serve as stop-gap measures,
but they will provide only temporary relief, perhaps mitigating some
of the worst consequences of a state's collapse. State failure, as has been
illustrated by the unfolding of events in Liberia, is the result of a confluence of forces—ancient ethnic tensions and stagnant politics, the end of
the cold war and economic deterioration, political repression and social
exclusion—that pushed the polity into collapse. It is, more often than
not, a case of what Charles Ragin has termed "multiple conjunctural
causation" whereby the historical outcome is the result of a complex
combination of structural and situational factors.[32]

Just as state failure has multiple causes, national identity is a multi-
dimensional phenomenon, involving not only the public institutions
and monopoly of coercive power in a given territory, but also the cultural and political bonds that unite different individuals into a single
community. Anthony Smith has defined the nation as "a named human
population sharing an historic territory, common myths and historical
memories, a mass, public culture, a common economy and common
legal rights and duties for all members."[33] In reverse, it could be said
that in a failed state one or more of these elements is found to be lacking. In Liberia, until recent times all of these constitutive elements were
found lacking, both *de iure* and *de facto*. Even after the reforms under
Presidents Tubman and Tolbert eliminated the *de iure* exclusion of the
majority of indigenous peoples from the national life, the *de facto* alienation persisted. Consequently, the state failed because the differentia-

tion permitted historical, ethnic-based communities to maintain stronger bonds, despite repeated attempts to depoliticize them and to eviscerate their traditional authority structures. In short, all the attributes of national identity were found at the level of the ethnic community, even while they were absent at the nation level, except among members the Americo-Liberian ruling class.

Ultimately, an effective and durable response to the phenomenon of state failure, however, will require that the citizens of the failed state itself take responsibility for their fate. Much emphasis has been made on "democratization." However, establishing a democratically elected government will not, by itself, be enough to build a free society out of a failed state, or anywhere else for that matter. Rather, a stable free society presupposes not only a democratic polity, but also a culture of liberty and a free economy. These three institutions are inherently interdependent: none can endure for long without the other two. The dependence of the economy on the basic rule of law and functional organs of government is relatively straightforward. Peruvian economist Hernando de Soto has, in recent years, clearly demonstrated that the principal obstacle to development in many countries is the lack of a access to clear legal property titles and, consequently, to credit markets. A government of laws insures this for the economy.[34] Likewise, as Francis Fukuyama, among others, has shown, the economy is also dependent on certain moral and cultural variables, including social trust and cohesion.[35] This culture, in turn, depends on the conditions established by a market-based economy and a democratic regime in order to ensure the freedom from want and fear necessary for it to thrive. And, of course, a stable democratic government requires material prosperity —or at least the reasonable opportunity to pursue it—and a culture that respects individual rights and encourages personal responsibility and tolerance for others.

In the case of Liberia, this requires the reconstruction of the nation's foundations if it is to ever overcome its failed state status and rejoin the international community as a viable sovereign entity. While hostilities in the Liberian civil war, now seen as a paragon of post-Cold War conflict in Africa and other developing regions, began in December 1989, violence had been systematic for years, predating even Doe's overthrow of the True Whig oligarchy. In retrospect, the structures and symbols of the Americo-Liberian dominated republic including the official motto, the national sense of historical mission and identity, and the general sense of community, as well as the institutions of government—contained within themselves the seeds of their own destruction, being perceived by the vast majority of the population as exclusionary and discriminatory. Consequently, no sense of shared community was ever cultivated except within very narrow groups—and the groups were often enough set against each other. No conciliation is possible between conflicting ethnic groups until the members of these groups themselves decide to adopt such a path: the will to peaceful coexistence cannot be imposed from above, much less from the outside. In Liberia, no amount of pressure will cause Krahns, Gios, Mandingos, and all the other tribes to set aside their ancient grievances and overcome their divisions—any more than three-quarters of a century of forced cohabitation convinced Bohemians, Moravians, and Slovaks that they were "Czechoslovaks," or Slovenes, Croats, Serbs, and Albanians that they were "Yugoslavs" or the UN Observer Mission in Congo will convince the Hemas and Lendus that they are *Congolaises*—until they themselves arrive at that conclusion, if they ever do. If the competing ethnic factions in Liberia are determined to settle their differences on the battlefield, there is little outsiders can effectively do without exacerbating the situation beyond exhorting the parties to hold their fire. As Madeleine Albright has observed: "True security will not come until there is a decisive political shift, which will not occur until the leaders doing the violence conclude that their tactics won't work."[36]

Reconstruction will also require the strengthening—if not wholesale overhaul—of the institutions of civil society that, if not destroyed during the years of fighting, remain compromised by either their involvement with previous rulers and regimes or their self-absorbed pursuit of individual interests. This charge, made by Liberians themselves, includes political parties, religious groups, and other non-governmental organizations. Only with civil society reinforced can a culture—and a truly national identity—be developed that can give hope to peace building and national reconciliation. Amos Sawyer, the academic who served as president of Liberia's Interim Government of National Unity from 1990 to 1994, recently made the same point when he argued that:

> No degree of external support can help Liberia in the long-run if Liberians are not the driving force in peace-building but are simply the beneficiaries of peace-building programs driven by others. And no peace-building approach can yield sustainable outcomes if it does not

empower Liberians by strengthening their individual and collective capacity to do things for themselves, to rely on their own resources, and then seek assistance from others.[37]

Liberia's problems were diagnosed with great clarity nearly four decades ago in an economic study whose conclusions were unambiguous, but whose recommendations remain, tragically enough, still await implementation:

> Despite its historic association with the United States, its rich resource base relative to population, and generous external assistance by foreign governments, Liberia must be placed among the least developed countries in Africa. In 1962, less than 10 percent of the population was literate, the quality of its educational establishment was low, the traditional divisions between tribal Liberians and the Americo-Liberian descendants of the colonial settlers remained in force, and traditional governmental procedures had not been appreciably revised to serve development needs.
>
> In 1962 there was nothing that could reasonably be called developmental planning. Neither effective plan nor personnel existed...Its most tenacious problems are institutional and require policies to reform traditional social and political organizations; to abolish forced recruitment of labor, to reform traditional land tenure arrangements, to reform the traditional administration of the tribal hinterlands in ways which provide incentives for tribal persons to enlarge their production for sale, and to allow them access to higher education and political expression.[38]

In the final analysis, every political community must accept responsibility for assuring its own viability. Liberian leaders should have long been aware of the precarious foundations on which their society existed: the fissure within the national sense of identity and the alienation, fed by fear and hatred, that resulted from the structures of what was essentially a colonial society, albeit one *sans* the stable ties to the metropolitan power. The over two decades of civil strife in Liberia present an example of how ancient and unresolved communal tensions—the fear of those in power that they will lose their position of dominance and suffer reprisals, the resentments of those exploited by or otherwise excluded from the oligarchy's exercise of power—not only increase the risk of state failure, but exacerbate the ensuing conflict. And once the spiral of violence starts a series of dormant, but ever present, factors takes on a life of its own, ensuring that the reduction in alienation and movement towards reconciliation that would be difficult enough in peace will be impossible in war.

LEARNING FROM EXPERIENCE

History has shown that the states that survived and prospered are not those that relied so much on being propped up, but rather those organic communities that were willing to carry out the internal reform and renewal demanded by the times. In contrast, those that litter the proverbial dustbins of history have been those that either were unstable artificial constructs to begin with or, even if they began as organic communities, were nonetheless unwilling to undertake the discipline necessary to change with the times. This harsh lesson applies, first and foremost, to the states that have either failed or are in danger of collapse. However, the lesson is likewise applicable to other states and international actors as well, for more is at stake in state failure than the destiny of the nations immediately effected by the crisis: in an increasingly globalized society, the entire international system is implicated.

The dramatic collapse in recent years of the Liberian state, a tragedy whose seeds were sown more than a century ago in the very foundations of the enterprise, and the spread of what began as a civil conflict into a regional conflagration represent, in many respects, a microcosm of the phenomena that—within the context of the epochal shifts that accompanied the end of the Cold War—have and will confront the international community for the foreseeable future. While like other countries in the unenviable category of the world's "failed states," Liberia's strategic importance to global society is *per se* non-existent, the collapse of even marginal states places additional stress on the international system that is already strained. Political will and visionary leadership will be needed within failed states in order to overcome their own internal difficulties – no amount of external involvement can substitute for national cohesion and self-responsibility. The peoples torn by the violence following state failure—especially in cases where the conflict takes on ethnic overtones—must themselves come to the conclusion that they must bind their own wounds, reconcile with their fellow countrymen, and heal their societies.

Nevertheless, more is required. Although primary responsibility for their destinies must repose with the effected countries and their peoples, the great powers—especially the United States which is *the* great power in the post-Cold War "unipolar moment"[39]—must inevitably be prepared to assume a leading role in formulating and supporting—if not directly leading—an appropriate response. Simply put, realism must admit that, notions of the sovereign equality of states notwithstanding, some nations are more "equal" than others: without the concurrence of these powers, things fall apart, as Chinua Achebe might put it. This is not to suggest that these powers, especially the United States, ought to directly intervene in every state failure, especially where no significant strategic national interests are directly at stake. However, neither the powers nor the world at large is ultimately unaffected by the collapse of nation states, no matter how remote the conflict may appear to be. In a sense, the problem of state failure confronting the statesmen of the world at the dawn of the twenty-first century is the geopolitical equivalent of the never-totally-resolved dilemma of the commons that economists face.

In this regard, American policy makers face a particularly difficult quandary. The extraordinary political, economic, and military power of the United States—especially the latter—is likely remain unchallenged, at least in the intermediate term.[40] Hence, U.S. leadership is a virtual prerequisite for any international intervention in failed state situations. The example from Liberia's neighbors neatly illustrates this point: contrast the relative success to date of the British-led intervention in Sierra Leone, which has enjoyed the political and economic support of both the Clinton and Bush administrations, with the lackluster record of the French intervention in the former crown jewel of francophone West Africa, Côte d'Ivoire, which hardly registers on the consciousness of the U.S. foreign policy establishment. On the other hand, there are limits even to America's diplomatic, financial, and military resources. Hyperactivity, especially in areas where a core geopolitical interest of the United States is not at stake, not only will fail to garner the support of the American leadership and people, it may well threaten the strategic hegemony the country currently enjoys by dissipating its relative and absolute strength. The resolution of this dilemma will require a process of national discourse and dialogue within the U.S. that has barely begun—and which, in the case of the crisis in Liberia during the summer of 2003, was almost entirely drowned out by a chorus of often ill-informed advocacy and moral posturing.

And even in the cases where intervention is ultimately judged necessary—perhaps on the basis of a rational criterion such as whether the state failure in question, as well as the intervention proposed, will increase or decrease the tensions elsewhere, particularly those affecting the powers—those intervening to "heal" ought to bear in mind the ancient principles that were enshrined for the medical profession in the Hippocratic Oath: to enter only for the good of those afflicted and, where conditions cannot be stabilized, to do nothing that would worsen matters. A case could be made—as outlined above—that the ECOMOG intervention in the Liberian civil conflict failed in both respects and paved the way for the sad events that followed.

It should be borne in mind, however, that, for better or worse, the qualitative lessons of historical and political experience differ from the normative quantitative postulates of the physical sciences. History is never repeatable in the manner that scientific experiments have traditionally been understood to be. The lessons of history and politics are, at best, analogical in nature. They must be painstakingly recognized and then carefully contextualized historically, culturally, and socially. Consequently, the conclusions to be drawn concerning state failure from recent episodes such as the Liberian experience require even a greater effort to evaluate, to say nothing of what is required to correctly apply such principles as might be culled. Many years before he ventured into practical statecraft, Henry Kissinger observed that: "States tend to be forgetful. It is not often that nations learn from the past, even rarer that they draw the correct conclusions from it."[41] The proper recognition and application of the lessons to be gleaned from the failure of the Liberian state will, in the coming months and years, require the true craft of the statesman.

ENDNOTES

1. See Andrew S. Natsios, *U.S. Foreign Policy and the Four Horsemen of the Apocalypse: Humanitarian Relief in Complex Emergencies* (Center for Strategic and International Studies "Washington Paper" 170; Westport, Connecticut/London: Praeger, 1997), 7.
2. See Steven Majstorovic, "Ancient Hatreds or Elite Manipulation? Memory and Politics in the Former Yugoslavia," *World Affairs* 159/4 (Spring 1997): 170–183.
3. See D. Elwood Dunn, Amos J. Beyan, and Carl Patrick Burrowes, *Historical Dictionary of Liberia*, 2nd ed. (Lanham, Maryland/London: Scarecrow Press, 2001), 108–109.
4. Wole Soyinka, *The Open Sore of a Continent: A Personal Narrative of the Nigerian Crisis* (1996; Oxford/New York: Oxford University Press, 1997), 21.
5. *Ibid.*, 142.

6. Quoted in Nathaniel R. Richardson, *Liberia's Past and Present* (London: Diplomatic Press, 1959), 117.

7. Ryszard Kapuściński, *The Shadow of the Sun*, trans. Klara Glowczewska (New York/ Toronto: Alfred A. Knopf, 2001), 239.

8. See Madeleine Albright (with Bob Woodward), *Madam Secretary: A Memoir* (New York: Hyperion, 2003). Albright mentions Liberia in passing as part of list of countries in conflict (149), noting that it has "no federal income tax" (174), and records a stopover there in January 1996 (520). In fairness to Albright, Liberia finds no mention at all in the 320-page and 687-page, respectively, memoirs of her immediate two predecessors. See Warren Christopher, *Chances of A Lifetime: A Memoir* (New York: Scribner, 2001); and James A. Baker III, *The Politics of Diplomacy: Revolution, War and Peace, 1989–1992* (New York: G.P. Putnam's Son's, 1995).

9. Graham Greene, *Journey Without Maps* (1936; New York: Penguin Books, 1980), 231.

10. Abba Eban, *Diplomacy for the Next Century* (New Haven/London: Yale University Press, 1998), 173–174.

11. Amos Sawyer, *The Emergence of Autocracy in Liberia: Tragedy and Challenge* (San Francisco: Institute for Contemporary Studies, 1992), 304.

12. Michael W. Foley and Bob Edwards, "The Paradox of Civil Society," *Journal of Democracy* 7/3 (July 1996): 38.

13. See Augustine Toure, *The Role of Civil Society in National Reconciliation and Peacebuilding in Liberia* (New York: International Peace Academy, 2002), 9.

14. One of the exceptions was the Peace and Justice Commission, sponsored by the Catholic Church in Liberia. Notwithstanding the troubling entanglements of members of the hierarchy in the political history of the country, the Commission, under the leadership of its energetic lay directors — most recently former Supreme Court Chief Justice Frances Johnson Morris, who succeeded the harassed James Verdier and the exiled Samuel Kofi Woods — has managed to maintain its independence and its reputation as one of the better sources of human rights documentation in Liberia.

15. Dave Peterson, "Liberia: Crying for Freedom," *Journal of Democracy* 7/2 (April 1996): 154.

16. Quoted in Robert A. Smith, *The Emancipation of the Hinterland* (Monrovia: Star Magazine and Publishing, 1964), 5.

17. For a detailed discussion of the relevant legal questions, see Klaas van Walraven, *The Pretence of Peace-keeping: ECOMOG, West Africa and Liberia (1990–1998)* (The Hague: Netherlands Institute of International Relations *Clingendael*, 1999), 19–33.

18. Adekeye Adebajo, *Liberia's Civil War: Nigeria, ECOMOG and Regional Security in West Africa* (Boulder, Colorado/London: Lynne Rienner Publishers, 2002), 64.

19. For a discussion of both the political and logistical issues, see Herbert Howe, "Lessons of Liberia, ECOMOG, and Regional Peacekeeping," *International Security* 21/3 (Winter 1996–1997), 1–31.

20. Stephen John Stedman, *International Actors and Internal Conflicts* (New York: Rockefeller Brothers Fund Project on World Security, 1999), 10.

21. See Stephen Ellis, *The Mask of Anarchy: The Destruction of Liberia and the Religious Dimension of an African Civil War* (1999; New York: New York University Press, 2001), 313

22. See William Reno, "Reinvention of an African patrimonial state: Charles Taylor's Liberia," *Third World Quarterly* 16/1 (1995): 109–120.

23. Michael Barnett, *Eyewitness to a Genocide: The United Nations and Rwanda* (Ithaca/ London: Cornell University Press, 2002), 29.

24. Michael Ignatieff, *Human Rights as Politics and Idolatry*, edited by Amy Gutmann (Princeton/Oxford: Princeton University Press, 2001), 45, 47.

25. See Chester A. Crocker, "Engaging Failing States," *Foreign Affairs* 82/5 (September/ October 2003): 32–44.

26. Henry Kissinger, *Does America Need a Foreign Policy? Toward a Diplomacy for the 21st Century* (2001; New York: Touchstone, 2002), 208.

27. William Jefferson Clinton, "Remarks to the 48th Session of United Nations General Assembly" (September 27, 1993), *Federal Register* 29/3 (1993): 1906.

28. Ryan Lizza, "Ace of Diamonds: Charles Taylor's terror ties," *The New Republic* (July 21, 2001): 14.

29. See William Langewiesche, "Anarchy at Sea," *The Atlantic Monthly* 292/2 (September 2003): 50–80.

30. Hans J. Morgenthau, *Politics Among Nations: The Struggle for Power and Peace*, 5th rev. ed. (New York: Alfred A. Knopf, 1978), 15.

31. Michael Ignatieff, "Why Are We in Iraq? (And Liberia? And Afghanistan?)," *New York Times Magazine* (September 7, 2003), 41.

32. See Charles Ragin, *The Comparative Method: Moving Beyond Qualitative and Quantitative Strategies* (Berkeley: University of California Press, 1987), pp. 23–30.

33. Anthony D. Smith, *National Identity* (London: Penguin, 1991), 14.

34. See Hernando de Soto, *The Mystery of Capital: Why Capitalism Triumphs in the West and Fails Everywhere Else* (New York: Basic Books, 2000).

35. See Francis Fukuyama, *Trust: The Social Virtues and the Creation of Prosperity* (New York: Free Press, 1995).

36. Albright, *Madam Secretary*, 451.

37. Amos Sawyer, "Peace-building in Liberia: Foundational Challenges and Appropriate Approaches" (Memorandum, August 21, 2003). The text has been posted to a website run by a group of U.S.-based Liberian exiles; see <www.thepersective.org>.

38. George Dalton and A. A. Walters, "The Economy of Liberia," in P. Robson and D.A. Lury (eds.), *The Economies of Africa* (Evanston, Illinois: Northwestern Univeristy Press, 1969), 314–315.

39. See Charles Krauthammer, "The Unipolar Moment," *Foreign Affairs* 70/1 (Winter 1990–1991): 23–33; also idem., "The Unipolar Moment Revisited," *The National Interest* 70 (Winter 2002–2003): 5–17.

40. See William C. Wohlforth, "The Stability of a Unipolar World," *International Security* 24/1 (Summer 1999): also Barry R. Posen, "Command of the Commons: The Military Foundation of U.S. Hegemony," *International Security* 28/1 (Summer 2003): 5–46.

41. Henry Kissinger, *A World Restored: Metternich, Castlereagh and the Problems of Peace 1812–1822* (1957; London: Phoenix Press, 2000), 331.

NOTES ON ANOTHER
PEACE PLAN

O N AUGUST 11, 2003, Charles Ghankay Taylor resigned the
Liberian presidency and, after a defiant farewell address in
which he promised to return, left for exile in the southeastern Nigerian coastal town of Calabar. Despite occupying a luxury villa
owned by the Nigerian government and put at his disposal by Nigerian
President Olusegun Obasanjo, Taylor will not be the most eminent figure in the resort community. That distinction belongs to Edidem Otu
Ekpe Nyong, Effa IX, Obong of Calabar and King of the Efik of Cross
River, scion of the Atai dynasty that traces its roots to the tenth century
and whose family has ruled the environs of Calabar since 1472—a poignant reminder of the potential stability of tribal ties to a modern warlord who exploited ethnic tensions for chaos.

Under United Nations Security Resolution 1497, the Nigerian-led ECOMIL peacekeeping force was to be joined by a UN stabilization force to support the transitional national authority and to assist in the implementation of an eventual comprehensive peace agreement. The UN force was to be deployed no later than October 1 and was to number some 15,000 personnel, although it remained unresolved from where they would be drawn or who would foot the bill. Earlier, on July 8, in a bid—ultimately unsuccessful—to enlist United States participation for the a multinational military intervention in Liberia, UN Secretary-General Kofi Annan appointed a retired U.S. Air Force major-general, Ambassador Jacques Paul Klein, then serving as the Special Representative of the Secretary-General in Bosnia-Herzegovina, as his Special Representative *for* Liberia. The nomination was typical of the machinations of UN institutions. There already was a Representative of the Secretary-General *in* Liberia, the ineffectual Chadian Abou Moussa, who headed the bloated UN bureaucracy. Rather than remove Abou Moussa and replace him with Klein, the Chadian functionary was left in place as Annan's representative *in* Liberia while the American was appointed to the newly created post of representative *for* Liberia.

At the time of Taylor's mid-August departure from Liberia, the country was one of the poorest and least developed in the world. The rapid economic growth experienced after the 1997 cessation in open hostilities, with annual growth rates between 20 and 30 percent, slowed sharply with the expansion of the attacks by LURD in 2001. Estimates are that the economy experienced a negative growth of five percent in 2002, a loss rate that was expected double over the course of the next year.[1] The country's GDP for 2002 was estimated at $561.8 million, or $169.20 per capita—a figure that represented just 45.9 percent of the precivil war GDP.[2] According to observers, more than three-quarters of the Liberian population subsists on less than $1 per day. In fact, Liberia risks falling off the world's economic map altogether: the UN Development Program (UNDP) did not even include Liberia in its *Human Development Report 2003*, an all-too-poignant twist given that the document subtitled *Millennium Development Goals: A compact among nations to end human poverty*.[3] The UNDP Human Development Index, which measures development by factoring life expectancy, educational attainment, and standard of living, on a scale of zero to one, listed Norway as the highest ranked with an index of 0.944 for 2001 and Sierra Leone with the lowest at 0.275 (the average for sub-Saharan Africa was 0.468).[4]

UNDP's Liberia office estimated that the Human Development Index for Liberia for 2001-2002 was 0.313—which would rank it third it third from the bottom, above only Niger and Sierra Leone—compared with 0.325 just a decade earlier.[5]

Taylor's resignation left his vice president, Moses Zeh Blah, as the country's constitutional head of state. An unknown figure to most Liberians, Blah is a fifty-six-year-old Gio from Toweh Town, a remote hamlet in northeastern Nimba County, near Liberia's border with Côte d'Ivoire. Like other Gios, he had fled the persecutions of the Krahn-dominated dictatorship of Samuel Doe and spent the 1980s training in Libya. Joining Taylor's National Patriotic Front of Liberia (NPFL) insurrection against Doe, he served the movement in several capacities, including inspector-general, adjutant-general, and finally as Taylor's special envoy. When Taylor's National Patriotic Party (NPP) won the 1997 presidential elections, he appointed Blah as Liberia's ambassador to Libya (with concurrent accreditation as ambassador to Tunisia). Blah was appointed to the vice presidential position when the elected incumbent, Enoch Dogolea, died suddenly on June 23, 2000.

Although under provisions of the existing Liberian constitution, Blah was empowered to remain in office until after the president elected in the elections mandated for October 2003 was sworn into office in January 2004, he quickly entered into negotiations with the principal armed rebel movement, the Guinea-based Liberians United for Reconciliation and Democracy (LURD), and its smaller, more recent, Côte d'Ivoire-based offshoot, the Movement for Democracy in Liberia (MODEL). With the mediation of the former Nigerian head of state, General Abdulsalami Abubakar, a "comprehensive peace agreement" that paved the way for the installation of a transitional government was signed on August 18.[6]

The agreement establishes a National Transitional Government of Liberia (NTGL) that will take office from interim President Blah on October 14, 2003. The NTGL, Liberia's sixth[7] transitional constitutional arrangement in less than a decade, will remain in office until January 16, 2006, when it will be expected to cede power to a government to be elected on October 15, 2005.

The NTGL will be presided over by a chairman, assisted by a vice chairman, neither of whom will be eligible to contest the eventual national elections. Three days after signing the accord, the assembly in Accra elected businessman Charles Gyude Bryant, a fifty-four-year-old

Grebo with family roots in Maryland County who heads the Liberian Action Party (LAP), as the chairman of the NTGL, with Wesley Momo Johnson, leader of the United People's Party (UPP), as his vice chairman. Not surprisingly, both leaders come from political parties with little following since leaders of more influential groups want to save themselves for a future contest. Between themselves, the two parties represented by Bryant and Johnson won barely won 10 percent of the popular vote in the last elections. Both are products of the old oligarchy, Bryant having begun his professional career in the early 1970s as manager for the Mesurado Group of Companies, the virtually monopolistic conglomerate controlled by President William Tolbert and his brother, Finance Minister Stephen Tolbert.

The most recent peace agreement parcels out positions in the cabinet and the rest of the government between the remnants of Taylor's NPP government, LURD, and MODEL, with some civil society representatives thrown in. The NPP will retain five ministries: post and telecommunications, health and social welfare, national defense, planning and economic affairs, and internal affairs. LURD will receive five ministries: finance, justice, labor, transport, and state. MODEL will likewise receive five ministries: agriculture, commerce, lands, mines and energy, public works; and foreign affairs. The remaining six ministries—national security, education, gender and development, information, rural development, and youth and sports—will be allocated to civilian political parties and civil society organizations.

A unicameral National Transitional Legislative Assembly (NTLA) was also created, with seventy-six members. The NPP government, LURD, and MODEL are each allocated twelve seats in the NTLA. Each of Liberia's fifteen counties will elect one representative. The eighteen registered political parties are allocated one seat each. The remaining seven seats will go to representatives of undefined "civil society and special interest groups."

The existing judiciary will be considered vacated upon the inauguration of the NTGL. New members of the Supreme Court will be appointed to by chairman of the NTGL, subject to confirmation by the NTLA.

Finally, and perhaps most controversially, the twenty-two most important public corporations in Liberia are also portioned out in by the agreement. The outgoing NPP government will receive the Liberia Broadcasting System, the Liberia Electricity Corporation, the Liberia

Petroleum Refining Corporation, and the Liberia Water and Sewer Corporation. LURD will be allocated the Liberia Free Zone Authority, the Liberia Telecommunications Corporation, the Liberia Produce Marketing Corporation, and the National Ports Authority. MODEL will be given the Agriculture Corporative Development Bank, the Forestry Development Authority, Roberts International Airport, and the National Social Security and Welfare Corporation. The civilian political parties and civil society organizations will manage the Agriculture Industrial Training Board, the Liberia Domestic Airport Authority, the Liberia Mining Corporation, Liberia National Lotteries, the Liberia Rubber Development Unit, the Liberia National Oil Company, the Monrovia Transit Authority, the National Housing and Savings Bank, the National Housing Authority, and the National Insurance Corporation of Liberia.

Likewise, twenty-two autonomous government agencies and commissions are to be parceled out. The NPP government will retain control of the Bureau of the Budget and the National Security Agency. The LURD will receive the General Service Agency and the National Investment Commission. MODEL receives the Bureau of Maritime Affairs and the Liberia Refugee and Resettlement commissions. The remaining sixteen agencies —the Bureau of Immigration and Naturalization, the Bureau of General Auditing, the Bureau of State Enterprises, the Center for National Documents and Records, the Civil Service Agency, the John F. Kennedy memorial Medical Center, the Independent National Human Rights Commission, the Liberia National Police Force (LNP), the Truth and Reconciliation Commission, the National Bureau of Investigation, the National Fire Services, the National Food Assistance Agency, the Contracts and Monopoly Commission, the National Elections Commission, and the Governance Reform Commission—are allocated to civilian political parties and representatives of civil society.

While the situation remains fluid, the arrangements in this latest "comprehensive peace agreement" tie the authority of the leaders of the various political groups directly to their ability to let their subalterns exploit profitable opportunities at the expense of the state. As William Reno has observed, such a condominium "points to a basic dilemma: What can reformers do if a government has a vested financial interest in shielding illicit transactions?"[8] When the very institutional structures of government shift public officials interests away from public service toward personal gain, the ability of the regime to provide for the common good is compromised, the legitimacy of the state itself is eroded, and democracy itself is threatened.

Under the cover of the 3,500 ECOMIL peacekeepers—who, on October 1, 2003 donned the trademark blue berets of UN peacekeepers—and whose number is expected to increase, Gyude Bryant and the other members of the NTGL were sworn into office on October 14. Whether the NTGL will deliver on its promises to the Liberian people remains to be seen. As with the interim authorities that preceded it during the 1989–1997 civil war, the new government's writ only runs as far as the fire range of the peacekeepers propping it up, if at that. Just days prior to Bryant's inauguration, fighting broke out on the outskirts of Monrovia between gunmen accompanying LURD leader Conneh into Monrovia and government soldiers, leaving several dead. Even as the transitional leadership was being installed, reports continue to filter in from the interior of continued LURD and MODEL incursions probing the positions of soldiers loyal to the government in Monrovia. None of this bodes well for Bryant's administration.

However, aside from the poor record of Liberia's past transitional governments to deliver on their promises, the agreement's principal difficulty is that replaces the constitutional government of Liberia with an *ad hoc* arrangement put together by warlords—the agreement actually refers to its signatories as "the warring parties"—who represent no one other than themselves. The very factions that have wrecked havoc with Liberia over the course of recent years have, with the assistance of a former military ruler, awarded themselves not just the government but the entire Liberian state as well, dividing the spoils among themselves in a fashion that would appear straight out of the Tammany Hall era. The formerly warring factions will now have more than two years – provided the peace lasts that long (reports of continued fighting in the interior are not encouraging)—to carve fiefdoms out of the remnants of the Liberian state. One would not be unreasonable to suspect that the various parties will be loath to vacate these acquired domains once they—and their tribal constituents—have settled in. While one hopes for the best, the observer is left wondering whether the bazaar of spoils was the nobler destiny to which a nation long forlorn was to be roused.

October 15, 2003

ENDNOTES

1. See Economist Intelligence Unit, *Guinea, Sierra Leone, Liberia Country Report* (June 2003).

2. United Nations Secretary-General, *Report of the Secretary-General in pursuance of paragraph 19 of resolution 1478 (2003) concerning Liberia* (S/2003/793, August 5, 2003), 2.

3. See United Nations Development Program, *Human Development Report 2003. Millennium Development Goals: A compact among nations to end human poverty*, edited by Sakiko Fukuda-Parr (New York/Oxford: Oxford University Press, 2003).

4. See *ibid.*, 237–240.

5. United Nations Secretary-General, *Report of the Secretary-General...concerning Liberia* (S/2003/793, August 5, 2003), 4.

6. For the text of the agreement, see <www.usip.org/library/pa/liberia/liberia_08182003_cpa.html >.

7. The 1989–1997 civil war created the circumstances for a series of interim arrangements. The Interim Government of National Unity (IGNU) headed by Amos Sawyer represented Liberia internationally from 1990 until 1994, although its exercise of authority within the country was limited. During the same period, the National Patriotic Reconstruction Assembly Government set up by Charles Taylor's National Patriotic Front of Liberia (NPFL) effectively governed up to 90 percent of national territory. The Cotonou agreement set up a five-member Council of State, chaired by David Kpomakpor, that presided over the Liberian National Transitional Government (LNTG) that governed from 1994 to 1995. The Abuja I accord set up yet another Council of State, this time with six members, that governed from 1995 until 1996, under the titular chairmanship of Wilton Sankawulo. The 1996 Abuja II agreement shuffled this government again, replacing Sankawulo with Ruth Perry. This last transitional authority ceded place to Charles Taylor's presidency when he won the July 19, 1997, elections.

8. Cited in Nicholas Shaxson, "Transparency in the international diamond trade," in Robin Hodess (ed.), *Global Corruption Report 2001* (Berlin Transparency International, 2001), 216.

THE QUESTION OF A "FAILED STATE"

THE DATE OF SEPTEMBER 11 will forever be associated with the attacks on the United States by the terrorists of Osama bin Laden's al-Qa'eda, attacks that shattered any illusions of American homeland's immunity from the wave of a new type of violence that had been sweeping across the globe over the course of the preceding decade. The violence was "new" in the sense that its perpetrators did not use it, to borrow the metaphor that Ambassador Paul Bremmer coined at the time, so much as a means for obtaining a seat at the table than as one to overturn the table itself and kill everybody at it.[1] The violence—which constituted the single most dramatic day in the history of the United States, claiming the lives of three times as many *civilians* in New York, Washington, and Pennsylvania, as *military personnel* who died at Pearl

Harbor—was also "new" to many Americans in its indiscriminate brutality, the nature of which, while commonplace in many third world conflicts, American society had never before encountered. In these circumstances, it is understandable that an eerie coincidence might be forgotten: exactly eleven years before, on September 11, 1990, U.S. President George H.W. Bush delivered an address to a joint session of Congress in which he introduced a new expression into the lexicon of international affairs. Referring to the crisis precipitated by the Iraqi invasion of Kuwait, the president declared that:

> Out of these troubled times...a *new world order* can emerge: a new era—freer from the threat of terror, stronger in the pursuit of justice, and more secure in the quest for peace. An era in which the nations of the world, East and West, North and South, can prosper and live in harmony. A hundred generations have searched for this elusive path to peace, while a thousand wars raged across the span of human endeavor. Today that *new world* is struggling to be born, a world quite different from the one we've known. A world where the rule of law supplants the rule of the jungle. A world in which nations recognize the shared responsibility for freedom and justice. A world where the strong respect the rights of the weak.[2]

Of course, not everyone was in full accord with the president's optimistic vision. British Prime Minister Margaret Thatcher, whom Bush hailed in the same speech as America's "dependable ally," was skeptical, later noting that:

> This sort of stuff makes me nervous. President Bush, like any leader in time of war, was justified in raising the rhetorical temperature. But anyone who really believes that a "new order" of any kind is going to replace the disorderly conduct of human affairs, particularly the affairs of nations, is likely to be severely disappointed, and others with him.[3]

The euphoric optimism with which President Bush greeted the post-Cold War "new world order" faded as the following decade, which witnessed an upsurge of violent civil conflicts splintering—if not totally destroying—nation-states along ethnic lines, vindicated the Iron Lady's cold realism. In fact, rather than "new world order," another term, "failed state"—popularized during Bill Clinton's presidency, especially by Secretary of State Madeleine Albright during her tenure as U.S. ambassador to the United Nations—seemed better adapted to characterizing international concerns the ensuing years. During the succeeding administration of President George W. Bush, the new term was even elevated to the center stage. In the "National Security Strategy" released in September 2002, failed or failing states were identified as a major threat to America by providing haven (if not sponsorship) to terrorist groups, to say nothing of the bane that they are to their own people who are brutalized and whose resources are squandered and the menace they present to their neighbors through regional destabilization if not actual invasion.[4]

For all of the term's current usage, however, there has surprisingly little work done to actually define what constitutes a "failed state." Consequently, it is necessary first to define what is meant by the expression "failed state," including the attributes that characterize a modern state as well as its survival or collapse. This effort leads naturally into an examination of some of the explanations that can be advanced for state failure. In reality, the normative and the causal factors form a hermeneutical circle: knowing the characteristics of a given situation can facilitate the individuation of its causes, recognizing the causes of a phenomenon can help predict the symptoms that it will manifest. With these parameters in mind, it will then be possible to examine Liberia, its history, and the crisis that confronts it, and assess the prospects for the West African nation. This, in turn will facilitate reflections the lessons that Liberia presents both scholars and policy makers—and the informed public to which both are responsible—regarding state failure in general.

CONCEPTS OF STATE AND STATE FAILURE

One of the earliest treatments of the "failed state" phenomenon employed terms reminiscent of the classical juridical concept of *debellatio* that treated subjugated states that disappeared,[5] defining the failed nation-state as one that is "utterly incapable of sustaining itself as a member of the international community" and whose "governmental structures have been overwhelmed by the circumstances."[6] However, that study—like many that followed—defined neither the state nor the functions those collapsed structures were supposed to carry out.

The traditional diplomatic definition of a state is that it is "a polity controlling fixed territory with defined borders."[7] Jurists have refined this classical formulation to specify three elements constitutive of the state: population, territory, and a monopoly over the legitimate means of coercion within that territory that is recognized (or at least acquiesced to) by the population and the international community.[8] The modern consensus, however, that the state is also responsible for the provision of a number of public goods:

> Protection from the hazards of fire, garbage collection, mail delivery, road construction and public utility services—e.g., electricity and telephone—are usually undertaken by public authorities, or regulated by them, to secure adequate supply, prevent price gouging and reduce the magnitude of the "free rider" problem. The state is also increasingly recognized as the "natural" guardian of what the French call *"le patrimoine national,"* meaning that it is expected to protect the environment and the nation's natural resources.[9]

In more developed countries, in addition to the exercise of authority over territory and population and the provision or protection of public goods, some sort of expectation also exists that the state also engage in some sort of redistribution or social safety net in favor of the less fortunate members of society, although what this consists of is the subject of often fierce policy debates, as America's rancorous debates over welfare reform have shown. However, given the realities of developing world, this last aspect of statehood should probably be excluded from the discussions of failed states since most developing countries have enough difficulty providing even the most minimal public goods and services including concepts from the realm of Western "welfare" states would stretch the notion of statehood so far as to empty the express "failed state" of any purposive meaning. Political scientist Jean-German Gros has proposed a useful "taxonomy of failed states" that measures state failure across a spectrum using fairly unambiguous tests:

> Is there a well-defined territory that is internationally recognized? Is there a polity whose social boundaries can be more-or-less delineated and which has a general sense of belonging to the country and the state in question? How effective is the control exercised by whatever authority structure lays claim over the territory and the polity? In

other words, do public authority figures have a monopoly over the means of coercion nationally, or are there parts of the country that are off-limits? Are taxes – as opposed to tributes paid to local lords acting in the name of the state – collected, and do they make their way into state coffers?[10]

Based on this, Gros identifies five types of failed states: the anarchic state, where no centralized government exists and where armed groups act under orders from warlords contest control; the phantom (or mirage) state, where a semblance of authority remains with efficacy in a very limited area; the anemic state, whose energy is sapped by insurgency or by a breakdown in effective control by the central government over regional and local agents; the captured state, where the state embraces only an often-insecure ruling elite rather than the entire *polis*; and the aborted state, that never fully consolidated.[11]

The distinctions made by this taxonomy—or any similar model that could be constructed—are particularly useful if one must contemplate anything other than the *laissez-faire* attitude that is ethically unacceptable to the international consensus. Where a collapsed state falls on the spectrum necessarily determines the approach that is ultimately adopted to dealing with it. An anarchic state will require an entirely different response than an aborted state. The chosen solution, if not adequate to the nature of the state failure in question, runs the risk of not only being ineffectual, but also being outright disastrous, as the experience of recent years has shown. A good case can be made that the Rwandan genocide happened because the UN actually *learned* the lessons of the imbroglio in Somalia: the problem was that the former was a failed state of the captured variety whose organizational machinery, alas, worked *too* well, while the latter was one of the anarchic kind, with its governmental structures completely disintegrated.[12]

WHAT CAUSES FAILED STATES

One of the most popular explanations advanced is that failed states are such because "the support they received from one or both superpowers as proxy allies during the Cold War withered away after the fall of Berlin."[13] The implicit argument is that with the collapse of the Soviet Union as a hegemonic power, the U.S. as the world's lone *hyperpuissance* (to recall former French foreign minister Hubert Védrine's less-than-affectionate designation for an America he viewed as too worryingly powerful to be designated a mere "superpower") had little interest in maintaining its former clients, much less picking up the tab for those of its former rival. With their sources of aid dried up, many of these states quickly revealed how shaky their foundations really were all along, manifesting deeply rooted national malaise as well as political and economic weaknesses. As one analyst summarized it:

> The end of bipolar competition has also reduced dramatically the motivation to use aid and trade as political instruments to obtain allies and keep them in power. One consequence has been that superpower or major-power patrons have withdrawn the foreign financial and military support on which some governments had come to rely for their power and capacity to govern. Dependent more on foreign resources than on a domestic tax base, and more on skills in obtaining foreign resources than on those of winning allegiance at home, controlling factional fights, and generating and collecting tax revenues, such regimes collapse rapidly when external resources disappear. Verbal support has replaced the funds, arms, and bases of legitimacy that had been used to neutralize or co-opt other contenders for power, buy domestic support, and distribute the minimal welfare necessary to social equity and to the peaceful resolution of conflicts provoked by inequalities. One need mention only the former Yugoslavia, Afghanistan, Somalia, Liberia, and Zaire/Congo.[14]

As Michael Ignatieff put it, in the aftermath of the Cold War, "huge sections of the world's population have won the right of self determination on the cruelest possible terms: they have been simply left to fend for themselves. Not surprisingly, their nation-states are collapsing."[15]

Alongside the transition from the bipolar system of the Cold War to the American dominated "unipolar moment"[16] with the attendant disappearance of external resources that the regimes of many underdeveloped countries had become dependent upon in the absence of a domestic base, another cause that has been suggested for state failure has been the set of phenomena known collectively as "globalization." The overall increase in international trade has created business opportunities throughout the developing world, bringing jobs and consequent rises in the standard of living.[17] On the other hand, what *New York Times* columnist Thomas Friedman calls the "three democratizations"[18]—technology, finance, and information—that were brought by globalization constitute a double-edged sword: while unleashing economic opportunities, they also erode traditional state sovereignty. While cutting away of the shackles on economic development is usually a positive change, often those same shackles are the only civil bonds in some countries. The often-painful adjustments during economic transitions are—thanks to almost instantaneous communications—even more acutely felt and widely resented, especially if inequities within a given society, whether relative or absolute, are increased. UN Under-Secretary-General Shashi Tharoor has commented:

> Conversion to free markets has exacerbated the problem of economic inequality in underdeveloped countries, many of which have underdeveloped regions which correspond to specific ethnic groups or segments of society...Indeed, some of the poster children for globalization proved that they were more, not less, vulnerable to civil strife as a result. The riots, lootings, and rapes that occurred in Indonesia in May-June 1998 provided a stark example of civil conflict – albeit fortunately not civil war – sparked by an economy's inability to cope with the demands as well as the opportunities of globalization.[19]

In fact, the economic and technological innovations brought by the creation of a global market make it possible to develop regional markets and "war economies" such as the diamonds and arms trade that drove the West African regional conflict. These "shadow states," as they have been called by William Reno, who has perhaps become the leading authority on the subject, are characterized by the concentration of power in the hands of an individual who is not bound by conventional laws and procedures, although these may be present even as the "shadow state" may operate alongside traditional governmental structures.[20] Those who control these regionalized "war economies" manipulate access to both formal and informal markets, using the access to resources to enrich themselves and control their societies and, in the process, undermining formal state structures. In short, politics becomes "criminalized" – rather than simply corrupt – when the government ultimately exists to benefit either the ruling elite or the competing warlords who might succeed the collapse of such an oligarchy, carving up fiefdoms for themselves.[21]

However, in addition to the external factors that have been suggested, state failure is also driven by a variety of internal physical and social factors. In 1993, Samuel Huntington proposed in the pages of the influential journal *Foreign Affairs* his celebrated thesis—later expounded in book-length form—that with the end of the Cold War, the conflicts between the ideological blocs led by the superpowers, would be replaced by the "clash of civilizations" between cultural blocs.[22] Then, in a now-famous essay entitled "The Coming Anarchy," published in the February 1994 issue of *The Atlantic Monthly* coincidentally just a few weeks before the onset of the Rwandan genocide,[23] journalist Robert Kaplan painted a depressing Malthusian panorama of environmental degradation and high birthrates creating a mass movement of alienated youth that lent a very real face to the Harvard University professor's thesis:

> West Africa is becoming the symbol of worldwide demographic, environmental, and societal stress, in which criminal anarchy emerges as the real "strategic" danger. Disease, overpopulation, unprovoked crime, scarcity of resources, refugee migrations, the increasing erosion of nation-states and international borders, and the empowerment of private armies, security firms, and international drug cartels are now most tellingly demonstrated through a West African prism...Sierra Leone is a microcosm of what is occurring, albeit in a more tempered and gradual manner, throughout West Africa and much of the underdeveloped world: the withering away of central governments, the rise of tribal and regional domains, the unchecked spread of disease, and the growing pervasiveness of war...[I]t is Thomas Malthus, the philosopher of demographic doomsday, who is now the prophet of West Africa's future. And West Africa's future, eventually, will also be that of most of the rest of the world.[24]

In short, according to this account, having been unleashed by the fall of communism in Central and Eastern Europe, the forces of primordial ethnic bonds made themselves felt. As one author has noted: "Collective identities in underdeveloped societies are particularly conflict prone because identities are derived from fundamental, incontrovertible, and non-negotiable values such as language, history, and religion."[25] That this politically incorrect assertion is vindicated in those sad cases where, even against the economist's rational interest-maximization, brutal civil conflict tears apart potentially wealthy societies, does nothing to mitigate its lack of popularity within many circles, who have branded its advocates as proponents of sort of "new racism" that they label the "New Barbarism thesis."[26]

Even those who argue that ethnic identity is at least partially determined by social and economic circumstances – a more sophisticated version of the "nurture versus nature" preference – have to admit that ethnicity is nonetheless exploitable as an effective means to the ends of political and economic gain, as UN Secretary-General Kofi Annan has noted:

> Weak Governments – and, of course, so-called failed States – have little capacity to stop the eruption and spread of violence that better organized and more legitimate Governments could have prevented or contained.
>
> The shift from war-proneness to war itself can be triggered by the deliberate mobilization of grievances, and by ethnic, religious or nationalist myth mongering and the promotion of dehumanizing ideologies, all of them too often propagated by hate-media. The widespread rise of what is sometimes called identity politics, coupled with the fact that fewer than 20 percent of all States are ethnically homogeneous, means that political demagogues have little difficulty finding targets of opportunity and mobilizing support for chauvinist causes. The upsurge of "ethnic cleansing" in the 1990s provides stark evidence of the appalling human costs that this vicious exploitation of identity politics can generate.
>
> In other cases armed conflict has less to do with ethnic, national or other enmities than the struggle to control economic resources. The pursuit of diamonds, drugs, timber concessions and other valuable commodities drives a number of today's internal wars. In some countries, the capacity of the State to extract resources from society and to allocate patronage to cronies or political allies is the prize to be fought over. In others, rebel groups and their backers command most of the resources—and the patronage that goes with them.[27]

Annan's deputy, Tharoor, is even more explicit in describing the "postmodern tribalism" that leaders use to "distract their citizens from other domestic failures, often when ethnic division is nowhere as profound as being claimed."[28] Even a scholar who dogmatically refuses to accept the thesis that ethnic ties are of a different order than other social bonds, Charles Kupchan, who served as director for European affairs at the National Security Council during the Clinton administration, has conceded its significance in that "precisely because nationalism is not primordial or essentialist, it is malleable and its trajectory is susceptible to influence through policy instruments."[29] In his study on ethnic conflicts in Africa, while he argued against the tendency to read the "exotic" into the continent's tribal strife, Bill Berkeley made the case that, despite the differences among them, the countries he examined—Liberia, Congo-Zaire, South Africa, Sudan, Uganda, and Rwanda—shared a history of ethnic (or racial) discrimination that "relied on institutionalized mechanisms of coercion and co-optation that were inherently divisive"[30] and that the subsequent ethnic conflict was a product of that tyranny. Consequently, even where ethnic tensions are not the initial grievance, the combination of ethnic differences and socio-economic inequality is a lethal one that can assume a life of its own once conflict is ignited. This is particularly true in polities where the fundamental features of national identity—an historic territory, common historical memories or myths, a common public culture, common and equal legal rights and duties for all members of society, and a common economy with freedom of movement[31] – are weak, if not altogether absent.

Taking into account the valid contributions of these different perspectives, it is possible to present a sketch, in four parts, a rough profile of the chain of causality of recent state failures in Africa and elsewhere:

• First, the Cold War rivalry between the Western and the Soviet blocs permitted the ruling elites in many countries to essentially engage in what economists politely call "rent-seeking," thus receiving aid that permitted them to maintain states that were essentially already failing. In fact, the reason some of these states had not already failed was that state failure went counter to the interests of both power blocs in the bipolar international system. Consequently, the Cold War created a set of circumstances where state failure was avoided by timely infusions of assistance by an international system committed—whether or not it articulated it as explicitly or eloquently as Henry Kissinger has—to a balance of power. North Korea's present continuing existence is an example of a failed state being maintained by other states—including the United States, China, Russia, Japan, and South Korea—with a vested interest in avoiding the vacuum that its total collapse would entail, irrespective of whether Kim Jong-Il's modern Hermit Kingdom possesses weapons of mass destruction or not.

• Second, circumstances have altered the landscape of the post-Cold War world, leading to the withdrawal of international patronage that had been the "artificial life support" to states that should have faltered and are now, however reluctantly, being allowed to fail. As economic conditions worsen and their relative impacted magnified by both the pressures of globalization abroad and increased competition for scarce resources at home, tensions inevitably rise in many of these former client states even as the authority of state institutions is weakened. The meltdown of Somalia when the U.S. pulled the plug on Mohammed Siad Barre after the Cold War—an action that was itself a response to the collapsing Soviet Union cutting off Ethiopian dictator Mengistu Haile Mariam—is an example of a state that could never realistically carry its own weight being allowed to fail.

• Third, cultural and ethnic identity, however repressed in the past, remain important factors in self and group identification. If governmental institutions are sufficiently weakened and the cultural and ethnic ties sufficiently correlated—statistically, even if not causally—to political and economic grievances, the potential for civil conflict is heightened. This is particularly true in those cases where the weakened nation-state either is an artificial construction rather than the product of historical, organic evolution, or where the unifying vision of society does not include all segments of the population within the mythological *polis*. Ironically, "ethnicity is an effective means of mobilizing around common material interests precisely because it is non-material, that is symbolic, content, which masks or 'mystifies' those interests for group members themselves."[32] The deeply rooted origins of the tensions and the rather superficial common bonds between the competing groups can both provoke and feed the frightening levels of brutality witnessed in recent years. The rampage of the Hutu *génocidaires* against the formerly dominant Tutsi in Rwanda is an example of the dangerous potential of residual ethnic resentments that may continue to seethe beneath the surface of "modernity."

• Finally, the end of the Cold War has created an international market in relatively inexpensive military equipment whose sale—in Conakry, Guinea, for example, the going price in late 2002 for a surplus Eastern European knockoff of the Russian AK-47 assault rifle at the Madina market was about thirty U.S. dollars—is facilitated by globalization's creation of regional markets for resources that are no longer protected by the faltering governments of many failing states.

Thus warlords can finance their armed conflicts by doubling as merchant princes. Those same regional markets create conditions where ethnic conflicts are not only confined to one country, but can be spread to neighboring countries and can even engulf an entire region. While the end of the Cold War cannot be blamed for the phenomenon of state failure, the rash of failed states seen in recent years is attributable to the removal of the constraint that the balance between the two superpowers had previously imposed upon their collapse. The high incidents of state failure in the past decade might, consequently, be ascribed to a delayed release of pent-up tensions. Furthermore, the combination of the four preceding conditions also renders any attempt to intervene in the process exceptionally difficult, if not ultimately futile. As brutal as it may seem, realism forces the admission that a "natural" entropy is involved, breaking down complex artificial constructions that have long repressed more fundamental group identifications—and the moment that the diplomatic or military intervention is withdrawn, the process will continue. In fact, as the present work shows with respect to Liberia, intervention may even exacerbate and prolong the woeful consequences of state failure.

THE CONSEQUENCES OF STATE FAILURE

State failure leads to a particularly insidious and destructive form of conflict precisely because it is the collapse of the very *polis* to which all members of a given society—to whatever degree, greater or lesser—have a stake in the outcome. The post-state failure conflict, whether contained in a localized setting or spread across a wider geographic area, creates the conditions for the "complex humanitarian emergency" that galvanize the attention of the international community. Andrew Natsios, administrator of the U.S. Agency for International Development, has defined the characteristics of these emergencies:

> First, the most visible characteristic, civil conflict, is rooted in traditional ethnic, tribal, and religious animosities. Such conflict is generally accompanied by widespread atrocities.
> Second, the authority of the national government deteriorates to such an extent that public services—to the degree they ever existed – disappear, and political control over the country passes to regional centers of power: warlords, provincial governors over whom the cen-

tral government has lost control, and occasionally traditional authority figures at the village level.

Third, mass population movements occur because internally displaced people and refugees want to escape the conflict or search for
food. Public health emergencies arise as dislocated civilians congre-
gate in camps.

Fourth, the economic system suffers massive dislocation resulting
in hyperinflation and destruction of the currency, double-digit de-
clines in the gross national product, depression-level unemployment,
and the collapse of markets.

Finally, these first four characteristics, sometimes exacerbated by
drought, contribute to a general decline in food security. This frequently leads to severe malnutrition that, although at first localized,
may degenerate into widespread starvation.[33]

In a failed state, these characteristics can feed off one another, creating a vicious cycle with catastrophic consequences, especially if the conflict is prolonged. The devastating upheaval in Liberia over the course
of the past decade has shown that much. In fact, the events in that unfortunate country are, most regrettably, indicative of phenomena are
only slowly penetrating into the consciousness of most of the developed
world.

ENDNOTES

1. See L. Paul Bremmer III, "A New Strategy for the New Face of Terrorism," *The National Interest* 65 (Autumn 2001): 23–30.
2. George H.W. Bush, *Address Before a Joint Session of the Congress on the Persian Gulf Crisis
and the Federal Budget Deficit* (September 11, 1990) (emphasis added). The complete text
of the address can be found at the website of the George Bush Presidential Library and
Museum at <bushlibrary.tamu.edu/>.
3. Margaret Thatcher, *Statecraft: Strategies for a Changing World* (New York: HarperCollins
Publishers, 2002), 29.
4. *The National Security Strategy of the United States of America* (September 17, 2002).
5. See Alfred Verdross and Bruno Simma, *Universelles Völkerrecht. Theorie und Praxis*, 3rd
ed. (Berlin: Dunker, 1984), 391.
6. Gerald B. Helman and Steven R. Ratner, "Saving Failed States," *Foreign Policy* 89 (Winter 1992–1993): 1–20, here 1 and 5.
7. Charles W. Freeman, Jr., *The Diplomat's Dictionary*, rev. ed. (1997; Washington, D.C.:
United States Institute of Peace, 2001), 273.
8. See Hans Kelsen, *Pure Theory of Law*, 2nd ed., trans. Max Knight (Berkeley/Los Angeles/
London: University of California Press, 1967), 286–290.
9. Jean-Germain Gros, "Towards a taxonomy of failed states in the New World Order: decaying Somalia, Liberia, Rwanda and Haiti," *Third World Quarterly* 17/3 (1996): 456.

10. *Ibid.*, 457.
11. See *ibid.*, 458–461.
12. See Michael Barnett, *Eyewitness to a Genocide: The United Nations and Rwanda* (Ithaca, New York/London: Cornell University Press, 2002).
13. David Carment, "Assessing state failure: implications for theory and practice," *Third World Quarterly* 24/3 (2003): 407.
14. Susan L. Woodward, "Failed States: Warlordism and 'Tribal' Warfare," *Naval War College Review* 52/2 (1999), at <www.nwc.navy.mil/press/Review/nwcrlisting.htm>.
15. Michael Ignatieff, *Blood and Belonging: Journeys into the New Nationalism* (New York: Farrar, Straus, and Giroux, 1994), 8.
16. See Charles Krauthammer, "The Unipolar Moment," *Foreign Affairs* 70/1 (Winter 1990–1991): 23–33; also idem., "The Unipolar Moment Revisited," *The National Interest* 70 (Winter 2002–2003): 5–17.
17. See Francis Fukuyama, "Why the Left Should Love Globalization," *The Wall Street Journal* (December 1, 1999).
18. See Thomas L. Friedman, *The Lexus and the Olive Tree: Understanding Globalization*, rev. ed. (New York: Anchor Books, 2000), 44–71.
19. Shashi Tharoor, "The Future of Civil Conflict," *World Policy Journal* 16/1 (1999): 3.
20. See William Reno, "Clandestine Economies, Violence and States in Africa," *Journal of International Affairs* 53/2 (2000): 433–460.
21. See Jean-François Bayart, Stephen Ellis, and Beatrice Hibou, *The Criminalisation of the State in Africa* (Bloomington, Indiana: Indiana University Press, 1999).
22. See Samuel P. Huntington, "The Clash of Civilizations?," *Foreign Affairs* 72/3 (1993): 22–49; also idem., *The Clash of Civilizations and the Remaking of World Order* (New York: Simon and Schuster, 1996).
23. See Robert D. Kaplan, "The Coming Anarchy: How Scarcity, Crime, Overpopulation and Disease are Rapidly Destroying the Social Fabric of Our Planet," *The Atlantic Monthly* 273/2 (February 1994): 44–76.
24. *Ibid.*, 46.
25. David Carment, "Modeling Ethnic Conflict: Problems and Pitfalls," *Politics and the Life Sciences* 16/2 (1997): 249.
26. Paul Richards, *Fighting for the Rain Forest: War, Youth, and Resources in Sierra Leone*, rev. ed. (1998; Oxford/Portsmouth, New Hampshire: James Currey/Heinemann, 2002), xiv.
27. Kofi A. Annan, "Facing the Humanitarian Challenge," introduction to the *Annual Report of the Secretary-General on the Work of the Organization 1999* (A/54/1, August 31, 1999), at <www.un.org/Docs/SG/Report99/intro99.htm>.
28. Tharoor, "The Future of Civil Conflict," 1–2.
29. Charles A. Kupchan, "Introduction: Nationalism Resurgent," in Charles A. Kupchan (ed.), *Nationalism and Nationalities in the New Europe* (Ithaca, New York: Cornell University Press, 1995), 3.
30. Bill Berkeley, *The Graves Are Not Yet Full: Race, Tribe and Power in the Heart of Africa* (New York: Basic Books, 2001), 11.
31. See Anthony D. Smith, *National Identity* (London: Penguin, 1991), 8–15.
32. David Turton, "Introduction," in David Turton (ed.), *War and Ethnicity: Global Connections and Local Violence* (Rochester: University of Rochester Press, 1997), 11.
33. Andrew S. Natsios, *U.S. Foreign Policy and the Four Horsemen of the Apocalypse: Humanitarian Relief in Complex Emergencies* (Center for Strategic and International Studies "Washington Paper" 170; Westport, Connecticut/London: Praeger, 1997), 7.

SELECTED
BIBLIOGRAPHY

THIS BOOK RELIED HEAVILY on its author's own experience as a diplomat covering the West African sub-region from 2001 through 2002, during which time he had direct contact many of the principals in the conflict as well as the extensive and lively coverage of events by the local press. In addition, he had access to a number of official documents and unofficial briefings, some of which have not yet been made public. For obvious reasons of the diplomat's craft, with one exception, these have not been referenced within the present work.

For those interested in first-hand documentation, regrettably, the offices of the Center for National Documents and Records Agency, the official archival agency of the Liberian state, were badly damaged during the first battle for Monrovia in 1990. The subsequent looting of the

National Archives has destroyed what was perhaps the best collection in the world of historical material on Liberia. The Justice and Peace Commission, an agency of the National Catholic Secretariat of Liberia, maintained an extensive collection of documents and other reference material. Sadly, the recent sacking of the offices of Catholic Secretariat, located behind Sacred Heart Cathedral in Monrovia, has deprived scholars of this valuable resource.

While books, scholarly essays and other publications are included in the bibliography that follows, articles from newspapers and other periodicals as well as public documents, both official and unofficial, and reports by non-governmental organizations are not listed as they have been adequately referenced in the notes to the text.

ON LIBERIA

Adebajo, Adekeye. *Liberia's Civil War: Nigeria, ECOMOG, and Regional Security in West Africa*. Boulder, Colorado: Lynne Rienner Publishers, 2002.

Armon, Jeremy, and Andy Carl, eds. *Accord: The Liberian Peace Process, 1990-1996*. London: Conciliation Resources, 1996.

Atkinson, Philippa. *The War Economy in Liberia: A Political Economy*. London: Overseas Development Institute, 1997.

Azango, Bertha B. "The Historical and Philosophical Development of *Liberian Education*." *Liberian Historical Review* 1 (1968): 28-37.

Best, Kenneth. *Cultural Policy in Liberia*. Paris: UNESCO, 1974.

Beyan, Amos J. "The American Colonization Society and the Socio-Religious Characterization of Liberia: A Historical Survey, 1822-1900." Liberian Studies Journal 10/2 (1984-1985): 1-11.

Clapham, Christopher. *Liberia and Sierra Leone: An Essay in Comparative Politics*. African Studies Series 20. Cambridge: Cambridge University Press, 1976.

Dalton, George, and A.A. Walters. "The Economy of Liberia," 287-315, in P. Robson and D.A. Lury (eds.), *The Economies of Africa*. Evanston, Illinois: Northwestern University Press, 1969.

Dick, Shelly, and Wiebe Boer. "The Spirits are Angry: Liberia's secret cults in the service of civil war." *Books and Culture* 7/1 (January/February 2001): 26-27.

Draman, Rasheed, and David Carment. *Managing Chaos in the West African Sub-Region: Assessing the Role of ECOMOG in Liberia*. Centre for Security and Defence Studies Occasional Paper 26. Ottawa: Norman Paterson School of International Affairs/Carleton University, 2001.

Dunn, D. Elwood, and S. Byron Tarr. *Liberia: A National Polity in Transition*. Metuchen, New Jersey: Scarecrow Press, 1988.

Dunn, D. Elwood, Amos J. Beyan, and Carl Patrick Burrowes. *Historical Dictionary of Liberia*. 2nd ed. Lanham, Maryland/London: Scarecrow Press, 2001.

Ellis, Stephen. *The Mask of Anarchy: The Destruction of Liberia and the Religious Dimension of an African Civil War*. 1999; New York: New York University Press, 2001.

Foley, David M. "British Policy in Liberia, 1862-1912." Ph.D. diss., University of London, 1965.

Fraenkel, Merran. "Social Change on the Kru Coast of Liberia." *Africa* 36/2 (1966): 154-172.

Gifford, Paul. *Christianity and Politics in Doe's Liberia*. Cambridge: Cambridge University Press, 1993.

Greene, Graham. *Journey Without Maps*. 1936; New York: Penguin Books, 1980.

Harrington, Patrick Joseph. "Secret Societies and the Church: An Evaluation of the Poro and Sande Secret Societies and the Missionary among the Mano of Liberia." Th.D. dissertation, Pontifical Gregorian University, 1975.

Harris, David. "From 'warlord' to 'democratic' president: how Charles Taylor won the 1997 Liberian elections." *Journal of Modern African Studies* 37 (1999): 431-455.

Howe, Herbert. "Lessons of Liberia, ECOMOG, and Regional Peacekeeping." *International Security* 21/3 (Winter 1996-1997), 1-31.

Huberich, Charles Henry. *The Political and Legislative History of Liberia, 1847-1844*. New York: Central Book Company, 1947.

Hyman, Lester S. *United States Policy Towards Liberia, 1822-2003: Unintended Consequences*. Cherry Hill, New Jersey: Africana Homestead Legacy Publishers, 2003.

Johnson, Charles S. *Bitter Canaan: The Story of the Negro Republic*. Edited with an introduction by John Stansfield. 1987; New Brunswick, New Jersey/London: Transaction Publishers, 1992.

Johnston, Harry Hamilton. *Liberia*, 2 vols. New York: Dodd, Mead & Company, 1906.

Kufuor, K. Otent. "The Legality of the Intervention in the Liberian Civil War by the Economic Community of West African States." *African Journal of International and Comparative Law* 5 (1993): 523-560.

Kuhn, Gary C. "Liberian Contract Labor in Panama, 1887-1897." *Liberian Studies Journal* 6/1 (1975): 43-52.

Kulah, Arthur. *Liberia Will Rise Again: Reflections on the Liberian Civil Crisis*. Nashville, Tennessee: Abingdon Press, 1999.

Liebenow, J. Gus. *Liberia: The Evolution of Privilege* (Ithaca, New York: Cornell University Press, 1969

———. *Liberia: The Quest for a Democracy*. Bloomington, Indiana: Indiana University Press, 1987.

Lyons, Terrence. *Voting for Peace: Post-Conflict Elections in Liberia*. Washington, D.C.: Brookings Institution, 1999.

McDaniel, Antonio. *Swing Low, Sweet Chariot: The Mortality Cost of Colonizing Liberia in the Nineteenth Century*. Chicago: University of Chicago Press, 1995.

Magyar, Karl, and Earl Conteh-Morgan, eds. *Peacekeeping in Africa: ECOMOG in Liberia*. New York: St. Martin's Press.

Martin, Jane Jackson. "The Dual Legacy: Government Authority and Mission Influence among the Grebo of Eastern Liberia, 1834-1910." Ph.D. diss., Boston University, 1968.

O'Neill, William. "Liberia: An Avoidable Tragedy." *Current History* 92/574 (May 1993): 213-217.

Peterson, Dave. "Liberia: Crying for Freedom." *Journal of Democracy* 7/2 (April 1996): 148-158.

Porte, Albert. *Liberianization or Gobbling Business?* Crozierville, Liberia: Porte, 1974.

Reno, William. "Reinvention of an African patrimonial state: Charles Taylor's Liberia," *Third World Quarterly* 16/1 (1995): 109-120.

_____. "The Business of War in Liberia." *Current History* 95/601 (1996): 211-215.

Richardson, Nathaniel R. *Liberia's Past and Present*. London: Diplomatic Press, 1959.

Sawyer, Amos. "The Making of the 1984 Liberian Constitution: Major Issues and Dynamic Forces." *Liberian Studies Journal* 12/1 (1987): 1-15.

_____. "Proprietary Authority and Local Administration in Liberia." In Wunsch, James S., and Dele Olowu, eds. *The Failure of the Centralized State: Institutions and Self-Governance in Africa*. Boulder, Colorado: Westview Press, 1990.

_____. *The Emergence of Autocracy in Liberia: Tragedy and Challenge*. San Francisco: Institute for Contemporary Studies, 1992.

Sesay, Max Ahmadu. "Bringing Peace to Liberia." *Accord: An International Review of Peace Initiatives* 1 (1996): 9-26, 75-81.

Shick, Tom W. "A Quantitative Analysis of Liberian Colonization from 1820 to 1843 with Special Reference to Mortality." *Journal of African History* 12/1 (1971): 45-59.

Smith, Robert A. *The Emancipation of the Hinterland*. Monrovia: Star Magazine and Publishing, 1964.

Staudenraus, Philip John. *The African Colonization Movement, 1816-1875*. New York: Columbia University Press, 1961.

Toure, Augustine. *The Role of Civil Society in National Reconciliation and Peacebuilding in Liberia*. New York: International Peace Academy, 2002.

van Walraven, Klaas. *The Pretence of Peace-keeping: ECOMOG, West Africa and Liberia (1990-1998)*. The Hague: Netherlands Institute of International Relations *Clingendael*, 1999.

Wickstrom, Werner T. "The American Colonization Society and Liberia: An Historical Study in Religious Motivation and Achievement, 1817-1867." Ph.D. diss., Hartford Seminary, 1958.

Williams, Gabriel I.H. *Liberia: The Heart of Darkness*. Victoria, British Columbia: Trafford Publishers, 2002.

Woods II, Samuel Kofi. "Civic Initiatives in the Peace Process." *Accord: An International Journal of Peace Initiatives* 1 (1996): 27-32.

Zamba Liberty, Clarence E. "Butuo: A Lilliputian Testament to a Struggle – The NPFL Journey to State Power: How Charles Taylor Upset the Bowl of Rice and Took Home the Whole Hog." *Liberian Studies Journal* 23/1 (1998): 135-207.

ON AFRICA AND OTHER GENERAL AND COMPARATIVE WORKS

Adebajo, Adekeye. *Building Peace in West Africa: Liberia, Sierra Leone, and Guinea-Bissau*. International Peace Academy Occasional Papers Series. Boulder, Colorado/London: Lynne Rienner Publishers, 2002.

Achebe, Chinua. *A Man of the People*. 1966; New York: Anchor Books, 1989.

Agetua, Nkem. *Operation Liberty: The Story of Major General Joshua Nimyel Dogonyaro*. Lagos: Hona Communications, 1992.

Alexander, Archibald. *A History of Colonization on the Western Coast of Africa*. 1846; New York: Negro Universities Press, 1969.

Ayittey, George B.N. *Africa Betrayed*. New York: Macmillan, 1992.

_____. *Africa in Chaos*. New York: St. Martin's Press, 1997.

Barnett, Michael. *Eyewitness to a Genocide: The United Nations and Rwanda*. Ithaca, New York/London: Cornell University Press, 2002.

Bayart, Jean-François, Stephen Ellis, and Beatrice Hibou. *The Criminalisation of the State in Africa*. Bloomington, Indiana: Indiana University Press, 1999.

Berkeley, Bill. *The Graves Are Not Yet Full: Race, Tribe and Power in the Heart of Africa*. New York: Basic Books, 2001.

Buell, Raymond Leslie. *The Native Problem in Africa*, 2 vols. 1928; Hamden, Connecticut: Archon Books, 1965.

Chabal, Patrick, and Jean-Pascal Daloz. *Africa Works: Disorder as Political Instrument*. International African Institute "African Issues" Series. Bloomington, Indiana: Indiana University Press, 1999.

Clapham, Christopher. *Africa and the International System: The Politics of State Survival*. Cambridge Studies in International Relations 50. Cambridge: Cambridge University Press, 1996.

Clapham, Christopher, ed. *African Guerillas*. Oxford: James Currey/ Bloomington, Indiana: Indiana University Press, 1998.

Conrad, Joseph. *Heart of Darkness*. 1902; New York: Penguin Books, 1995.

Davidson, Basil. *The Black Man's Burden: Africa and the Curse of the Nation State*. London: James Currey, 1992.

Ellis, Stephen. "The Old Roots of Africa's New Wars." *Internationale Politik und Gesellschaft* 10/2 (2003): 29–43.

Engelbert, Pierre. *Burkina Faso: Unsteady Statehood in West Africa*. Boulder, Colorado/Oxford: Westview, 1996.

Funke, Nikki, and Hussein Solomon. *The Shadow State in Africa: A Discussion*. DPMF Occasional Papers 5. Addis Ababa: Development Policy Management Forum, 2002.

Goldsborough, James O. "Dateline Paris: Africa's Policeman." *Foreign Affairs* 33 (Winter 1978–1979): 174–190.

Gros, Jean-Germain. "Towards a taxonomy of failed states in the New World Order: Decaying Somalia, Liberia, Rwanda and Haiti." *Third World Quarterly* 17/3 (1996): 455–471.

Hirsch, John L. "War in Sierra Leone." *Survival: The International Institute for Strategic Studies Quarterly* 43/3 (Autumn 2001): 145–162.

_____. *Sierra Leone: Diamonds and the Struggle for Democracy*. Boulder, Colorado/London: Lynne Rienner Publishers, 2001.

Ignatieff, Michael. *Human Rights as Politics and Idolatry*. Edited by Amy Gutman. Princeton/Oxford: Princeton University Press, 2001.

Huliaras, Asteris. "Qadhafi's comeback: Libya and sub-Saharan Africa in the 1990s." *African Affairs* 100/1 (2001): 5–25.

Kaplan, Robert D. "The Coming Anarchy: How Scarcity, Crime, Overpopulation and Disease are Rapidly Destroying the Social Fabric of Our Planet." *The Atlantic Monthly* 273/2 (February 1994): 44–76.

_____. *The Ends of the Earth: From Togo to Turkmenistan, From Iran to Cambodia – A Journey to the Frontiers of Anarchy*. 1996; New York: Vintage, 1997.

_____. *The Coming Anarchy: Shattering Dreams of the Post Cold War*. New York: Vintage Books, 2000.

Kapuściński, Ryszard. *The Shadow of the Sun*. Translated by Klara Glowczewska. New York/Toronto: Alfred A. Knopf, 2001.

Keen, David. "Greedy Elites, Dwindling Resources, Alienated Youths: The Anatomy of Protracted Violence in Sierra Leone." *Internationale Politik und Gesellschaft* 10/2 (2003): 67–94.

Levgold, Robert. *Soviet Policy in West Africa*. Cambridge: Harvard University Press, 1970.

Mays, Terry, and Mark W. DeLancey. *Historical Dictionary of International Organizations in Sub-Saharan Africa*. Historical Dictionary of International Organizations 21. Lanham, Maryland/London: Scarecrow Press, 2002.

Melady, Thomas Patrick. *Profiles of African Leaders*. New York: Macmillan, 1961.

Montague, Dena. "The Business of War and the Prospects for Peace in Sierra Leone." *The Brown Journal of World Affairs* 9/1 (2002): 229–237.

Museveni, Yoweri K. *What is Africa's Problem?* Edited by Elizabeth Kanyongo-nya. Minneapolis: University of Minnesota, 2000.

Reno, William. *Warlord Politics and African States*. Boulder, Colorado/London: Lynne Rienner Publishers, 1998.

_____. "Clandestine Economies, Violence and States in Africa." *Journal of International Affairs* 53/2 (2000): 433–460.

_____. "Political Networks in a Failing State: The Roots and Future of Violent Conflict in Sierra Leone," *Internationale Politik und Gesellschaft* 10/2 (2003): 44–66.

Richards, Paul. *Fighting for the Rain Forest: War, Youth, and Resources in Sierra Leone*. Rev. ed. 1998; Oxford/Portsmouth, New Hampshire: James Currey/ Heinemann, 2002.

Richburg, Keith B. *Out of America: A Black Man Confronts Africa*. Rev. ed. San Diego/New York/London: Harcourt, 1998.

Shagari, Shehu. *My Vision of Nigeria: Selected Speeches*. London: Frank Cass Publishers, 1981.

Soyinka, Wole. *Open Sore of a Continent: A Personal Narrative of the Nigerian Crisis*. Oxford/New York: Oxford University Press, 1996.

Woodward, Susan L. "Failed States: Warlordism and 'Tribal' Warfare," *Naval War College Review* 52/2 (1999): online at <www.nwc.navy.mil/press/ Review/nwcrlisting.htm>.

Tchidimbo, Raymond-Marie. *Noviciat d'un évêque. Huit ans et huit mois de captivité sous Sékou Touré*. Paris: Éditions Fayard, 1987.

Touré, Ahmed Sékou. *Expérience guinéenne et unité africaine*. Paris: Éditions «Présence africaine», 1961.

van de Walle, Nicholas. *African Economies and the Politics of Permanent Crisis, 1979–1999*. Cambridge/New York: Cambridge University Press, 2001.

OTHER REFERENCES

Albright, Madeleine, with Bob Woodward. *Madam Secretary: A Memoir*. New York: Hyperion, 2003.

Bremmer III, L. Paul. «A New Strategy for the New Face of Terrorism.» *The National Interest* 65 (Autumn 2001): 23–30.

Carment, David. "Modeling Ethnic Conflict: Problems and Pitfalls," *Politics and the Life Sciences* 16/2 (1997): 249–250.

_____. "Assessing state failure: implications for theory and practice." *Third World Quarterly* 24/3 (2003): 407–427.

Carment, David, and Patrick James. *Peace in the Midst of Wars: Preventing and Managing International Ethnic Conflicts*. Columbia, South Carolina: University of South Carolina Press, 1998.

Crocker, Chester A. "Engaging Failing States." *Foreign Affairs* 82/5 (September/ October 2003): 32–44.

Devey, Muriel. *La Guinée*. Paris: Éditions Karthala, 1997.

Eban, Abba. *Diplomacy for the Next Century*. New Haven/London: Yale University Press, 1998.

Foley, Michael W., and Bob Edwards. "The Paradox of Civil Society." *Journal of Democracy* 7/3 (July 1996): 38–52.

Franklin, John Hope. *The Free Negro in North Carolina, 1790–1860*. Rev. ed. Chapel Hill: University of North Carolina Press, 1995.

Freeman, Jr., Charles W. *The Diplomat's Dictionary*. Rev. ed. 1997; Washington, D.C.: United States Institute of Peace, 2001.

Frei, Hans. *Hans J. Morgenthau: An Intellectual Biography*. Baton Rouge, Louisiana: Louisiana State University Press, 2001.

Friedman, Thomas L. *The Lexus and the Olive Tree: Understanding Globalization*. Rev. ed. New York: Anchor Books, 2000.

Fukuyama, Francis. *Trust: The Social Virtues and the Creation of Prosperity*. New York: Free Press, 1995.

Helman, Gerald B. and Steven R. Ratner. "Saving Failed States." *Foreign Policy* 89 (Winter 1992–1993): 1–20.

Huntington, Samuel P. "The Clash of Civilizations?" *Foreign Affairs* 72/3 (1993): 22–49.

_____. *The Clash of Civilizations and the Remaking of World Order*. New York: Simon and Schuster, 1996.

Ignatieff, Michael. *Blood and Belonging: Journeys into the New Nationalism*. New York: Farrar, Straus, and Giroux, 1994.

_____. *Human Rights as Politics and Idolatry*. Edited by Amy Gutmann. Princeton/Oxford: Princeton University Press, 2001.

Kelsen, Hans. *Pure Theory of Law*. 2nd ed. Translated by Max Knight. Berkeley/Los Angeles/London: University of California Press, 1967.

Kissinger, Henry. *A World Restored: Metternich, Castlereagh and the Problems of Peace 1812–1822*. 1957; London: Phoenix Press, 2000.

_____. *Diplomacy*. 1994; New York: Touchstone, 1995.

_____. *Does America Need a Foreign Policy? Toward a Diplomacy for the 21st Century*. 2001; New York: Touchstone, 2002.

Krauthammer, Charles. "The Unipolar Moment." *Foreign Affairs* 70/1 (Winter 1990–1991): 23–33.

_____, "The Unipolar Moment Revisited." *The National Interest* 70 (Winter 2002–2003): 5–17.

Kupchan, Charles A., ed. *Nationalism and Nationalities in the New Europe*. Ithaca, New York: Cornell University Press, 1995.

Majstorovic, Steven. "Ancient Hatreds or Elite Manipulation? Memory and Politics in the Former Yugoslavia." *World Affairs* 159/4 (Spring 1997): 170–183.

Morgenthau, Hans J. *Politics Among Nations: The Struggle for Power and Peace*. 5th rev. ed. New York: Alfred A. Knopf, 1978.

Natsios, Andrew S. *U.S. Foreign Policy and the Four Horsemen of the Apocalypse:*

Humanitarian Relief in Complex Emergencies. Center for Strategic and International Studies "Washington Paper" 170. Westport, Connecticut/London: Praeger, 1997.

Ragin, Charles. *The Comparative Method: Moving Beyond Qualitative and Quantitative Strategies*. Berkeley: University of California Press, 1987.

Rehnquist, William H. *The Supreme Court*. Rev. ed. 2001; New York: Vintage Books, 2002.

Smith, Anthony D. *National Identity*. London: Penguin, 1991.

de Soto, Hernando. *The Mystery of Capital: Why Capitalism Triumphs in the West and Fails Everywhere Else*. New York: Basic Books, 2000.

Stedman, Stephen John. *International Actors and Internal Conflicts*. New York: Rockefeller Brothers Fund Project on World Security, 1999.

Thatcher, Margaret. *Statecraft: Strategies for a Changing World*. New York: HarperCollins Publishers, 2002.

Tharoor, Shashi. "The Future of Civil Conflict." *World Policy Journal* 16/1 (1999): 1–11.

Thomas, Hogh. *The Slave Trade: The Story of the Atlantic Slave Trade*, 1440–1870. New York: Simon & Schuster, 1997.

Turton, David, ed. *War and Ethnicity: Global Connections and Local Violence*. Rochester: University of Rochester Press, 1997.

Verdross, Alfred, and Bruno Simma. *Universelles Völkerrecht. Theorie und Praxis*. 3rd ed. Berlin: Dunker, 1984.

INDEX

ABOUT THE AUTHOR

JOHN-PETER PHAM, a scholar with advanced degrees in economics, history, theology, civil and canon law, and international affairs, is the author of over one hundred essays and reviews on a wide variety of subjects in scholarly and opinion journals on both sides of the Atlantic. He is also the author, editor, or translator of over a dozen books. From 2001 through 2002, Dr. Pham served as an international diplomat in Liberia, Sierra Leone, and Guinea.